Relational database principles

Relational database principles

Colin Ritchie
Lecturer
Computer Studies Department,
Glasgow Caledonian University

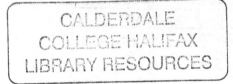
Letts Educational
Aldine Place
London W12 8AW
0181 740 2268

1998

A CIP catalogue record for this book is available from the British Library

ISBN 1-85805-363-3
Copyright Colin Ritchie © 1998

First edition 1998

Typeset by Tech Set Limited, Gateshead, Tyne & Wear.

Printed in Great Britain by
Ashford Colour Press, Gosport, Hants.

Contents

|102417

Preface

Overview

This text provides an introductory treatment of the principles and practice of relational databases and is intended for students in HND and degree courses in computing or information technology in which the students are expected to develop competence in designing practical database systems.

No previous knowledge of databases is assumed but some knowledge of the general principles of a computer and a little programming experience would be helpful. The text is not a guide to any particular database system although Microsoft Access and Oracle are used as exemplar systems.

Database design properly forms part of the broader process of systems analysis and design; however, data modelling and the consequent construction of a database are sufficiently distinct tasks that are worthy of treatment in a separate textbook. In addition to aspects of database design, this book also deals with other aspects of databases such as integrity and concurrency.

The structured query language (SQL) is one of the more important elements of modern database technology. It is used very extensively by virtually all database systems and is a major vehicle in facilitating inter-database communication. Accordingly, it is important that students studying database principles obtain a good grounding in the language. To this end, the last chapter in the book contains a tutorial on SQL. Other laboratory exercises on SQL are available in the lecturer's supplement.

Objectives

The objectives of the text are to provide

- an introduction to the principles underlying relational databases
- instruction in the techniques used to design and develop practical database systems
- instruction in the use of the Structured Query Language (SQL)
- an introduction to other database technologies that are becoming important.

Treatment

In order to make the text as readable as possible, the following principles were adopted in the construction of the chapters. Each chapter (except for Chapter 13) is

ix

of limited length so that the student's knowledge and appreciation can be tested at regular intervals. Within each chapter three forms of assessment are employed.

1. A series of in-text questions appear throughout the text. These provide an immediate check on the student's understanding of the foregoing section of work and are intended to focus the student's mind on particular aspect of the topic.
2. At the end of the chapter a set of review questions are presented. These are questions requiring a short answer and are intended simply to test the student's recall of the material covered. The review questions are answered in Appendix C.
3. Also at the end of the chapter, a set of exercises are presented. These are either practical exercises, where appropriate, and/or questions that might appear in examination papers. Answers to selected exercises appear in Appendix D (these exercises are flagged with an asterisk at the start of the question); the answers to the other questions are available in a lecturer's supplement.

Chapter 13 is a tutorial on SQL and is organised somewhat differently from the others. It consists of a series of instructional notes on aspects of SQL followed by sample queries based on the current topic. The chapter is divided into seven separate sessions. To obtain maximum benefit from the chapter it is suggested that the student tries to resolve the query before looking at the solution given. No additional exercises are given within the chapter but a set of laboratory exercises are available in the lecturer's supplement which correspond to sessions used in this chapter.

Summary of chapters

The text consists of thirteen chapters. The last chapter is somewhat distinct from the others in that it is a tutorial on SQL. The contents of the chapters are listed by chapter number below

1. Introduction and background: this chapter provides a non-technical intuitive introduction to the subject.
2. The relational data model: the underlying principles of relational databases are introduced.
3. Data modelling 1: introduces the entity-relationship (ER) data model which is used in the design of relational database tables.
4. Data modelling 2: describes the process of converting ER diagrams to relational tables.
5. Normalisation: the process of normalisation is used to ensure that tables are optimally designed.
6. Physical design: considers aspects of converting the conceptual design into a practical system implemented on a specific database platform.
7. Database management systems: describes the facilities one would expect to find in practical DBMS systems.
8. Database programming: describes various aspects of the use of programming in database construction.

9. Integrity and security: describes techniques used to ensure the integrity and security of the database.
10. Concurrency: discusses the problems that can arise when a multi-user database system is used.
11. Networked and distributed systems: the use of networked databases and, specifically, techniques for distributing a database over several computers are described in this chapter.
12. Beyond the relational model: discusses the limitations of relational databases and describes some alternative technologies.
13. SQL tutorial notes: a series of exercises designed to teach the basic principles of SQL programming.

Supplements

A lecturer's supplement is available that provides answers to some of the chapter exercises in addition to other material such as SQL lab exercises that can be used in the teaching of the subject. Other material such as a file of SQL statements to construct the sample tables used in Chapter 13 are also available in the supplement.

1

Introduction and background

Introduction

Most computer applications require a means of holding persistent data; i.e., data that preserves its value between successive invocations of the software that produces it and, indeed, between successive 'switch-ons' of the computer itself. For some systems, including commercial applications such as Order Processing and Personnel, the storage of data is a major part of their function, while for others it is perhaps more subsidiary to their purpose.

The need for persistent storage has traditionally been met by the use of magnetic storage devices such as tape and disk with magnetic 'hard disks' being the predominant form at the current stage of technology. Quite possibly, other forms of storage may become prevalent, with optical systems being the current most likely contender. However, the principles discussed in this book are likely to remain valid regardless of the storage technology used. For convenience, we will refer to 'disk' storage in this book, although this should be taken to mean any current or new form of mass storage.

The storage space on disks is generally controlled by file management software, which can be part of the operating system or a layer of software above the operating system or both. The basic tool provided is the 'file' abstraction; a file is a group of binary digits of arbitrary length, recorded on the disk surface, which the operating system treats as a unit of storage. To support the use of files as a storage medium, the system also provides a naming and categorisation mechanism (in the form of a hierarchical file and directory system), and reading, writing and positioning facilities. The file can have an arbitrarily complex internal structure but this is generally recognised only by the application software and is not visible to the operating system. For instance, the file may consist of purely text characters or it may be a binary image of a graphical picture. The operating system, however, views it purely as a series of bits and it is not aware of the interpretation placed on these bits by the application software.

The file system provides the user with the means to store programs and associated data (text and binary data such as graphics, sound, etc.) and as such is an indispensable part of the computer. End-user applications such as word processing, graphic design and spreadsheets extensively utilise the file system for storage of

1

documents, designs, etc. In doing so, such applications use their own specialised formatting of data, although many standard formats, such as TIFF, BMP, RTF are now in use.

Our main concern in this text is systems – databases – that provide generalised facilities for the storage and retrieval of data of arbitrary conceptual structure and format but predominantly textual and numerical. Databases are used extensively, but not exclusively, in commercial applications. In the earlier days of such systems, application programs normally used the file system directly to provide persistent storage, with each program using its own file formats. Of particular note in this respect is the COBOL language; this was the earliest commonly used language to provide the programmer with extensive file-handling facilities including, notably, the ability to store data in the form of records. A record is a compound data item consisting of a number of component fields, each of which is an elementary data item such as a text item or a numerical amount. This is a convenient format to use to represent 'real-world' entities such as orders, invoices, bank accounts and customers.

For instance, if we design a file to hold data on motion pictures, a possible record format, together with sample data, might be as detailed below.

Title	30 characters
Director	20 characters
Year	4 numeric digits
MainStar	20 characters
SupportStar	20 characters

The fields of this file are 'Title', 'Director', etc., and a typical record of this file might hold the values

| Titanic | James Cameron | 1997 | Leonardo DiCaprio | Kate Winslet |

If we were to write COBOL programs to create, read and update such a file, each such program would contain a description of the file format, which, in COBOL notation, would look something like this:

```
01 Film-Record.
    02      Title          PICTURE      X(30).
    02      Director       PICTURE      X(20).
    02      Year           PICTURE      9999.
    02      MainStar       PICTURE      X(20).
    02      Support        PICTURE      X(20).
```

This record definition effectively allocates main memory spaces, of the sizes indicated by the PICTURE clauses (e.g., X(30) specifies a field of thirty characters, 9999 specifies four numeric digits) in one contiguous sequence of bytes. This record space can then be populated with valid data values and transferred to disk using a WRITE instruction. Subsequently, the record could be retrieved using a READ instruction.

COBOL records can be arbitrarily complex; each record can have any required number of fields (within system limits) and, with some constraints, can have variable length fields and a variable number (i.e. an array) of fields. If we wanted to include a list of stars rather than just the two as used above, an alternative format might be:

```
01 Film-Record.
    02    Title       PICTURE    X(30).
    02    Director    PICTURE    X(20).
    02    Year        PICTURE    9999.
    02    Star        PICTURE    X(20) OCCURS 6 TIMES.
```

Different record formats within the one file are also possible, provided some record-type field is employed to enable the application programs to distinguish between the various formats. Additionally, COBOL provided very effective file organisation and accessing facilities including random, relative and indexed files. The merits of these facilities at that point in computing history account for COBOL's long-lived dominance of the commercial computing market.

However, technology marches on, and problems and limitations were soon encountered in file-based systems. The development of the concept of a database arose at this time to meet these difficulties and, later again, the relational database ultimately provided more effective solutions. In the rest of this chapter, we provide an overview of the database concept and, in particular, its implementation using the relational model. The treatment in this chapter is essentially intuitive; later chapters provide more detailed and formal descriptions of relational techniques.

The database concept

The problems with file systems that became apparent were:

1. The structure of the records is defined in the application program. This produced two unfortunate consequences:
   (a) In order to change a file format, every program using the file had to be modified.
   (b) At the same time, the file had to be rebuilt in the new format using 'one-off' conversion programs.
2. The files were designed to suit the application currently being developed. When attempts were made to integrate different applications, the files were often found to be incompatible.
3. Because files were created to meet the requirements of each separate application, the same data, such as customers' names and addresses were often duplicated. In addition to the waste of space implied by this, amendment of such data was made more complex and the possibility existed of the various versions of the data being different.
4. The ability to create files of arbitrary complexity made it difficult to provide generalised querying and maintenance facilities. For instance, the conversion process mentioned above could not be readily automated.

The database concept arose as an attempt to solve these problems. The conceptual leap made was to consider the data, instead of the application programs, of prime importance in the design of systems. Typically, file-based systems concentrated on the functionality of the programs, with files being constructed to serve the persistent storage needs of these programs. The alternative approach, the database approach, is to look first at the design of the application's data and then write programs to process it. This is illustrated in Figure 1.1.

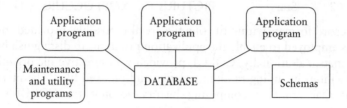

Figure 1.1   The database concept.

The diagram shows that the data is the centre of interest and is maintained independently of the application programs that access and update it. Note also that we can employ general maintenance and utility programs (the nature of these will be described later) which are concerned only with the database and are not associated with any particular application. To facilitate this, the database must contain, not just the data, but also descriptions of the data within the database. This takes the form of schemas that define the structure of records held in the database. A schema is roughly equivalent to the COBOL record definition but is stored separately from the application programs that use it.

In effect, we want the database to represent the application's data; i.e., the database models the application. The concept of modelling introduced here is very important in computing and recurs again elsewhere in this text.

Philosophical aside
It is too much to expect this process of modelling to be complete, i.e., fully representative of the system being modelled. Real systems are sufficiently complex that an exhaustive model is rarely possible. Attempts to capture every interrelationship, exception and dependency of the real system are likely to fail and are probably unnecessary. What we need to model is not the real system *per se* but the computer application that interacts with the real system.

Realisation of the features described above requires a software system that manages the data and the schema information and provides an interface to the user. This software is called a Database Management System (usually abbreviated to DBMS). The term 'database package' is often used; this is used to refer to a DBMS implementation offered by a particular vendor, such as Microsoft Access, Borland Paradox or Oracle.

1.1 How do older file systems and the database approach differ in terms of the relationship between the data and the application programs?

Definition of database

We can perhaps at this stage attempt a definition of 'database'; unfortunately, like many terms used in computer technology, there is considerable variation in interpretations placed on the word 'database'. These range from the least prescriptive, 'a collection of data' – to the over-specific: 'a large centralised shared data repository', which seems to exclude a database on a personal computer.

Rather than trying to capture the full import of the database concept in a single compact sentence, it is perhaps more productive to outline the essential features of a database and this can serve as a defining description. To be worthy of being called a database, a system must have two essential properties.

1. It holds data as an integrated system of records.
2. It contains self-describing information.

These properties are explained in more detail below.

Integrated organisation

We imply by this term that all the data pertaining to the application or applications being served by the database is held under the control of one software management system, so that any data relevant to an application transaction is directly available. Any interrelationships between the data can be exploited by application programs. For instance, an order-processing system might contain a set of customer records and a set of order records; integration implies that the order records that belong to each of the customers can be readily determined.

Self describing

The database must contain 'meta-data', i.e., descriptions of the data held in the database. These are referred to as schemas. In principle, a schema corresponds to a record description held in a COBOL or Pascal program: it defines the position, size and type of each component field of each database record type. Practical database systems vary in the techniques used to define schemas; some of these will be explored later in this text. The significance of the schema concept is that it enables the database to exist independently of any program. Programs can discover the format of the data from the schema and hence process the data appropriately. For instance, if the Motion Picture file illustrated earlier were transferred to a database, the schema would show that the first 30 bytes of the stored records were the name of the film, the next 20 were the Director's name, etc. The software can therefore 'unpack' the data according to the pattern supplied by the schema.

As we mentioned earlier, in order to implement these features in an application system, we require the assistance of appropriate software in the form of a DBMS. Application programs are not expected to probe unassisted into the schemas and the database data store; they must operate through the intermediary of the DBMS software. The DBMS presents a user interface to the users and to users' application programs and provides accessing facilities to the database data. We can now re-express the diagram of Figure 1.1 more precisely as in Figure 1.2.

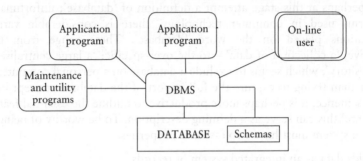

Figure 1.2   Conceptual view of database system.

Figure 1.2 is intended to illustrate the following important points

1.   Access to the database application data and to the schemas or 'meta-data' (i.e., the stored specification data that describes application data formats) is vested entirely in the DBMS. Direct access to the stored data, even in read-only mode, is not possible.

2.   The schemas are stored within the database itself so the database effectively contains its own description.

3.   Different modes of access to the DBMS are possible.
     (a) We can write a program in a high-level language that talks to the DBMS to provide the required services.
     (b) We can use interactive facilities provided by the user interface of the DBMS.

4.   Additional services can be provided by specially written maintenance and utility programs. These might include report generators, system documentors, etc.

The nature and facilities of DBMS packages is covered in more detail in Chapter 7.

?   **1.2** What are the two most significant properties of a database?

Earlier forms of database

The earliest databases were designed to meet the data processing demands of large organisations. In particular, large assembly type industries often required to manage data which had an inherently hierarchical structure. The classic example of this is in 'Bill of Materials' applications where the company's products are constructed from a number of component assemblies, each consisting of a number of sub-assemblies, which in turn contained further sub-assemblies and so on, eventually to the individual component parts. For instance, a car consists of 'top-level' assemblies such as the body, engine, wheels, etc.; the engine can be further broken down into the engine block, carburettor, air filter, etc. This process of subdivision continues until we reach the level of basic 'atomic' components such as nuts and bolts. If the structure of a car is represented in a database that can reflect this hierarchy, it can be used to yield useful information; one of its main tasks, for instance, is to generate a complete parts listing from which, given the individual costs of parts, the overall cost of the product can be produced.

The first type of database, therefore, was based on a hierarchical structure, the so-called 'Hierarchical Model Database', which could directly represent the structure of the data used in these applications. In fact, the data of many, if not most, applications have an inherent hierarchical structure; for instance, a sales order would consist of root information such as the customer involved, the date of the order, etc., but associated with this would be a set of data items representing the individual items of the order. We can visualise this as shown in Figure 1.3.

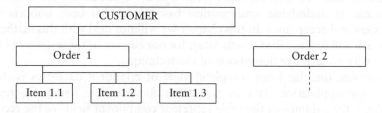

Figure 1.3   Hierarchical view of sales orders.

This technique meets the 'integrated' database criterion; it enables data pertaining to different entities (e.g., customers, orders, etc.) in the application domain to be united such that associations among these entities are reflected in the structure of the database: given a customer, it is possible to find data about that customer's orders.

It is perhaps less obvious how this type of database meets the 'self-describing' criterion. In fact, the hierarchical database uses a two-level architecture; the physical schema defines the physical structure of the full database, while the logical schema specifies different views of the data for the purposes of each application.

Following the hierarchical database architecture, the network model database was conceived. This is, in effect, a generalisation of the hierarchical database; in addition to the hierarchical association, connections indicating other relevant associations between entity types can be defined. This enables more semantics (i.e., interpretation of the meaning of the data) to be built into the database.

The main disadvantage of the hierarchical and network databases is that this structural information is embedded in the data; the connection between the Sales Order base data and the Order Detail is implemented by physical record address pointers within the data records, typically forming a chain of related data items. Consequently, retrieval of data from the database involved 'navigating'(by program) along these chains. It also meant that common requirements such as simple queries required the production of a special program.

In spite of these disadvantages, these databases were nevertheless a substantial improvement over conventional file processing for large applications. When the relational database was first proposed, it was not acknowledged by all experts in the database field to be a serious competitor to the established systems. One apparent drawback to the relational approach is that it is very processor intensive and it appeared initially that this would seriously damage its prospects. However, with the rapid growth in computer performance and the development of improved disk-accessing techniques, this disadvantage was soon overcome. The success of the relational database is such that it is the automatic choice for virtually all new development work.

? **1.3** What is the principal disadvantage of hierarchical and network databases?

The relational database

The invention of the relational database is largely attributed to Edward Codd who presented the idea in a seminal paper written in 1970 (Codd 1970). The relational database has an underlying mathematical basis which has been important in its development and acceptance. In this chapter we will not deal with this mathematical aspect which will be described briefly later; for our current purposes, we will content ourselves with an intuitive description of the technique.

The simplest (but far from complete) view of relational databases is that they represent the application data as two-dimensional tables. Using file-processing terminology, the columns of the table represent component fields of the record and each row details an instance of a record. An example is shown below.

Film table

Film title	Director	Year	Main star	Support star
Gone with the Wind	Victor Fleming	1939	Clark Gable	Vivien Leigh
Forbidden Planet	Fred Wilcox	1956	Leslie Neilson	Walter Pidgeon
Shane	George Stevens	1953	Alan Ladd	Van Heflin
Casablanca	Michael Curtiz	1942	Humphrey Bogart	Ingrid Bergman
Titanic	Cameron, James	1997	Leonardo DiCaprio	Kate Winslet
Schindler's List	Spielberg, Steven	1993	Liam Neeson	Ralph Fiennes

Note that as conventionally drawn, each column of the table has a heading, such as Film Title, that specifies the content of the column. The heading is part of the schema, the stored description of the data, and not part of the data itself. In physical terms, the headings and the data would be stored separately.

Film note

The sample data of Movie Titles shown above uses some classic films of recent times and older. As well as celebrating some of the great films, use of classic names prevents the data in this textbook from ageing quite so much!

Rather than the 'files', 'records' and 'fields' of file processing, relational database parlance introduces its own new terminology – in fact we have a choice! The most common terms in use are 'tables', 'rows' and 'columns' which are intuitively meaningful. More formal terms, which are derived from their mathematical basis are 'relation', 'tuples' and 'attributes'. These terms will be explained in Chapter 2.

The conceptually simple tabular arrangement can be readily understood by most people and this simplicity is an important factor in the popularity of relational databases. In particular, its ease of understanding for simple tasks has made the relational database amenable for use by end-users, in addition to professional system developers.

However, the apparent simplicity is perhaps misleading; the precise requirements for the construction of tables, the techniques employed in representing all the elements of a complex application and the practical problems of designing and using relational databases provide many interesting problems. Additionally, we need a supporting software environment to provide the necessary storage and access facilities and, importantly, to provide the aforementioned characteristics of integration and self description. Study of techniques that support these characteristics constitutes a major proportion of this text.

?

1.4 What is the most significant design feature of a relational database?

Tables in practice

Let us look in more detail at the way we construct a relational table. As we saw above, a table can be used to store data on some application topic, such as Films. However, in a more complex application environment, there may be more than one subject about which we need to hold data. For instance, in a video hire shop we would store data about videos available for hire and also data on the shop's customers who hire the tapes. In this context we refer to subjects such as films and customers as 'entity types' and the application environment (the video shop in this example) as the 'application domain'.

Terminological note

The term 'entity type' refers to the category of subject, e.g., 'customer'. We would refer to an actual instance of this entity class, such as Mr John Smith as an entity. In common with much terminology in computing, these terms are often used rather loosely; in particular, 'entity' is often used for both meanings described above, confusing the general with the specific. In most cases, this should not cause a problem in understanding what is intended; this note is provided to reassure those readers who may have already noticed the need for this distinction.

In general, each entity class is represented in a relational database by a separate table. In our video shop example above we would need two tables, the Film table (as shown above) and a Customer table.

Customer table

Customer number	Name	Address	Balance owing
5567	Jones	Cross Road	2.50
2913	Anderson	River Lane	0.00
4890	Murray	West Street	1.50
1622	Richards	Mill Lane	3.00

For each table there is a certain column (or possibly more than one column) that has a unique value and serves as an identifier for the row. This is called the 'primary key' of the table. For instance, the primary key of the Customer table above is the Customer number.

Notice, however, that the data in these two tables do not provide any information about which customer has hired which film and from the point of view of the video shop, it is clearly necessary that this information is represented somewhere. We say that there is a relationship between these two tables which we could call, 'Hired by'. This is the sort of inter-data information that was represented in the network and hierarchical databases as physical pointers in the data but such techniques are not used in relational databases. One tentative (and not very satisfactory) solution might be to add a column to the Customer table to indicate which film (if any) the customer currently has on hire.

Customer table version 2

Customer number	Name	Address	Balance owing	Film title
5567	Jones	Cross Road	2.50	Forbidden Planet
2913	Anderson	River Lane	0.00	Titanic
4890	Murray	West Street	1.50	Casablanca
1622	Richards	Mill Lane	3.00	Schindler's List

What is wrong with this arrangement? Well, since there is only one column to indicate the hired film, the tables as they stand can record only one hired film per customer; it is unlikely that either the video shop or the customer would be happy with that restriction!

An obvious solution to this difficulty, and one which might be adopted in a file-processing system, would be simply to add more Film title columns, say, allowing up to three films.

Customer table version 3

Customer number	Name	Address	Balance owing	Film title 1	Film title 2	Film title 3
5567	Jones	Cross Road	2.50	Forbidden Planet	—	—
2913	Anderson	River Lane	0.00	Titanic	Shane	Casablanca
4890	Murray	West Street	1.50	Casablanca	Titanic	—
1622	Richards	Mill Lane	3.00	Schindler's List	—	—

In principle, the number of titles could be extended indefinitely in this way. In effect, in programming terms, these columns constitute an array of titles.

While this appears to be an acceptable method of dealing with the situation, the use of an array of items like this is specifically disallowed in relational database tables. Certainly, there is nothing to prevent you from specifying a table as shown above with three title columns, but they would be treated as three distinct columns and not as a true array of values. Use of multiple columns in this way is not in the spirit of relational systems and would cause some difficulties and awkwardness in defining queries and in other operations. Note, in particular, that the relational system permits only a fixed number of columns in any one table.

How do we specify the films on loan to each customer? In effect, what we are trying to specify is a relationship between entities – customer and film. In relational systems, relationships are most often represented by another table; for instance, in our current example, we could use a Hired by table.

Hired by table

Customer number	Film title	Date hired
5567	Forbidden Planet	12/9/98
2913	Titanic	14/9/98
2913	Shane	10/9/98
2913	Casablanca	16/9/98
4890	Casablanca	25/9/98
4890	Titanic	20/9/98
1622	Shindler's List	29/9/98

Cautionary note

The description in this chapter is deliberately informal; the expression of relationships between tables is rather more involved than that implied by the above example. The later chapters of this book will, of course, deal with this topic in much more detail.

The video shop, therefore, can be represented by a set of three tables, one of which links the other two tables together. Note that the link values refer to the primary key columns of the tables (Customer number and Film title). We can illustrate this diagrammatically as shown in Figure 1.4, showing, for clarity, only one customer and one film.

Note that the database tables do not actually hold any representation of the links shown in Figure 1.4; linkage is achieved by having equal values in the linked fields of each table pair. If this point is not clear, look back at the customer tables shown earlier (page 10) and note how the Hired by table shows that Mr Murray (Customer Number 4890) has two films on hire given by the two rows:

4890	Casablanca	25/9/96
4890	Titanic	20/9/96

Customer table

Customer number	Name	Address	Balance owing
5567	Jones	Cross road	2.50

Hired by table

Customer number	Film title	Date hired
5567	Forbidden Planet	12/9/98

Film table

Film title	Director	Year	Main star	Support star
Forbidden Planet	Fred Wilcox	1956	Leslie Neilson	Walter Pidgeon

Figure 1.4   Video shop table system.

These correspondences are used by database software to extract required information from the respective tables. If, for example, we wanted to print out the titles and stars of all films currently on loan to Mr Murray, the database software would need to access all three tables.

We indicated earlier that one required feature of a database is integration; the above example shows how a set of separate tables are interrelated to provide a model of the application domain. This is one important aspect of data integration.

The other required database feature is self description; in terms of the above example, if we wanted to use the database software to access information from the video shop tables, the software would obtain the format of these tables from the table schemas stored (on disk) along with the tables.

What do we mean by 'specification of a table'? As we have seen, a table consists of a fixed number of columns, each of which represents some property or attribute of the entity being described and which is given a descriptive symbolic name, such as 'Film title'. Each column must hold values of one type only, i.e., each value in any one column must be all text or all numeric or all dates, etc. Specification of the table therefore consists of detailing the names and types of each of the columns of the table.

The actual method of doing this varies from system to system, although a standard database language exists called Structured Query Language (or SQL) which provides a system-independent way of specifying the schema information; SQL will be described in some detail in Chapter 13. In most database packages, the schema information is supplied to the system using a form- or table-based input routine.

In addition to the basic name and type information, database packages will also allow the specification of additional features such as validation criteria and formatting controls; these topics will be covered in Chapter 9.

? **1.5** Explain how separate tables in a relational database are linked together.

Further example of database design

In this section, we will derive an intuitive design for a simple application requiring the use of a database. The total data requirements of the application are first defined; this data is then intuitively organised into separate tables which avoid the duplication of information. In Chapter 5, a procedure called normalisation is described, which provides a formal basis for the process of table design and justifies the intuitive solution arrived at in this section.

Scenario
A small correspondence college offers courses in a range of topics. For each course, students complete a series of assignments which are sent to the college office; the assignments are gathered into batches, which are then dispatched by post to tutors for marking (i.e., complete batches of up to ten assignments are sent to tutors). Assume that there can be an indefinite number of tutors. The tutors mark the assignments, then return them, retaining them within the same batches. A system is required that enables tracking of the assignments, so that the college knows what assignments have been received, sent to tutors or marked. Also, the system should keep a running total of the number of assignments that have been marked by each tutor.

First we make a list of all of the data items that the system appears to require:

    Tutor Code
    Batch Number
    Student Code
    Course Code
    Assignment Number
    Total Assignments marked (per tutor)
    Date Batch sent to Tutor
    Date Batch returned from tutor

However, this list does not reflect the relative numbers of these items; for instance, one batch contains several assignments. We can illustrate the structure of the data using a diagrammatic approach; Figure 1.5 is intended to show the data representing one batch.

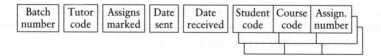

Figure 1.5   Table design – first attempt.

Note that Figure 1.5 shows one batch and that, for each batch, there is a single value for the first five items but that there can be several occurrences of the fields Student code – Course code – Assignment number. One possible way of storing this data is shown in Figure 1.6.

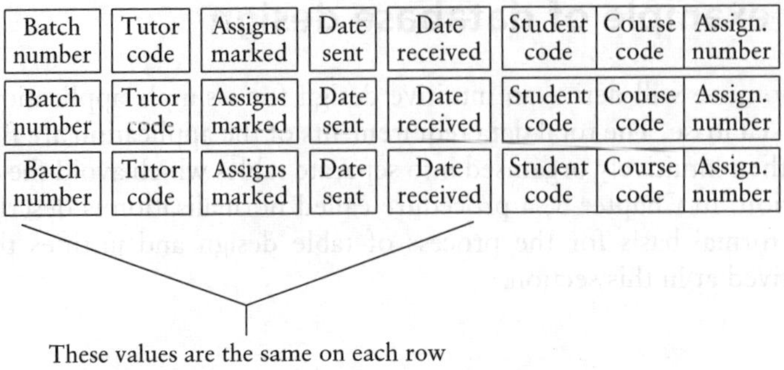

Batch number	Tutor code	Assigns marked	Date sent	Date received	Student code	Course code	Assign. number
Batch number	Tutor code	Assigns marked	Date sent	Date received	Student code	Course code	Assign. number
Batch number	Tutor code	Assigns marked	Date sent	Date received	Student code	Course code	Assign. number

These values are the same on each row

Figure 1.6   Possible data design.

At this stage it is possibly easier to visualise if we look at sample data in a tabular format.

Batch number	Tutor code	Assigns marked	Date sent	Date returned	Student code	Course code	Assign. number
23	JS	87	12/4/98	07/5/98	981230	PR007	3
23	JS	87	12/4/98	07/5/98	978001	AB003	1
23	JS	87	12/4/98	07/5/98	980239	PR009	7

This is clearly wasteful, since the first five fields are repeated in all the rows; there is considerable redundancy in this representation of the data. A better solution would be to separate the data into two tables; the batch information is stored in one row of the Batch table and the individual assignment data is stored in a separate Batch items table.

Batch table

Batch number	Tutor code	Assigns marked	Date sent	Date returned
23	JS	87	12/4/98	07/5/98

Batch items table

Student code	Course code	Assign. number
981230	PR007	3
978001	AB003	1
980239	PR009	7

A problem here though! There is now no indication in the Batch items table of which batch each row belongs to. To resolve this problem, we need an extra field in the Batch item table to specify the relevant batch number.

Batch items table

Batch number	Student code	Course code	Assign. number
23	981230	PR007	3
23	978001	AB003	1
23	980239	PR009	7

The data now looks quite efficient, with minimal duplication; the Batch number has to be repeated in each of the Batch item row pertaining to that batch, but otherwise no duplication occurs.

However, the limited scope of the above example data does not reveal another problem; if we were to show more of the Batch table data (more of the separate batches) the problem becomes more apparent.

Batch table

Batch number	Tutor code	Assigns marked	Date sent	Date returned
23	JS	87	12/4/98	07/5/98
24	GH	91	16/4/98	15/5/98
25	GH	91	19/4/98	24/5/98
26	CR	129	27/4/98	20/5/98
27	JS	87	05/5/98	25/5/98

The point to note is that every row pertaining to a particular tutor repeats the Assignments marked value for that tutor. For instance, every time GH appears in the Tutor code column, 91 will always appear in the Assigns marked column, because the Assigns marked value only depends on the Tutor. We can eliminate this duplication by, once more, factoring the table into two separate tables and removing the duplicate rows. For clarity, we show below the final version of all three tables; note that the Batch items table shows only one batch.

Batch table

Batch number	Tutor code	Date sent	Date returned
23	JS	12/4/98	07/5/98
24	GH	16/4/98	15/5/98
25	GH	19/4/98	24/5/98
26	CR	27/4/98	20/5/98
27	JS	05/5/98	25/5/98

Tutor table

Tutor code	Assigns marked
JS	87
GH	91
CR	129

Batch items table

Batch number	Student code	Course code	Assign. number
23	981230	PR007	3
23	978001	AB003	1
23	980239	PR009	7

As mentioned earlier, this process of factoring the data into a number of storage-efficient tables can be specified in a more formal procedure called 'normalisation', described in Chapter 5. It will also be shown that, in addition to reducing data duplication, normalised data also avoids certain difficulties or anomalies which can arise with un-normalised data.

Elements of a practical database system

The foregoing sections have shown how relational database tables can be used to represent the data in an application domain. For instance, the data in the Film, Customer and Hired by tables represents or models aspects of the video shop and its customers. Figure 1.4, for instance, represents the fact that customer Jones has the film Forbidden Planet on hire. When such information has been captured for a company's activities, it directly facilitates the development systems to drive the transactions of the company,

In order to facilitate the setting up, maintaining and accessing of a database, a DBMS would provide a range of facilities serving the needs of the application system developers and the endusers. A practical database package would typically provide facilities for

- the design and maintenance of database tables. This involves the schema specification previously described.
- the formulation of queries, i.e., requests for information from the database. This is a fundamental mechanism in database technology; having stored the data, it is important that retrieving it is made as convenient and efficient as possible. Hence, much of the study of databases is concerned with aspects of querying. A number of techniques are used for this including languages such as SQL and table-based methods such as Query-by-Example which is used in MS Access and other systems.
- the design of forms; a form is a full-screen display of data from a database table, normally showing a single row of the table at a time. This is a more convenient method for users to view, amend and enter data.
- the design of reports; a report is a printed presentation of data extracted from the database (typically a query) in a format convenient to the user.
- the construction of macros and programs; a macro is a method of automating a sequence of steps involved in implementing some database operation. A program written in a procedural language is sometimes required when the interactive facilities are inadequate for a special purpose.

The current database software market

In order to be able to utilise a database in an application, you will require a software package that provides the requisite facilities. Although some current systems still exist that use a network or hierarchical database, these are 'legacy' systems, running primarily on mainframe computers. The relational database has been so dramatically successful that it forms the heart of virtually all new development work in commercial information processing.

Some newer forms of database have recently appeared, notably object-oriented databases (e.g., ObjectStore, O2, Ontos, *et al.*), extended relational and object relational (e.g. UniSQL, Informix Datablades, Oracle 8). The object-oriented databases have achieved some success in specialised applications; typically, they perform best for applications with large volumes of relatively static data which require fast access. These newer forms of database are described in Chapter 12.

The current market can be roughly divided into large-scale and small-scale database packages; the former are designed to cater for more complex applications involving large numbers of users, tables and table rows. The principal vendors in this market are Oracle, Sybase, Informix, Ingres and IBM's DB2. Applications built with these packages would typically run on a mainframe or mini-computer running UNIX, or possibly a network of high-powered PCs. These database systems are intended primarily for systems development by professional system developers for use in commercial applications and are not used extensively by end-users.

End-user in this context refers to office staff, managers, and accountants who require access to the data held in the corporate database and also to personal users who design and build a database for their own applications. It is assumed that such users have a very good knowledge of their own field of work and, in particular, the application area of the intended database system, but they possibly lack the level of knowledge expected of a professional software engineer. The challenge in the design of database packages suitable for end users is to provide a system that makes it as easy as possible to develop a system while providing a reasonable level of assurance that the system will perform as intended.

Small-scale database packages are those running on personal computers. While many of these are now high-powered systems, suitable for the development of substantial multi-user applications, they have also been designed with the end user in mind. The particular features of such systems are

- use of a graphical user interface which facilitates the design of tables, forms and reports
- extensive interactive capability which minimises need for programming.

There are a large number of PC database packages currently available, but the most common are Microsoft Access, Borland Paradox, dBase IV for Windows and Lotus Approach. Examples used in this text are drawn from Microsoft Access.

Summary

The purpose of this chapter has been simply to provide a gentle intuitive introduction to the central concepts of relational databases; the rest of the book is spent delving deeper into these concepts. The most significant points introduced in this chapter are:

1. A database is an integrated and self-describing system of data storage.
2. The predominant form of database today is the relational database.
3. The relational database uses two-dimensional tables to represent application entities such as Customers, Orders, Parts, etc., and to represent relationships (i.e., associations) between entities.

4. The columns of a relational table represent properties or attributes of the entity class described by the table. For instance, in a Customer table, likely columns would be Name, Address, Credit limit, etc.

5. The rows of a relational table represent instances of the entity class; in a Customer table, each row represents one customer.

Answers to in-text questions

1.1 In file systems the application programs were designed first and the files organised to suit their purpose. In a database, the data is viewed as existing independently of the programs and forms the central pillar of applications built on the data.

1.2 The properties are self describing and integrated organisation.

1.3 In these databases, structural information (links between related records) are 'mixed up' with the data. This makes modification of the structure of the database rather complex.

1.4 Data is organised into two-dimensional tables where the columns represent attributes or properties of the entity being represented and each row represents one instance of the entity.

1.5 The linking is done by having a column value in one table that refers to a column value in another table.

REVIEW QUESTIONS
Answers in Appendix C.

1 Outline the basic structure of a relational database table.

2 Explain the meaning of the rows and columns of a relational database table.

3 What is meant by the term 'schema'?

4 List the main elements of a practical database management system.

2

The relational data model

Overview

In the first chapter, the basic notion of a relational database was introduced via informal examples. With these elementary ideas in place, the more formal principles underlying the relational model can now be readily examined. To put the idea of the relational model in context, we begin this chapter with a brief introduction to the general principles of data modelling; this also includes an overview of other data models described in this text. We then begin our description of the relational model by starting at its roots in the mathematical theory of sets. This leads us into the details of the principles and properties of relations and the techniques used to construct a database from a set of relations.

Data modelling

In general usage, a model of some 'real' system is another representation that shares certain relevant features with the real system. A model can be a set of equations, an actual physical scale model, a computer program, etc. Models are useful in that the characteristics of the real system can be analysed by studying the nature and behaviour of the model. The rationale for this approach will depend on the system being modelled; for instance, in order to examine the behaviour of a new ship design, a scale model is economically more feasible than building an actual ship. A computer model of a queuing system in a post office is more useful when investigating different queuing disciplines and number of service points than actually experimenting with a real post office.

In the study of databases, our interest is in data modelling. The role of data modelling is to provide techniques that allow us to represent, by graphical and other formal methods, the nature of data in real-world computer applications. The principal justification for the use of data modelling is to provide a clearer understanding of the underlying nature of information and the processing of information in this area. It provides analysts and designers with a means of characterising and describing the structure, relationships and transformations of information. It is expected that the use of data models will provide a better understanding of the application area being studied and hence will enable the design of better database systems.

There are a number of data models, some of which are covered in this text over a number of chapters. In an earlier chapter, the hierarchical and network models were mentioned briefly but will not be discussed further. The data models that are of interest to us are

- the relational model
- the entity relationship model
- the object-oriented model.

The relational model (RM) was first introduced by Codd in 1970 (Codd 1970) and forms the basis of most current database management systems. Its essential simplicity has been effective in fuelling its rapid rise in popularity; this has been tempered only by the fact that practical relational database systems can require considerable computer processing power.

The entity relationship (ER) model was devised by Chen in 1976 (Chen 1976). It is a diagrammatic technique that provides a generalised approach to the representation of data and which is particularly suitable and helpful in the design of relational database systems.

The object-oriented (OO) model has become more prominent in recent years, particularly its application to data management, in the form of the object-oriented database. The latter provides a competitor to the relational database and appears to have some advantages for certain applications.

In addition to these specific models, there are a number of general terms (pertaining to the representation and interpretation of data) in common use that require to be explained in the context of these models. In this and the next three chapters we cover the topics of the relational model and the entity relationship model. The object-oriented model, being less directly applicable to the relational database, is outlined in a later chapter.

General properties of data models

The first point to be made here is that the term 'data model' is something of a misnomer. Such models are not concerned with just the data but also the processing of the data and hence all models provide not only a conceptual view of the representation of data and data structures but also define allowable operations on these. For instance, the relational model not only represents data as a set of two-dimensional tables but also defines operations such as 'restrict', 'project' and 'join' on these tables.

The real-world system being modelled is usually referred to as an 'enterprise'. Elements within the enterprise, such as human workers, goods, transactions, etc., are modelled by concepts such as entities or objects.

One difficulty in data modelling is the difference between the human view of an information system and the way it has to be implemented within a computer system. To resolve the difficulties caused by this difference, we can view the architecture of a database system as a series of levels, that provide varying degrees of abstraction of the system.

To address the problem mentioned above, a standard architecture called the

ANSI/SPARC architecture has been widely adopted. The ANSI/SPARC architecture is divided into three levels, known as the internal, conceptual and external levels, as follows:

External level   This refers to the users' logical view of the enterprise; i.e., it refers to how the user perceives the data. A user view will consist of entities such as invoices, stock, employees, accounts, etc.

Conceptual level   The conceptual level provides a formal representation of the real data and procedures. It is essentially a 'mapping' between the internal and external views and describes the semantics of entities, relationships, constraints, etc.

Internal level   Refers to the physical database, i.e., how and where the data is stored and how it can be accessed. Terminology encountered in this area includes disk sectors and clusters, indexing, access time, etc.

On this basis, the relational model can be seen as a conceptual model. It expresses the data of the 'real' application in terms of a set of tables that define entities and relationships. However, it does not define how the tables are to be stored on disk nor how specific data is to be accessed. Earlier data models tended to smudge the distinction between these levels; for instance, the hierarchical model required explicit record pointers embedded in the data records to specify connections such as Order– OrderItem links. Thus the logical notion of data linking was implemented by actual physical links. In effect, the conceptual and internal layers are intertwined. Such an arrangement is deemed to be undesirable, since it ties the levels together too intimately, making modification and evolution of the system at any of the levels more difficult. This conflicts with the critical notion of data independence, i.e., it is deemed important to be able to effect changes at some level without being concerned with the ramifications of the change at some other level. For instance, in a relational system, we can alter the table structure (e.g., add a new column, change the size of a data item etc.) without having to attend directly to the physical reorganisation of the table.

Modelling concepts

Before we can proceed to work with a data model, we have to develop a set of semantic concepts to help us to describe 'the real world' and its relationship with the database. One must be warned that this area of study is fraught with difficulties, dealing as it does with philosophical notions that do not have precise definitions. For this reason, it is important to appreciate the limitations of the modelling process. We are not trying to produce a comprehensive representation of the real world; this would be too problematic and is not in any case necessary. In practice, we must be content to model those aspects of the application domain that are relevant to the database design.

A number of these modelling concepts are described below; in Chapter 4 some more advanced concepts are introduced.

Application domain
The application domain of an information system is the real-world environment in which the information system is to be applied. Common examples are university student management, company stock control, hotel room reservation, etc. An alternative term for this is 'universe of discourse'.

Entities
When we perceive the world, we see that it contains a number of recognisably separate 'things', such as people, vehicles, products, offices, etc. We can also appreciate the existence of less tangible notions such a sales order or hotel booking. In data modelling, we refer to these as 'entities'. A database application system will be concerned with a number of such entities, within the application domain. In effect, the database will contain a representation of each relevant entity. Additionally, relationships between entities would also be represented in some way within the database.

A problem presented by the entity concept is identifying what should be treated as an entity and what would be better viewed as a property of an entity. In many cases, there is no single 'correct' interpretation and more than one valid model of a situation may be possible. Generally though, one solution may stand out as being more natural and convenient than the others.

We really ought to distinguish between an entity and an entity type; the latter denotes a generic classification while the former refers to an instance of that type. Within a university, for instance, students could be identified as an entity type while Joe Bloggs on the BSc course for Chemistry is an instance of that entity type. In practice, these terms are not strictly applied and entity types such as student and lecturer are often referred to as entities.

Attributes
An attribute of an entity is some property or characteristic that is relevant to the application. An entity is essentially defined by a set of attributes. For instance, an Employee has attributes name, address, salary, department, etc.

Domain and type
The domain of an attribute is the range of possible values that the attribute can have. Some domains are very large (e.g., the domain of people's names) while others can be more precisely delineated (e.g., the range of possible salary values in a company).

Relationship
A relationship is an association or interaction between two (or more) entities. For instance, the relationship 'employs' exists between entities 'company' and 'employee', the relationship 'teaches' exists between 'teacher' and 'pupil'.

? | **2.1** Distinguish between: (a) an entity and the entity type (b) the application domain and the domain of an attribute.

The relational model

Sets and relations

Basic set principles

The concepts introduced in this section are perhaps not essential to an understanding of the relational model but it is helpful to be able to appreciate that the model has a strong theoretical underpinning. The relational model is based on the mathematical theory of 'sets'. A set can be viewed as a collection of zero or more items of similar type. For instance, a set of numbers could be {32, 5, 99, 1066}; another set of numbers could be {1}. A set of people could be {Thomas, Frank, Anne, Joe}. A subset is part of a full set. For instance {Frank, Joe} is a subset of the previous set. Set theory is not concerned with the nature of the contained items, only about the common properties of such sets and the ways in which sets can be processed mathematically. For instance, we can define operations on sets such as 'union' that combines two sets into one: the union of the sets {32, 5, 99, 1066} and {1} is the set {32, 5, 99 1066, 1}.

The three most important characteristics of sets for our purposes are

1. All members of the set are of the same type.
2. Only one instance of any item is held in a set. For instance, a set {Bob, Joe, Bob} is not a proper set and would be expressed correctly as {Bob, Joe}.
3. The sequence of items in the set is not significant. Therefore, the sets {Bob, Joe} and {Joe, Bob} are the same set.

These simple set principles can be used to develop the concept of a relation as described in the next section.

Relations

Given two sets X and Y, we can take any element from x from X and y from Y to form an 'ordered pair' (x, y). The set of all ordered pairs is called the 'product set' and is denoted by X.Y.

e.g.,   X = {1, 2}   Y = {A, B, C}
then   X.Y = {1A, 1B, 1C, 2A, 2B, 2C}

A subset of X.Y is called a 'relation' and can be denoted R(X, Y). A relation can be considered as a mapping from one set to another and given a functional name.

e.g.,   X = {Jones, Smith, Brown}
        Y = {Accounts, Sales, Despatch, Personnel}

and the relation R(X, Y) is to be interpreted as 'works in', so that the ordered pair (Jones, Sales) represents the fact 'Jones works in Sales'.

The set X could be mapped into a number of other sets, in addition to Y; for instance,

        Y1 = {Clerk, Accountant, Manager, Salesman}
        Y2 = {5, 10, 15, 20, 25}

to give ordered pairs like (Jones, Salesman) and (Jones, 15). These can be combined into a single expression such as

(Jones, Sales, Salesman, 15).

Such an expression is called an n-tuple (where n is the number of sets involved; e.g., the above example is a 4-tuple) or just tuple. Each of the elements of the tuple is called an attribute. Each attribute has a name identifying its meaning in the application area of the data. For the example above, we might use the attribute names:

Employee name, Department, Occupation, Years of service

A relation can now be viewed as a set of tuples:

Employee name	Department	Occupation	Years of service
Jones	Sales	Salesman	15
Smith	Accounts	Clerk	5
Brown	Accounts	Accountant	10

Hence, the data of an application can be modelled as a two-dimensional table; in effect, each relation/table defines and/or describes some area of the application and provides a mapping from some identifying value (in our example, the Employee name) to other descriptive or qualifying attributes (Department etc.). The identifying value is called the 'ruling part' while the rest of the attributes are called the 'dependent part'.

If we were to store data in this form, it is convenient to utilise the following correspondences between the relation concept and more conventional file processing notions:

Relation is synonymous with table or file
Tuple is synonymous with row or record
Attribute is synonymous with column or field.
Ruling part is synonymous with primary key (described in next section)

For example, while most file processing uses a record as a 'unit' of input/output, a relational system reads and writes one row at a time. Each row of a relation describes one entity within the application area. Unfortunately, all of the above terminology is found in current usage and not always within consistent groupings. In general, the terms 'relation' and 'table' tend to be used interchangeably. The term 'attribute' is used in preference to 'column' when talking about a property of an entity, while 'column' is used when referring to a specific column of a table. The term 'row' is definitely preferable to the alternatives.

Notice that each of the columns of a table is drawn from a set of similar values such as

$$Y1 = \{Clerk, Accountant, Manager, Salesman\}$$
$$Y2 = \{5, 10, 15, 20, 25\}$$

so that all items in any one column are all of the same data type (i.e., numeric, text, date, etc.). The range of available data types is dictated by the particular database software used.

You will recall that earlier in this chapter the concept of a domain was introduced. We can repeat the definition in terms of our current example: the domain of an attribute is the set of all possible values of that attribute. In the above example, the domains of Y1, Y2, etc., were assumed to be the enumerated list of values shown. In general, the domain of a column is prescribed by the column's data type; a column defined as an integer type is limited to values in the range (for a 16-bit representation) of –32,768 to +32,767. However, in a practical system, the actual domain of the data will often be more restricted. For instance, an attribute such as 'years of service' is notionally an integer value having the aforementioned domain, whereas a more realistic range of values would be, say, zero to 50 years. In current database packages, it is not possible to fine-tune a column's domain by defining a new data type, such as age; i.e., user-defined types are not available. (Note that this is a technique used in 'extended relational' systems which are now appearing in the market. This topic is covered in more detail in Chapter 12.)

However, most database packages allow the simulation of a narrower domain by means of column constraints which can be specified within a table definition. In effect, when a table structure is defined, the user can specify the range of admissible values that can be entered in the table for each column; for instance, a years of service column might be given a constraint of 'between 0 and 50'. The purpose of such constraints is to prevent invalid data being entered into the table; this topic is covered in much more detail in Chapter 9, which deals with security and integrity.

Properties of a relation

Based on the foregoing principles, a relation can be seen to have the following properties:

1. Columns in the relation are all single values, i.e., arrays of values or other compound structures are not allowable.
2. Entries in any column are all of the same data type, e.g., integer, real number, character, data, etc.
3. No two rows of the relation are identical.
4. The order of the rows in the table is immaterial.
5. The order of the columns in the table is immaterial.
6. Each table contains an identifying column or columns (the ruling part or primary key).

Some comments on the above items are worth making.

Property 3 This property is effectively saying it is meaningless to have two identical rows – both rows identify the same real entity.

Property 4 It is likely, in a particular application, that you might want to 'see' the data in a certain sequence, for instance, you might want to list a Customer table in order of surname. However, such ordering of the data is not achieved by reorganising the table rows into the required sequence. Instead, the data is extracted from the (unsorted) table in that sequence. Normally, the data in a database table is simply held in the order of physical writing to the table.

Property 5   Application programs access the table columns by name independently of the position or sequence of the columns.

Property 6   The primary key concept is covered in more detail shortly.

Practical database systems based on relational principles, by and large, conform to these criteria. In addition to these essential properties, there are a number of other issues contributing to relational theory which need our attention. Some of these are described in the remainder of this chapter, while the rest are covered in Chapter 5.

?   **2.2** The above properties of a relation indicate that the sequences of the rows and of the columns are immaterial. How can a particular row and column be located?

Other relational concepts and terminology

Primary key

In an earlier section, we introduced the idea of the ruling part and the dependent part of a table row. The ruling part, usually called the primary key, plays a very important role in relational database theory and practice. Note that the primary keys of each table are underlined.

The primary key of a table is a column (or a combination of two or more columns) that serves to identify the individual rows of the table. For instance, in the Customer table described in Chapter 1, the primary key is the Customer number; since this number has a unique value for each customer it can be used within the database to reference a specific customer. We can see from this definition that the non-key columns are dependent on the primary key. This leads to an important concept called functional dependency which is described in more detail later in this chapter.

Customer table

Customer number	Name	Address	Balance owing
5567	Jones	Cross Road	2.50
2913	Anderson	River Lane	0.00
4890	Murray	West Street	1.50
1622	Richards	Mill Lane	3.00

            Primary key   Dependent part

The adoption of a set of unique codes such as the Customer number in the above table is often used to simplify the definition of a primary key. Such codes are of course well established in general use, independent of their application in relational databases and for much the same reason – to guarantee proper identification of customers, products, orders, etc. Where there is no natural or existing code available for a relation, it is common practice simply to assign a sequential number to successive rows to serve as the key. Databases often provide a facility to generate these numbers automatically, for instance, the Autonumber 'data type' in Microsoft Access.

Composite primary key

Note that the primary key may consist of more than one column; the key value may effectively be a concatenation of two or more columns. The reasons for this occurring will be more evident later, but a simple example may clarify the nature of this usage. Suppose we have a table holding data on which engineers have been assigned to which projects and the date of the assignment. An extract of this table may appear as shown below:

Assignment table

Project number	Engineer name	Assignment date
A2367	Connelly	31-Nov-96
G0814	Chapman	22-Dec-96
G0814	McDonald	12-Jun-96
P9890	Connelly	01-Feb-96
V0122	McDonald	23-Apr-96
V0122	Stewart	15-Apr-96

This table represents assignment 'events'; each row records one instance of such events and hence has a unique identity. Neither Project number nor Engineer name can suffice as a primary key value on its own because the values in each column are not unique. For example, Project V0122 occurs twice and engineer Connelly occurs twice. The combination of Project number and Engineer name does produce a unique value which is suitable as a primary key.

It may be necessary to use more than two columns; to extend the previous example, let us assume that the name is not sufficient to identify the engineer, due to the possibility of duplicate names. We could of course adopt an 'engineer code' but if we wanted to persist with the name then some other distinguishing attribute must be found, say, a first name. If we assume that there are two McDonalds, namely Angus and Hamish, then our table would now appear as shown in the table below.

Assignment table

Project number	Engineer surname	Engineer firstname	Assignment date
A2367	Connelly	James	31-Nov-96
G0814	Chapman	David	22-Dec-96
G0814	McDonald	Angus	12-Jun-96
P9890	Connelly	James	01-Feb-96
V0122	McDonald	Hamish	23-Apr-96
V0122	Stewart	Alan	15-Apr-96

We now have a three column primary key. This example is somewhat contrived, but multiple column primary keys can occur quite naturally in practice. Examples of this will be encountered later in this text.

Functional dependency

The concept of functional dependence was mentioned briefly above in the description of primary keys. We can define functional dependence formally as follows: If we say that one column B of a table is functionally dependent on another column A (or group of columns) it means that every value of A uniquely determines the value of B. This is often written using the notation $A \rightarrow B$.

This concept is important in relational data theory and it is worth some thought to ensure that it is understood. If $A \rightarrow B$, then it means that every time a particular value appears in the A column, then another particular value must appear in the B column. If, in one row, the A column value is 999 and the B column value is POLICE, then if another row has A = 999, column B must be POLICE.

To consider another example; a car hire company. A representative sample of data from their rental charges table is shown in the table below. The charges are based on a daily rate assigned to each model and an additional mileage rate.

<u>Make</u>	<u>Model</u>	<u>Engine size</u>	Daily rental £	Mileage charge p.
Ford	Escort	1400	15	10
Ford	Mondeo	1600	20	15
Nissan	Almera	1400	16	10
Renault	Megane	1400	16	10
Vauxhall	Vectra	1600	22	15
Vauxhall	Vectra	2000	25	15

Note that for any value of engine size, say 1400, the mileage charge is always the same (in this case 10p). This is because the mileage charge is functionally dependent on the engine size. We would write this as:

Engine size $\rightarrow$ Mileage charge

? **2.3** Note that the mileage charge for 2000 cc engines is the same as that for 1600. Does this confirm or disprove the above functional dependence?

Functional dependency must be determined from knowledge of the application domain; it is important to understand that it is a feature of the real world domain of the database application and is not an observation of chance coincidence of column values. It follows from this that you cannot determine that a dependency exists simply by inspection of the table data – which is why we said in the above example that the table was a representative sample of data. In practice, such dependencies are often derived from 'business rules' of the application domain; in the car rental example, the company has decided that such a rule will apply.

Foreign keys

As indicated above, the primary key is used to refer to a specific row in a table. Primary key values can be included in a column of another table which is related in some way to the first table. Columns containing such values are called foreign keys. An example will clarify this concept.

In Chapter 1 we presented an example of a table system which included the following pair of tables:

Batch table

Batch number	Tutor code	Date sent	Date returned
23	JS	12/4/93	07/5/93
24	GH	16/4/93	15/5/93
25	GH	19/4/93	24/5/93
26	CR	27/4/93	20/5/93
27	JS	05/5/93	25/5/93

Tutor table

Tutor code	Assigns marked
JS	87
GH	91
CR	129

The Tutor code column of the Batch table contains values that refer to the Tutor table primary key values, and hence is a foreign key within the Batch table.

To put this definition more succinctly, a foreign key is a column in one table that refers to the primary key of another table. This is the basic linking mechanism that allows a set of tables to form an integrated database. Note that relational databases do not use any form of stored 'pointers' between foreign and primary keys; the linking is done purely on a match of values.

Candidate keys

In some tables, it is possible to find that more than one column, or combination of columns, could serve as a primary key. Such alternative primary keys are called candidate keys. One of the possible candidate keys is chosen to be the primary key. In most cases this choice is obvious; for example, a code (such as a customer number) is often specifically created to identify the instances within the table. Such codes will be guaranteed to be unique, will generally be compact and may be convenient for use outwith the database system, for example, a product sales catalogue would typically display the same codes as used within the database.

Within the basic data, however, it is often possible to identify other potential candidate keys. For example we may have a Lecturer table (from a university database) with the structure as shown in the table below:

Lecturer ID	Name	Department	Room no	Subject leader
123	Harrison	Finance	A029	Taxation
145	Cooper	Mathematics	M074	Algebra

The 'obvious' primary key is the Lecturer ID whose role in life is solely to act as a unique identifier for lecturing staff. However, depending on the particular conditions prevailing in the university, several other candidate keys are theoretically possible.

- The name is a possibility if we are sure that no duplicate names will occur.
- It may be that there is only one lecturer per room. In this case, the room number will be unique in the table.
- The Subject leader is (presumably) unique, at least per department (if not in the whole university) so Department–Subject leader is a candidate key.

On grounds of effectiveness and economy, none of these options is very appealing and would not be used in practice. The candidate key concept is not very significant in practical systems but is a factor in one of the higher normalisation forms.

Nulls

It often happens when inserting data into a database table that some of the attribute values cannot be entered for a variety of reasons. Possible reasons are that

- the data is not available, e.g., a new employee has failed to provide his date of birth. The rest of the employee information has to be added to enable the payroll program to proceed.
- the data is not applicable to this entity, e.g., the attribute is salesman's rate of commission but this salesman doesn't earn commission.

To provide a standard means of filling in columns of a table that are empty, the null concept was devised. Although sometimes referred to as a 'null value', a null is not a value but an indicator held in the column to specify that the attribute does not have a value! One merit of the null concept is that, since it is not a value, a null is type-less; hence, it can be used with a date, a text value, a number or any other data type.

The use of nulls in relational systems is very controversial; there is a strong school of thought that believes that its use is, at best confusing and awkward, and at worst, definitely dangerous in terms of accuracy in queries. While the idea may appear fairly innocent, it has far-reaching consequences that affect many aspects of using relational databases. Particularly in the area of database queries, one has frequently to take special account of the likely effect of null attributes within the query parameters.

What is the alternative to null? A technique used by some designers is to adopt a system of default values; within an attribute column, say a salesman's commission rate, values (not within the normal domain of values for the column) are adopted to represent 'missing' and 'inapplicable'. One problem here is that the default values must conform to the data type of the column, so that a 'missing' date would be some artificial date, while a 'missing' numerical amount must be a numeric value.

There are pros and cons for both the null and anti-null approaches but the inescapable fact is that for current database systems the null mechanism is well entrenched and cannot be completely avoided even if you want to. It figures significantly, for example, in the SQL query language. See the section dealing with joins in Chapter 13.

?   **2.4** How are separate tables in a relational database notionally connected together?

Entity integrity

It is a defining principle of relational tables that each row of a table uniquely represents one entity in the application domain; one row in the Customer table represents one Customer. It is also necessary that no two rows of the table are the same. If this were allowed it would mean that the same application domain entity was represented by two rows of the table. Preservation of this principle is referred to as entity integrity. In general, the use of unique primary key values guarantees that this principle is complied with. Note, however, that the use of any nulls within the primary key value would invalidate the principle; a null expresses some uncertainty about a value and hence is inappropriate for a key that serves as a unique defining label. Consequently, the definition of entity integrity is usually expressed as:

> 'Entity Integrity is the principle that no part of a primary key can be null.'

As an aside, it is interesting to note that the principle of 'one row – one entity' is routinely broken in relational database applications! The philosophical notion that real-world entities require one-to-one representation within a database breaks down when the individual entities being dealt with are sufficiently trivial. So, for example, if we had a database representing the stock within a hardware store, it is unlikely that we would record each nut and bolt individually. Instead, we would have one row per nut and bolt type and an associated 'quantity in stock' value. Thus, the row represents an entity type rather than the individual entities. This technique would be employed until the entities became worthy of separate identification on the grounds of value or other reason.

It is also perhaps worth noting that the uniqueness of rows in a relation applies specifically to 'base relations', i.e., the relations that constitute the designed database and not to relations created as intermediate answers within a query which can often contain duplicate values.

Referential integrity

Referential integrity is concerned with the linkages between tables defined by the foreign and primary key fields. As we indicated above, a foreign key is an attribute in one table that refers to the primary key in another table. For a set of database tables, every foreign key value in all tables must be matched by a row in some other table. A database table for which this is true is said to conform to referential integrity, otherwise it does not.

A typical situation is shown below; the primary key of each of the tables is underlined.

Course table

CourseCode	CourseTitle	CourseDept
A123	Maths	Mathematics
B654	Economics	Business
C299	Computing	Comp Science

Student table

MatricNum	StudentName	CourseCode
990134	Jones	B654
992011	Smith	333
992888	Brown	A123

The Course table defines courses offered by a college; the Student table holds information on each student. In the Student table, the column CourseCode is a foreign key referring to the primary key of the Course table.

In the first row of the Student table, the CourseCode value B654 is valid because it refers to an existing row in the Customer table (economics course). However, the CourseCode in the second row (D333) breaks referential integrity because there is no corresponding row in the Customer table. In application terms, it implies that the student Smith is on a non-existent course.

Note that the C299 CourseCode in the Student table is not matched with any value in the Student table; this is OK, however, since CourseCode is not a foreign key in the Course table. It simply implies that the Computing course has currently no enrolled students.

?   **2.5** Does the third row in the Student table comply with referential integrity?

A database that does not exhibit referential integrity is in an anomalous and impractical condition and will be likely to produce serious run-time failures. Hence, it is important that referential integrity be maintained throughout the database and most database systems now provide facilities to assist in complying with this. For instance, the current SQL standard provides clauses that define referential relationships, enabling the database software to check for consistency. In current interactive environments such as Microsoft Access, referential integrity can be enforced by defining to the system the relationships that exist between member tables of a database using a graphical interface. The screen shot shown in Figure 2.1 illustrates how the diagram shows the link between the two tables.

The example shows the referential link between the two tables using the CourseCode. The effect of establishing this link is that the database software will not permit any modification to the database that breaches this referential integrity requirement. For instance, we cannot delete a row of the Courses table if some row or rows of the Student table refer to it. This corresponds to the application domain restriction that you cannot cancel a course while there are still students on it.

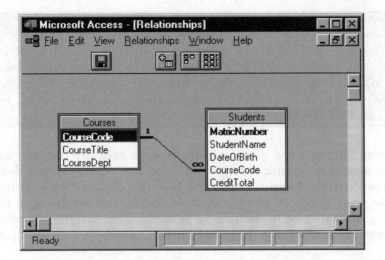

Figure 2.1   Referential relationships screen.

Relational algebra

Relational databases are based on the mathematical notion of a relation, i.e., a set of mappings from independent values (keys) to dependent values. The mathematical theory defines a number of algebraic operations on relations that produce new relations from one or more originals. The fact that the algebra operates on a relation or relations to produce a new relation (i.e., the operations exhibit 'closure') is important because it means that a succession of operations can be applied to 'output' relations in order to implement a compound operation.

The operations defined are as follows:

RESTRICT   form new relation from selected rows of input relation.

PROJECT   form new relation from selected columns of input relation.

JOIN   form new relation by 'joining' rows of two or more input relations.

UNION   form new relation by combining rows from both input tables.

PRODUCT   form new relation by joining every row in one table with every row of a second; i.e. the Cartesian product of the relation members.

DIFFERENCE   the difference of two relations is a third relation containing rows that occur in the first relation but not in the second. Also known as MINUS or COMPLEMENT.

INTERSECTION   the intersection of two relations is a third relation containing rows that appear in both the first and second relations.

> **Note:**
>
> The RESTRICT operator is often (and probably better) known as SELECT; however, SELECT is used extensively as a command in the SQL query language but with a much broader meaning than that used in the relational algebra. To avoid confusion, the operator will be called 'RESTRICT'.

For Union, Difference and Intersection the relations must have the same structure, i.e., they must have the same number of attributes drawn from the same domains.

Of the above, the Restrict, Project and Join operations are the most significant from the point of view of practical database working and are described first. The following tables are used to illustrate the principles. Note that the expressions used in the examples are not in any recognised standard format – they are descriptive only.

Orders

OrderNo	CustNo	OrdDate	Carrier
AJ123	5567	12/12/93	DHL
GK300	3488	13/12/93	TNT
NN125	5567	10/12/93	SEC

OrderItems

OrderNo	ItemCode	Quantity	Size
AJ123	A/23	100	L
AJ123	F/12	250	M
AJ123	M/66	30	M
GK300	B/10	500	S
GK300	F/12	300	L
NN125	M/66	50	M

Principal operators

RESTRICT

RESTRICT Orders WHERE CustNo='5567' would give the relation:

OrderNo	CustNo	OrdDate	Carrier
AJ123	5567	12/12/93	DHL
NN125	5567	10/12/93	SEC

PROJECT

PROJECT Columns OrderNo, OrdDate FROM Orders would give the relation:

OrderNo	OrdDate
AJ123	12/12/93
GK300	13/12/93
NN125	10/12/93

JOIN

JOIN Tables Orders, OrderItems

   Matching Columns Orders.OrderNo with OrderItems.OrderNo

would give:

OrderNo	CustNo	OrdDate	Carrier	ItemCode	Quantity	Size
AJ123	5567	12/12/93	DHL	A/23	100	L
AJ123	5567	12/12/93	DHL	F/12	250	M
AJ123	5567	12/12/93	DHL	M/66	30	M
GK300	3488	13/12/93	TNT	B/10	500	S
GK300	3488	13/12/93	TNT	F/12	300	L
NN125	5567	10/12/93	SEC	M/66	50	M

Note: This is technically known as a natural join. There are other forms of join; in particular, there is an equi-join which is the same as the natural join but with the 'matching' columns left in. In the above example, this would give a relation with two OrderNo columns.

The join can be considered as a combination of a product (i.e., a 'perm' of all rows in one table with all rows in the other table) with a restriction (extracting rows with equal values in the 'join' columns) and, for a natural join, a projection eliminating the duplicate matching column. Joining of tables in this way is a fundamental part of relational database working; in effect, it is a 'drawing together' of data held in a number of separate entity and relationship tables. There are other variations on the theme of joining that will be described in Chapter 13.

As noted earlier, all these operations yield another relation so that, for example, a Restriction could be applied to the result of the Join. Notionally, this involves using compound statements containing two or more of the above operations.

?   **2.6** What is the essential nature of the relational algebra?

Other relational operators

From a practical point of view, the Restrict, Project and Join operations are by far the most significant. In this section we examine the other operators, namely, Union, Difference, Intersection and Product which are used less frequently.

The operators Union, Difference and Intersection can be applied only to tables of identical structure. For the purposes of describing these, let us suppose that two departments within a university keep their own separate database table of students called STUDENT1 and STUDENT2, (with, fortunately, identical structure).

Student1

Matric no	Name	Address
951234	Smith	Glasgow
952356	Jones	Aberdeen
953388	Brown	Dundee
954001	Adams	Edinburgh

Student2

Matric no	Name	Address
952991	Gray	Paisley
953777	White	Glasgow
953388	Brown	Dundee

Note that Mr Brown has managed to get himself onto both tables.

UNION

A Union forms a new relation by combining rows from both input tables, removing any duplicate rows. Hence, STUDENT1 UNION STUDENT2 would yield

Matric no	Name	Address
951234	Smith	Glasgow
952356	Jones	Aberdeen
953388	Brown	Dundee
954001	Adams	Edinburgh
952991	Gray	Paisley
953777	White	Glasgow

Note that the duplicate row is dropped. Such an operation might be useful if the two departments were merged and a single table formed from the two originals. A Union can also be useful in combining two (or more) of intermediate results (with the same structure) obtained from other queries.

DIFFERENCE

The Difference of two tables A and B (sometimes written A – B) is the set of all rows in A that do not appear in B. Note that A – B is different from B – A. Another way of looking at this is that A – B is what is left of A after rows common to A and B are removed.

Matric no	Name	Address
951234	Smith	Glasgow
952356	Jones	Aberdeen
954001	Adams	Edinburgh

INTERSECTION

The Intersection of two tables contains the rows that are in both tables. Again, it is essential that the two input tables have the same structure.

Matric no	Name	Address
953388	Brown	Dundee

In terms of our two student tables, this operation would immediately reveal which students were in both tables.

PRODUCT

The Product, also known as the Cartesian Product, is the result of combining each row of one table with every row of a second table; in other words, it is a condition-less join of the two tables. It would normally be applied to tables of different structure. The Product has limited practical application. Note that a relation is defined as a sub-set of a Product as explained earlier in this chapter.

Relational algebra and SQL

Relational algebra provides a useful mathematical basis for relational databases, demonstrating that complex processing can be performed on such databases with a relatively small number of basic set operations. It could, in principle, be implemented as a 'language' which could be used to manipulate relational database tables. However, in practice, the operations provided by this algebra are implemented in a more user-friendly form by declarative query languages such as SQL. The basic SQL SELECT command can be used to perform Restrict, Project and Join operations. Extended formats of SELECT are also available that implement the other operations.

Relational views

A view is a virtual relation, i.e., it appears to the user (end-user or programmer) as a named table but it does not in fact exist as an actual stored table. It is, in effect, a relation created by a query on actual tables; the 'result' table of this processing is managed by the DBMS software to provide the illusion of a real table. The system will store the definition of the view (as a query specification) and it can hence be used as if it were a real table.

Reasons for using a view are

- It provides a mechanism for hiding sensitive parts of actual tables from certain users.
- It simplifies certain processing such as the production of reports by providing a predefined virtual table as the source of the report.
- It enables the same data to be 'seen'in different ways by different classes of users, suited to their individual needs, without any effort on their part.

To provide a transparent view service, the DBMS has to ensure that any changes to the underlying base relations of a view are reflected consistently in the view. Since a view is based on execution of a query, changes in the base tables will necessitate re-evaluation of the query. While this has potential time/processing implications, it is essentially easy to comply with. The converse, namely, to propagate changes to a view through to the base tables is much more problematic and is not, in fact, always possible.

Views are considered again later when practical query systems such as SQL and QBE are covered.

Summary

In this chapter, we have covered a number of very important concepts which we meet again in later work.

1. A data model is a representation of data within some application domain. In this chapter we have looked at the relational model.

2. An application domain is a real-world environment within which an information system and/or a database is being employed.

3. The relational model is based on the theory of sets. A relation represents a mapping of one set into one or more other sets.

4. Null is a presentation used in relational databases to indicate that an attribute value is missing.

5. The primary key of a relation is a column or columns of a relation that uniquely defines the rows of the table.

6. A candidate key is a column (or columns) of a relation that could potentially be used as a primary key.

7. Relations are associated with one another by means of a foreign key in one relation that holds the value of a primary key in another relation.

8. Referential integrity is the principle that within a database a (non-null) foreign key in one table must be matched with an existing primary key in the referenced table.

9. Entity integrity is the principle that no part of a primary key can be null.

10. Relational algebra is a system of algebraic operators that operate on relations. These operations define the ways in which data in relations can be retrieved and transformed. In practice, relational algebra is implemented using the SQL language.

11. The common relational operators are Restrict, Project and Join. Others are Union, Intersection Difference and Product.

12. A view is a virtual table; the DBMS can treat it (in many respects) like a real table but it is generated from the execution of a query.

Answers to in-text questions

2.1 (a) An entity type is a generic classification of 'things in the real world' (e.g., people, city, country, etc.). An entity is an instance of an entity type (e.g., Joe Bloggs, London, England).

(b) The application domain is the real world environment in which the database is to be employed. The domain of an attribute is the range of possible values of the attribute.

2.2 The row is identified by the 'ruling part' (or primary key) attribute. The column is located by the column name, not by the position of the column.

2.3 Neither! If there were other 2000cc cars in the table we would expect that their mileage rate was also 15p. The fact that the mileage charge for both the 1600 and 2000 is the same has no bearing on the functional dependency. The test is: given an engine size, does this size always have the same mileage charge?

2.4 The relations are notionally connected by means of a foreign key attribute in one relation having the value of a primary key in the other relation.

2.5 Yes. For the Course Code of A123, there is a matching row in the Course table – row 1.

2.6 It is a system of operations, derived from the set theory roots of relational databases, that can be performed on and between relations. These operations each produce another relation as a result value.

REVIEW QUESTIONS

Answers in Appendix C.

1 List the properties of a relation.

2 Distinguish between terms primary key, candidate key and foreign key.

3 What does it mean to say that one attribute of a table is 'functionally dependent' on another?

4 Explain the purpose of nulls in database tables and indicate why it is not quite correct to talk of a 'null value'.

5 Explain the concept of referential integrity and its importance in relational database practice.

6 Define the term 'view'.

EXERCISES

Answers to exercises flagged with an asterisk appear in Appendix D.

1 *Using the following tables, evaluate the relational algebra operations listed below

Table A

Order number	Company	City
A1002	Rentokil	London
A3333	Eurotunnel	Paris
B0987	Kwikfit	Glasgow
C7521	BT	Edinburgh
E0102	Halifax plc	Halifax

Table B

Order number	Company	City
E0102	Halifax plc	Halifax
D2489	Hanson	London
B0987	Kwikfit	Glasgow

(a) Union of A and B
(b) Difference A – B

(c) Difference B – A

(d) Intersection of A and B

2   The following Tutor and Student tables show tutors who are assigned to students. The student's tutor is identified by the Tutor column of the Student table. The primary keys are underlined. Do these tables conform with (a) entity and (b) referential integrity? If they do state why you think so. If not, identify where their integrity is lacking.

Tutor table

Tutor ID	Tutor name
21	Newman
34	Martin
56	Wright
78	Adams

Student table

Student ID	Student name	Tutor
990199	Young	56
990278	Fletcher	56
990445	Chung	45
null	Cohen	21
990721	Kennedy	78

3

Data modelling 1

Entity-relationship (ER) model

Introduction

The nature of entities and relationships was described in the previous chapter. To recap, an entity is a term used to denote any real thing or abstract notion that we wish to recognise as a separate object within the domain of a database application. A relationship is some association that exists between these entities.

Entity-relationship (ER) modelling is a diagrammatic technique used by analysts as a top-down method for analysing the nature of an application system, its objective being to help in understanding the nature and relationships that exist within the data of the system. The ER diagrams can then be used to derive a set of relational tables that model the data of the application system.

The first requirement before any attempt is made to design an ER diagram is a proper understanding of the problem domain. No design methodology can compensate for a lack of knowledge and/or understanding of the problem that is being tackled. Analysis and design techniques are outwith the scope of this book and the methods covered in this chapter assume that a proper study of the problem domain has taken place.

While general and intuitive rules can contribute to the ER design, many of the factors to be taken into account in this respect can be called 'business rules', i.e., stipulations and /or restrictions on how things will be done within an enterprise. For example, management of a company may decide 'each client will only be dealt with by one salesperson' or 'every project will have at least two engineers but each engineer will work on only one project'.

This chapter describes the nature of ER diagrams and how they are produced. Chapter 4 will explain how ER diagrams are used in the design of relational database tables.

Entities and relationships

Entity types and relationships are expressed diagrammatically in ER diagrams, using suitable drawing conventions that distinguish clearly between entities and relationships. There are, unfortunately, several different conventions used in drawing ER diagrams. In this text, the conventions we use are similar to those used in CASE tools and by other authors and are perhaps more easily interpreted than alternatives. An example of a basic ER diagram is shown in Figure 3.1.

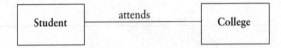

Figure 3.1   Simple ER diagram.

Entities Student and College are shown as rectangles; the relationship 'attends' is shown as a labelled connecting line between the entities. We can 'read' this diagram as 'Student attends College' and in its inverse sense, 'College is attended by Student'.

It is important to realise that, in general, ER diagrams express relationships between entity types (such as Student); another way of looking at it is that each entity box in an ER diagram refers to a set of entities (e.g. a set of Students) of the given type and that every member of that set is potentially involved in the specified relationships. Figure 3.2 shows a more elaborate system (School/Head/Teacher/Child).

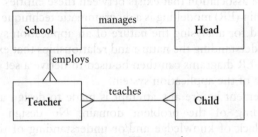

Figure 3.2   ER example.

You will note that some of the connecting lines terminate in a splayed fashion, commonly referred to as a 'crowsfoot'. This device is used to specify the 'cardinality' of the relationship; the cardinality specifies, for one member of the first entity set, the possible number of members it can be related to in a second entity set. There are three flavours of cardinality:

1. 1:1   One to one   e.g., Head manages school
2. 1:n   One to many   e.g., School employs teacher
3. m:n   Many to Many e.g., Teacher teaches child

The 'crowsfoot' line is used to indicate the 'many' end of a relationship.

Each of the relationships can be 'read' in two directions and each interpretation depends on the type of line ending, one or many. The sense of the relationship name has to be suitably reversed to suit the direction of reading; for instance, 'teaches' becomes 'is taught by'. Thus, a complete interpretation of Figure 3.2 is

- One head manages only one school and each school has only one head.
- One school employs many teachers but one teacher is employed by only one school.
- One teacher teaches many children and each child is taught by many teachers.

Note that we interpret each relationship from the point of view of one instance of the entity; for example, even for the many–many relationship, we refer to 'one teacher teaches many children'. To emphasise this point, the entity names are always expressed in the singular: 'teacher', not 'teachers'.

To interpret a relationship within a diagram, for instance, school employs teacher, we start at one end and move towards the other end, interpreting the relationship and the terminal crowsfoot, if any:

- starting at the school end we say – **one** school employs (crowsfoot=) **many** teachers.
- starting at the teacher end we say – **one** teacher is employed by (no crowsfoot=) **one** school.

We emphasise again that we always read the relationship by starting with 'one . . .' and we ignore the crowsfoot, if any, at the starting end.

3.1 Draw an ER diagram to model the following set of conditions pertaining to Students, Courses and Lecturers:

Each student is on only one course.
Each course must have one or more students.
Each course is taught by one or more lecturers.
Each lecturer teaches on one or more courses.

Optionality and participation

Consider the relationship between School and Teacher originally defined in Figure 3.2 and shown again in Figure 3.3.

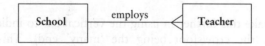

Figure 3.3   School–teacher relationship.

As already described, this expresses the rules:

'one School employs one or more Teachers'
'one Teacher is employed by one School'

However, it may be that some teachers are not employed by any school. This might be the case where a specialist teacher was employed by the central education authority and visited many schools. Thus the second rule given above is incomplete – it should really indicate the 'zero school' possibility. For instance, the rule could be expressed as

'one Teacher is employed by one school or by no School'

We need some additional convention for use in ER diagrams that allows us to express this kind of condition. Regrettably, this topic has produced a variety of different terminology and diagramming conventions in the database literature. In an area that is already potentially quite confusing, it is unfortunate that database literature is so inconsistent in its handling of the topic. In our explanation below we try to cover the more common terminology and conventions in current use.

Optionality
The School–Teacher rule given above could be viewed as expressing the fact that the relationship, from the point of view of the Teacher, is optional; i.e., a Teacher may or may not be employed by a School. This can be indicated on an ER diagram as shown in Figure 3.4. The circle is intended to indicate 'zero' or 'optionally'.

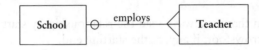

Figure 3.4   Example of optionality.

We read Figure 3.4 as:

'One Teacher is employed by one School or (circle) zero School'

This convention permits convenient reading of the diagram but has the unfortunate aspect that the zero indicator (the circle) is at the opposite end of the relationship line from the entity concerned in the optionality.

Note on alternative notations

An alternative convention makes the optionality indicator explicit; if an entity is not optional a vertical bar is used instead of the circle. Figure 3.4 above would then be changed to that shown in Figure 3.5(a); this means that a school must have at least one teacher.

Other authors take this further in using the vertical bar to indicate the 'one' end of a relationship (the crowsfoot being the 'many' end). This would produce Figure 3.5(b).

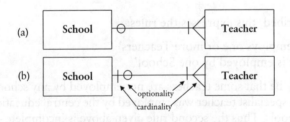

Figure 3.5   Alternative conventions.

Another common ER diagram convention in this respect is to use a broken line to optionality in the relationship. This convention is used in many CASE design tools and is illustrated in Figure 3.6

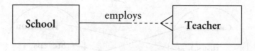

Figure 3.6   May be–must be convention.

The usual way of reading this is to use the phrase 'may. . .' or 'may be . . .' for the dotted line and 'must. . .' or 'must be . . .' for the full line. Hence Figure 3.6 can be read as:

'One School must employ one or more Teachers'
'One Teacher may be employed by one School'

The second line also implies: '. . . but may be employed by no School'

3.2 Would it be meaningful to have both ends of the School/Teacher relationship optional? This is illustrated in Figure 3.7. If so, express the full diagram in English.

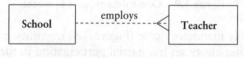

Figure 3.7   Diagram for question 3.2.

Participation
An alternative approach is to highlight the fact that some instances of the Teacher entity set do not participate in the relationship; there are Teachers that are unconnected (through the Employs relationship) with any School. This is expressed by saying that the Teacher entity class has partial participation in the relationship. The alternative is total participation. Using the convention shown in Figure 3.6, partial participation is indicated by the broken line (at the end of the relationship line nearer to the entity with partial participation) and total participation by the full line. Thus we would say that the Teacher entity class exhibits partial participation in the Employs relationship.

Visualisation of relationships

Relationships represent a mapping from one entity set to another. For instance, a one-to-many relationship is one where an entity in one set 'maps to' one or more entities in the other set. Mapping diagrams can help in visualising the notions of cardinality and optionality. These illustrate the mapping by means of explicit connecting lines between entities in example sets. Here are a few examples using the School model above.

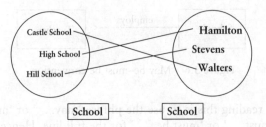

Figure 3.8   One-to-one, mandatory.

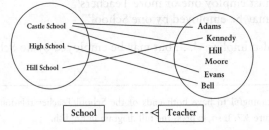

Figure 3.9   One-to-many, part optional.

Notice that in the fully mandatory case (Figure 3.8) no entity is left 'unattached'. In Figure 3.9, the Teacher entity set has partial participation in the relationship; this is illustrated by teacher Moore who is not connected to any school. In Figure 3.10 the School entity set is partially involved; in particular, we can see that the High School does not participate in the relationship.

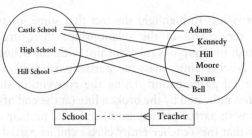

Figure 3.10   One-to-many, part optional.

3.3 Express Figure 3.10 fully in English.

Attributes

The first level ER diagrams show only the general structure of the system; the next step is to identify attributes or properties of the entity. In the school example, possible attributes are name, address, type of school and name and number of teacher. These can be represented in the ER diagram as ellipses as shown in Figure 3.11.

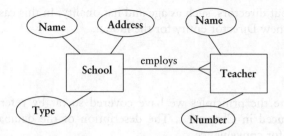

Figure 3.11   Entity attributes.

For most practical systems, displaying the attributes in this fashion would make the diagrams too complicated. At the risk of confusing the reader with yet another notation, it is worth noting that the attributes can be represented more neatly using the box convention shown in Figure 3.12. The entity name is shown at the top with the attributes listed in the section below. Diagrams similar to this are used in many CASE tools such as SELECT. It is important to identify attributes at this stage as it helps to clarify what we mean by each entity and often reveals alternative formulations of the model. It is also helpful in highlighting certain particular cases, namely, multi-valued attributes and time-varying attributes. Discussion of these is included in Chapter 4.

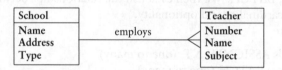

Figure 3.12   Attribute display.

Another difficulty that often arises at this stage in ER design is that in some situations there is uncertainty about whether something should be treated as an entity or an attribute. In most cases, the attributes of an entity can be readily identified; a person's name and age, the colour of a car, the cost of a refrigerator are all fairly clear. However, consider the case of a film catalogue which could be represented as in Figure 3.13; we make the assumption that a Film has only one Director.

Figure 3.13   Film catalogue.

The Director certainly seems to be a valid entity in this scenario but in practice the only attribute of this that we would probably record would be his/her name, a single value. In this case it could be absorbed into the Film entity with no serious effect on the model. Conversely, we may initially have decided that Director was to be modelled by a simple attribute but later decided that we wanted to store other information about directors, such as age and nationality. In this case, it would make sense to form a new Director entity for the model.

Example

We can illustrate the principles we have covered so far by referring back to the example introduced in Chapter 1. The description of the database application is repeated below for convenience.

> A small correspondence college offers courses in a range of topics. For each course, students complete a series of assignments which are sent to the college office; the assignments are gathered into batches, which are then dispatched by post to tutors for marking (i.e. complete batches of up to ten assignments are sent to tutors). Assume that there can be an indefinite number of tutors. The tutors mark the assignments, then return them, retaining them within the same batches. A system is required that enables 'tracking' of the assignments, so that the college knows what assignments have been received, sent to tutors or marked. Also, the system should keep a running total of the number of assignments that have been marked by each tutor.

In designing an ER diagram, we try to identify the distinct 'entities' in the application. In the above scenario, we appear to have entities STUDENT, TUTOR, ASSIGNMENT, BATCH. We then establish the relationships between these entities, including their cardinality and optionality.
Relationships are

STUDENT sends ASSIGNMENT (one to many)
TUTOR processes BATCH (one to many)
ASSIGNMENT contained in BATCH (one to many)

Note
A commonly asked question at this point is: the 'college' is mentioned in the scenario description; why does it not appear in the ER diagram? In effect, the diagram models the 'whole college' so it is not appropriate for it to appear *in* the diagram. This is a general rule: the environment being modelled should not appear in the ER diagram; it is represented by the whole diagram.

From this information, the basic diagram can be derived; see Figure 3.14.

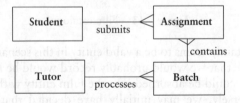

Figure 3.14   Correspondence college example.

? **3.4** You should satisfy yourself at this point about the cardinalities indicated in Figure 3.14. Read each relationship both ways and express in English.

The question of which relationships to include often arises; for instance, do we need a relationship between TUTOR and ASSIGNMENT called 'marks'? From our understanding of the situation, we can see that the relationship between TUTOR and ASSIGNMENT is implied through the TUTOR–BATCH–ASSIGNMENT relationships; it tells us that the tutor marks all the assignments in a batch. An additional marks relationship would not define anything new.

In our example, we also have to establish optionality. Examine each relationship and determine whether either (or both) entities are optional or mandatory in the relationship. As in all aspects of the ER modelling process, this can only be determined from a knowledge of the application domain. Take each relationship in turn:

STUDENT submits ASSIGNMENT: an Assignment must be submitted by a Student, so Assignment participation is total. A Student may send no Assignments so Student participation is partial.

BATCH contains ASSIGNMENT: an Assignment is always part of a Batch and a Batch must have at least one Assignment, so both entities are mandatory.

TUTOR processes BATCH: a Tutor may have no Batches to process, so Tutor involvement is partial. A Batch must have an associated Tutor Batch so participation is total.

We can now draw the ER diagram incorporating the optionalities as illustrated in Figure 3.15.

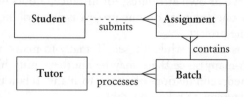

Figure 3.15   College model with optionalities.

Many-to-many relationships

Some relationships appear at first analysis to be many to many. When we study the process of conversion of an ER diagram into relational tables (Chapter 4), we will find many-to-many relationships present us with a problem. It helps at the ER design stage, to see if the relationship can be converted naturally to two one-to-many relationships. This process is shown in Figure 3.16.

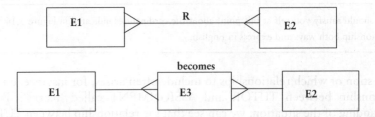

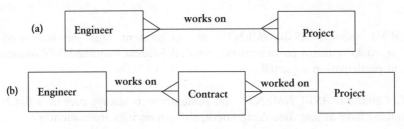

Figure 3.16   Redefinng many-to-many relationships.

In effect, the original relationship R has become an entity. In many situations, this new entity corresponds to some valid concept in the application domain, albeit abstract. If we take the case of engineers and projects within an engineering company, it may be the rule that each engineer works on many projects at once and each project employs several engineers, giving us the ER diagram shown in Figure 3.17(a)

Figure 3.17   Example of many-to-many conversion.

The relationship here can be interpreted as a noun 'Contract' which could be modelled by an entity. There now arise two new relationships, which could be interpreted as 'Engineer works on many Contracts' and 'Project worked on by many Contracts', see Figure 3.17(b).

We can see that this is probably an entity that should have been adopted in the first place, since it can have its own attributes; for instance, 'hours worked' – the number of hours worked by one engineer on one project is an attribute of the contract, not of the engineer or the project.

In summary, it is worth while to see if many-to-many relationships can be converted to one-to-many since there may be another entity hidden there. Also, as previously mentioned, elimination of many-to-many relationships simplifies the conversion of ER diagrams to relational tables.

?   **3.5** Consider the entities FILM and STAR, with the many-to-many relationship STARS IN. Devise another entity that allows modelling of the situation appropriately as two one-to-many relationships. What attributes might the new entity have?

Weak entities

A weak entity is one which cannot exist without the existence of some other entity. In a video hire shop, for instance, we would have entities FILM, representing actual films such as Braveheart, and FILM COPY, which represents physical tape copies of that film. Clearly, each FILM COPY instance must correspond to an instance of a FILM entity; it makes no sense to have a tape which has no associated film. In ER diagrams, a weak entity is represented by double box as shown in Figure 3.18.

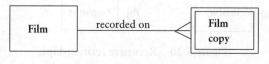

Figure 3.18   Weak entity.

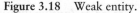

3.6 How about a blank tape? Does a blank tape not represent a 'copy' without a 'film'?

A little thought will show that weak entities arise in mandatory many-to-one relationships; the FILM entity in the above diagram is the 'one' end and must exist for any corresponding FILM COPY instance.

A normal or 'non-weak' entity is sometimes called a strong entity. Weak entities have an important bearing on the integrity of a database. Within a database, we must maintain consistency between entities related in this way; for instance, if a FILM is to be deleted from the video shop database, all related FILM COPYs must also be deleted or the database will contain weak entities with no related 'owning' entity. This is the concept known as referential integrity which was described in Chapter 2.

An alternative terminology for expressing this concept is to say that the weak entity is existence dependent on the other entity.

3.7 Is the diagram in Figure 3.19 a valid possibility? If so, what is its practical interpretation?

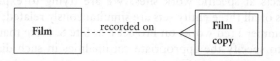

Figure 3.19   Question 3.7 diagram.

More unusual relationships

The ER models described so far are all based on straightforward binary relationships. In practice, this is not sufficient for some situations.

Unary relationships

We should recall that an ER model represents relationships between entity sets; i.e. it expresses relationships between each member of one set with one or more members of another set. However, we may wish to show a relationship between two members of the same set. Typical examples are shown in Figure 3.20.

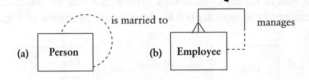

Figure 3.20   Recursive relationships.

Figure 3.20(a) says that each Person is (optionally) married to one other Person. Figure 3.20(b) says that each employee manages zero or more other employees and that each employee is managed by one other employee. These are sometimes referred to as recursive relationships.

Ternary relationships

Some situations call for a ternary relationship, i.e., three entities are involved in the one relationship. Figure 3.21 illustrates one possibility.

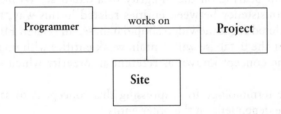

Figure 3.21   Ternary relationship.

The situation represented here is of a set of programmers who are working on a number of projects at specific work sites. We are trying to express the fact that specific members of all three entity sets are simultaneously related; for instance, that a specific programmer Fred works on Project P at Site S. Note that it is not possible unambiguously to specify the appropriate cardinalities in such diagrams, since the line terminating at an entity, say Site, connects to two other entities, Programmer and Project.

If we split this relationship into two binary relationships, we might produce the diagrams shown in Figure 3.22, adopting an *ad hoc* set of cardinalities.

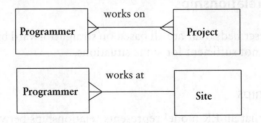

Figure 3.22   Ternary conversion.

Figure 3.22 certainly shows that Fred works on Project P and that he works at Site S, but they fail to indicate which project at which site. Project P may be worked on at a number of sites, while each site might host several projects.

It is desirable to transform a ternary relationship into something more manageable; the recommended technique is to change the relationship itself into an entity, with relationships with the other entities. This is illustrated in Figure 3.23.

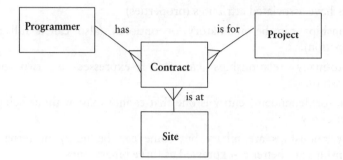

Figure 3.23   Ternary relationship re-expressed.

More than one relationship between entities

Although not explicitly stated earlier, there is nothing in the 'rules' of ER diagrams that prevent entity types being related by more than relationship. This is of course necessary to reflect real-life situations. A typical example is shown in Figure 3.24

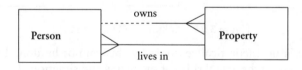

Figure 3.24   Multi-relationship.

This diagram indicates that any person can own zero or more properties and any person lives in one property. Also, one property can be occupied by one or more people and is owned by one person. It is worth noting at this point that the diagrams are expressing general relationships, between members of the specified sets of entities, which should be treated independently. For instance, the 'owns' and 'lives in' relationships are independent and do not imply, for instance, that a person necessarily lives in one of the properties that he/she owns.

Summary

1. Entity Relationship (ER) diagrams are used to model the nature of data within
    the domain of a database application.

2. Entities are identifiable objects or concepts that are relevant to the application. These are modelled in the ER diagrams by boxes. The entity box represents a set of entities of one type.

3. Relationships express associations between entities. They are drawn as lines connecting the related entity boxes.

4. Relationships can be one-to-one, one-to-many or many-to-many. This is referred to as the cardinality of the relationship.

5. Entities have associated attributes (properties).

6. Relationships can be mandatory or optional (also called full and partial participation).

7. Many-to-many relationships can be re-expressed as two one-to-many relationships.

8. A weak (or dependent) entity is one that cannot exist without being related to another entity.

9. Most relationships are binary but some can be unary or ternary. Ternary relationships are better re-expressed as three binary ones.

Answers to in-text questions

3.1 See Figure 3.25

Figure 3.25   Solution to Question 3.1.

3.2 Yes. There is no theoretical reason why this cannot be done but it would of course depend on the actual rules of the real world situation. The diagram could be expressed as:

'one teacher is employed by zero or one school'
'one school employs zero or more teachers'

3.3 One School employs zero or more Teachers. One Teacher is employed by one School.

or

One School may employ zero or more Teachers. One Teacher must be employed by one School.

3.4 One Student submits many Assignments, one Assignment is from one Student. One Tutor processes many Batches, one Batch is processed by one Tutor. One Batch contains many Assignments, one Assignment is in one Batch

3.5 The most appropriate intermediate entity would be ROLE, with possible attributes of description (e.g., Leading Male) and role name (e.g., James Bond).

3.6 No. The point is that every weak entity must be related to another entity. Within the meaning of the situation we are modelling it makes no sense to have a weak entity without an associated independent entity. A blank tape by its nature is not associated with any film.

3.7 Figure 3.19 says that a film may have zero or more copies. The zero is probably acceptable within the application; it implies that we can record the existence of a Film (perhaps to take advance bookings for it) without having an actual copy of it.

REVIEW QUESTIONS

Answers in Appendix C.

1 Distinguish between an entity and an entity set. Which one is represented in an ER diagram?

2 List the possible variants of cardinality.

3 How is the 'many' end of a relationship denoted in ER diagrams?

4 Explain what is meant by saying that a relationship is 'optional'.

5 Explain what is meant by saying that an entity set may have 'partial participation' in a relationship.

6 What is meant by the term 'weak entity'?

7 Explain what is meant by a unary and a ternary relationship.

EXERCISES

Answers to exercises flagged with an asterisk appear in Appendix D.

1 Express the diagrams shown in Figure 3.26 in English.

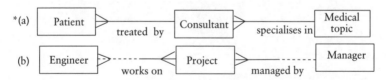

Figure 3.26   Exercises 1 and 2 diagrams.

2 *For Figure 3.26(b), replace the many-to-many relationship with two one-to-many relationships.

3 Construct ER diagrams to represent the following scenarios:

*(a) Order processing system: A company processes ORDERS each of which consists of a number of ORDER ITEMS. Each ORDER refers to a particular CUSTOMER and an order date. Each ORDER ITEM specifies a PRODUCT and a quantity.

(b) Diet system: A hospital prepares, for PATIENTS, special DIETS for which the nutrient value must be known. Each diet consists of a number of INGREDIENTS (meat, potatoes, carrots etc.), each of which have a number of NUTRIENT VALUES (calorific value, protein, vitamins, fibre etc.). Each patient has a recommended daily amount (RDA) of each nutrient value.

(c)   University Courses: A university offers COURSES each of which consist of one or more
      MODULES. Each course is managed by one DEPARTMENT. Each module has a MODULE
      LEADER who is a LECTURER in one of the university departments. A module can be taught by
      any lecturer in any department. A module may have a prerequisite module.

(d)   Programming projects: A software development company hires out programmers to work
      on clients' computing projects. At any one time each programmer works on zero or one
      project but each project may have one or more programmers. Each project belongs only to
      one client; each client may have zero or more current projects. The project work is carried out
      at a number of sites; each site may be involved with one or more projects and any one
      project may be worked on at one or more sites. It is necessary for the programmers to
      account for work carried out at each individual site.

4

Data modelling 2

Introduction

In Chapter 3, we looked at how ER diagrams can be designed to model the data of an application system. In this chapter, we investigate the important topic of deriving a design for a relational database from the completed ER model. A full treatment of database design would require a textbook of its own as well as some reference to other topics such as general systems analysis and design techniques. The objective here is simply to provide an introduction to some of the factors that must be considered when designing a database and to show how the techniques of data modelling and ER diagrams can contribute to the design process.

ER diagrams and database design

As mentioned earlier, in addition to providing a general data modelling facility, ER diagrams can be used to assist in the design of relational databases; indeed, this is their main function in practice. It is found by many designers that a diagrammatic approach facilitates visualisation of the overall application domain and assists in identifying relationships between entities that must be represented in the database.

If the process of developing the database tables is carried out correctly, then we have taken the first important step in producing an effective database application. The database forms the foundation stone on which the application system can be built.

Deriving a table design from an ER diagram

We can use an ER diagram (together with details of the entity attributes) to produce a set of relational tables that model the data requirements of the application. We begin, in the next section, with an overall summary of the procedure then in the subsequent sections we examine each step in more detail.

For the purposes of illustration, we will use the simple example shown in Figure 4.1, based on a scenario wherein Engineers are assigned to work on Projects.

Figure 4.1   Example ER diagram.

In Figure 4.1, we have not indicated any cardinality or optionality at this stage as various alternatives for these are examined later.

Summary of design process

The following stages define the conversion process:

1. Entity tables: Create a table to represent each entity.
2. Relationships: Represent relationships according to their cardinality and optionality. Some relationships will generate another table while some can be represented within the entity tables,
3. Primary and foreign keys: Linkages between the tables must be established by the design of suitable primary and foreign keys. This process actually occurs in parallel with the other two.

Detailed process

1. Entity tables

This process is relatively straightforward. The attributes of the entity set determined at the ER design stage simply become the column attributes of the table. It is necessary to adopt one (or more) of the columns as a primary key. Frequently, this choice is obvious; there is often some identification code such as a Product code, Order number, Matriculation number, etc., already in use in the application domain that will serve this purpose. Where no such code is available, it is necessary to choose from one of the candidate keys of the relation or to invent a new identity code. A common practice is to use an automatic number generator to assign a unique number to each row. Such a facility is provided by most DBMSs; Microsoft Access provides a datatype called Autonumber that adopts a new value for every row created. Oracle does not provide an actual attribute datatype but offers a CREATE SEQUENCE command that defines a variable that increments by 1 each time it is referenced.

The essential requirement, of course, is that the primary key must have a unique value for each row of the table.

4.1 Why is it essential that the primary key is unique for each row of a table?

For our Engineer-Project model our tables would appear as follows:

Engineer

Eng ID	Name
12	Jones
34	Anderson
56	Murray

Project

Proj Code	Title
S03	Mercury
X99	Venus
Z22	Apollo

The primary keys are shown underlined.

2. Relationships

Incorporating the ER relationships into the tables can be somewhat more complex. In the notes below, we consider separately the different cases of cardinality, namely, one-to-one, one-to-many and many-to-many.

Case 1: One-to-one relationship

(a) Using a single table   In principle, the two tables can be combined into one. Using our sample model and arbitrary assignments, this might produce the table shown below:

Engineer-Project

Eng ID	Name	Proj Code	Title
12	Kelly	X99	Venus
34	Ross	S03	Mercury
56	Smith	X22	Apollo

Note that we have two candidate keys (Eng ID and Proj Code) and one would have to be adopted as primary key. If the relationship is mandatory in both directions then either candidate key can be used; the choice would be made purely on grounds of convenience.

However, if the relationship is optional in one direction, then a free choice is not available and the primary key depends on the optionality. If it is possible to have an Engineer not assigned to any Project, then the situation shown below could arise.

Engineer-Project

Eng ID	Name	Proj Code	Title
12	Kelly	X99	Venus
34	Ross	S03	Mercury
45	Jones	*null*	*null*
56	Smith	Z22	Apollo

The Proj Code column can be null and hence cannot be used as a primary key; the only choice therefore is the Eng ID. Conversely, if it is possible for there to be a project with no assigned engineers, then the Eng ID is not valid as primary key and the Proj Code must be used:

Engineer-Project

Eng ID	Name	Proj Code	Title
12	Kelly	X99	Mercury
34	Ross	S03	Venus
null	*null*	T15	Zeus
56	Smith	Z22	Apollo

(b) Using two tables   In many, if not most examples, it is advisable to use a separate table for each entity. This clarifies the entity-table representation and is more amenable to amendment. The two tables have to be 'linked' and a foreign key must be inserted in one of the tables. In the Engineer-Project model, we can put the Proj Code in the Engineer table

Engineer

Eng ID	Name	Proj Code
12	Kelly	X99
34	Ross	S03
56	Smith	Z22

Project

Proj Code	Title
X99	Venus
Z22	Apollo
S03	Mercury

or the Eng ID in the Project table:

Engineer

Eng ID	Name
12	Kelly
34	Ross
56	Smith

Project

Proj Code	Title	Eng ID
X99	Venus	12
Z22	Apollo	56
S03	Mercury	34

The foreign keys in the above tables are shown with dotted underline.

Case 2: One-to-many relationship
One-to-many relationships can be represented by two or three tables. The design decisions are described below. We will assume for this section that the relationship is one Project to many Engineers.

(a) Using two tables   Since any one Engineer is only associated with one project, it is possible to adopt a foreign key of Proj Code for the Engineer table:

Engineer

Eng ID	Name	Proj Code
12	Kelly	X99
29	Brown	S03
34	Ross	Z22
56	Smith	Z22
62	Adams	Z22

Project

Proj Code	Title
X99	Venus
Z22	Apollo
S03	Mercury

Note that Brown and Ross both work on S03 (Mercury) and Smith and Adams both work on Z22 (Apollo).

?   **4.2** If the relationship was one engineer to many projects (and one project to one engineer) how would the above tables change?

(b) Using three tables   The most general way of dealing with one-to-many relationships is to form a third table, a 'relationship' or 'association' table, that specifies the assignment of engineers to projects. The three tables would look like this:

Engineer

Eng ID	Name
12	Kelly
29	Brown
34	Ross
56	Smith
62	Adams

Project

Proj Code	Title
X99	Venus
Z22	Apollo
S03	Mercury

Assignment

Eng ID	Proj Code
12	X99
29	S03
34	S03
56	Z22
62	Z22

The primary key of the Assignment table can be formed by concatenating the Eng ID and the Proj Code. The Eng ID and the Proj Code columns in the Assignments table are each foreign keys linking with the primary keys in the other two tables.

Note that the table designs would be the same regardless of whether the relationship was one engineer to many projects or one project to many engineers.

Case 3: Many-to-many relationship
In a many-to-many relationship, we have no choice: we must form a third table to represent the relationship.

Engineer

Eng ID	Name
12	Kelly
29	Brown
34	Ross
56	Smith
62	Adams

Project

Proj Code	Title
X99	Venus
Z22	Apollo
S03	Mercury

Assignment

Eng ID	Proj Code
12	X99
29	S03
34	S03
34	X99
56	Z22
62	Z22
62	S03

We can see from the above table that engineer 34 (Ross) is working on two projects (S03 and X99) and engineer 62 (Adams) is working on two projects (Z22 and S03). An attempt to condense this information into two tables will fail; these multiple project assignments cannot be expressed within the Engineer table because it would require multiple values in the Proj Code (foreign key) column.

Engineer

Eng ID	Name	Proj Code
12	Kelly	X99
29	Brown	S03
34	Ross	S03 X09
56	Smith	X99
62	Adams	Z22 S03

These multiple values in the Proj Code column are not allowed; hence, three tables must be used.

It is possible that the Assignment table as shown above could itself be viewed as an 'entity' table; i.e. the allocation of engineers to projects could be considered a distinct concept within the application domain which merits its own table. Recall that we have encountered this idea before in the context of ER diagrams: many-to-many relationships can often be interpreted as two one-to-many. This is especially true where additional information pertaining to the assignment (as opposed to either the engineer or the project separately) can be represented; e.g. we might want to record Hours Worked per engineer per project:

Assignment

Eng ID	Proj Code	Hours Worked
12	X99	210
29	S03	35
34	S03	90
34	X99	200
56	Z22	65
62	Z22	15
62	S03	47

This shows, for example, that a total of 290 hours were worked by engineer 34, 90 on project S03 and 200 on X99. We could not represent the Hours Worked figure without using a separate table for Assignments.

? **4.3** Using the above example, try to 'make do' with two tables by putting the Eng ID into the Project table. Why will this not succeed?

---

3. Primary and foreign keys

We have noted, in the sections above, that we have to insert foreign key columns into certain tables to implement a link to another table. In general, a foreign key value must be the same as a primary key value in the linked table. This is the principle of referential integrity that has been mentioned before. However, a foreign key value is allowed to be null if the relationship is optional. While it is possible to be very prescriptive about the combinations of cardinality and optionality that would allow a null to be used, it is easier to manage if the basic principle is understood: if a relationship is not mandatory, the foreign key value can be null.

The Engineer–Project example given earlier in this chapter illustrates this point. If the relationship 'works on' between Engineer and Project is mandatory then the Proj Code column of the Engineer table cannot be null, every engineer must connect to some project.

Engineer

Eng ID	Name	Proj Code
12	Kelly	X99
34	Ross	S03
56	Smith	Z22

Project

Proj Code	Title
X99	Venus
Z22	Apollo
S03	Mercury

If, however, the relationship is optional (Engineer has only partial participation) then the Proj Code column of the Engineer table can be null. The table below shows that Smith is not currently assigned to a project and hence has a null Proj Code.

Engineer

Eng ID	Name	Proj Code
12	Kelly	X99
34	Ross	S03
56	Smith	null

Project

Proj Code	Title
X99	Venus
Z22	Apollo
S03	Mercury

Database systems typically allow you to specify whether or not a foreign key attribute can be null; SQL, for instance, provides a NOT NULL clause in the CREATE TABLE command for this purpose. The NOT NULL clause would always be used in respect of the primary key and it should also be specified for foreign keys within a mandatory relationship.

Example

We will describe an example to illustrate the conversion process. A software company employs a number of programmers who are assigned to work on specific projects. Each project is controlled by one manager. Each programmer works on only one project but contributes to the writing of several programs. Each program may be written by one or more programmers. Construct an ER diagram to represent this scenario and hence construct suitable relational tables. Assume that the entities shown have (at least) the following attributes:

Manager: Employee number, name
Project: Project code, start date, planned finish date

Programmer: Employee number, name, programming language,
Years experience in language.
Program: Program number, title, language

Solution: the ER Diagram is shown in Figure 4.2.

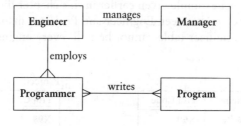

Figure 4.2   ER diagram solution.

Table design

The first step is to create a table for each of the entities shown and to identify their attributes. This yields the following tables:

Manager

Employee Number	Name

Project

Project Code	Project Name	Start Date	Finish Date

Programmer

Employee Number	Name	Language	Years Experience

Program

Program Number	Title	Language

We now have to examine the relationships to determine the requirements for additional tables and the placement of foreign keys.

Manager–Project Relationship
This is a one-to-one relationship where we have chosen to keep the entity information in separate tables. The only requirement is to establish a foreign key to link the tables. The most natural representation is probably to put the manager's employee number in the Project table. This is based on the principle that a project is unlikely to have more than one manager. It is more likely that the system could be modified to allow one manager to have more than one project; in this event, no modification to these tables would be necessary. So the Project table gets an additional column to hold the manager's employee number as a foreign key, indicated by a dotted underline:

Project

Project Code	Project Name	Start Date	Finish Date	Manager Number

Project–Programmer Relationship

This is a one-to-many relationship and will require a foreign key column in the table at the 'many' end of the relationship, i.e., the Programmer table. This table now becomes

Programmer

Employee Number	Name	Language	Years Experience	Project Code

It is important to appreciate why the foreign key must go in the Programmer table and not the Project table: there are potentially several Project → Programmer links so they cannot all be specified by one foreign key in the Project table.

Programmer–Program Relationship

This is a many-to-many relationship as it currently stands. As we noted earlier, we must convert this to two one-to-many relationships. We will introduce a new relationship entity called Assignment that shows the assignment of programmers to programs. The relevant part of the ER diagram now looks like Figure 4.3.

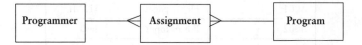

Figure 4.3   Resolving a many-to-many relationship.

Since the new Assignment table is at the 'many' end of both of the new relationships, it will contain both of the foreign keys. The Assignment table will have the following structure:

Assignment

Programmer Employee Number	Program Number

Each of the columns are individually foreign keys linking to the other tables. The two columns combined form the primary key of the table.

This completes the design of the tables. It is worth while at this point to try to build the tables using sample test data (either invented or better still, drawn from the real application environment) to verify that the structure is correct. Below we have composed a set of tables using sample data.

Manager

Employee Number	Name
432	Morrison
512	Kennedy

Project

Project Code	Project Name	Start Date	Finish Date	Manager Number
P001	Website	12/02/99	30/09/99	512
P002	Sales	5/04/99	20/11/99	432

Programmer

Employee Number	Name	Language	Years Experience	Project Code
127	Jones	Oracle	4	P001
258	Green	Oracle	8	P001
361	Allen	Java	2	P002
677	Orr	Java	10	P001
780	Grant	Oracle	4	P002

Program

Program Number	Title	Language
A001	Home pages	HTML
A002	Forms input	Java
A003	Database interface	Java
S101	Enter New Sales	Oracle
S102	Invoicing	Oracle
S103	Sales Enquiry	Oracle

Assignment

Programmer Employee Number	Program Number
127	S102
258	S101
361	A002
677	A003
780	S103

The reader should examine these tables to confirm that the data is consistent with the ER model.

? **4.4** If the database were to allow for programmers having more than one language experience, how could this be accommodated into the above structure?

Additional techniques

In this section we examine some additional techniques that can be usefully employed when building relational tables. These include

- an alternative approach to primary keys
- multi-valued attributes, already mentioned in the previous section
- time-varying attributes
- generalisation.

Primary keys – an alternative approach

In our treatment of relational database tables so far, we have adopted the usual practice of utilising what could be called 'natural' primary key values such as codes and identifiers that would be used in the application domain. Sometimes, it is necessary to invent new attributes for the purposes of identification in a database table where no suitable value exists in the current domain. As mentioned earlier, a common technique is to use a sequential counter, such as the Microsoft Access Autonumber datatype, to generate unique key values.

An approach which is adopted by some database designers is to utilise a sequential number for the primary key of every table. Sometimes, this key value will be adopted as a conventional key within the application but frequently it can be superfluous to the application and exists only to provide a unique key value. To show how this would affect the structure of tables, we have redefined the tables of the example given in the previous section.

Manager

Row ID	Employee Number	Name
1	432	Morrison
2	512	Kennedy

Project

Row ID	Project Code	Project Name	Start Date	Finish Date	Manager ID
1	P001	Website	12/02/99	30/09/99	2
2	P002	Sales	5/04/99	20/11/99	1

Programmer

Row ID	Employee Number	Name	Language	Years Experience	Project ID
1	127	Jones	Oracle	4	1
2	258	Green	Oracle	8	1
3	361	Allen	Java	2	2
4	677	Orr	Java	10	1
5	780	Grant	Oracle	4	2

Program

Row ID	Program Number	Title	Language
1	A001	Home pages	HTML
2	A002	Forms input	Java
3	A003	Database interface	Java
4	S101	Enter new Sales	Oracle
5	S102	Invoicing	Oracle
6	S103	Sales Enquiry	Oracle

Assignment

Row ID	Programmer ID	Program ID
1	1	5
2	2	4
3	3	2
4	4	3
5	5	6

This is an extreme example that assumes that none of the generated key values (Row ID) is used in the application domain and they are used purely to interconnect the tables. The following points can be made about this method of working:

1. For a given table, a generated key value is never reused, even a value used in a row that is deleted. This guarantees life-time (of the table) uniqueness of the key values.
2. The technique is similar to the use of 'identity' codes used in object-oriented systems where the system generates a unique identifier for every object created. We will return to this point when object systems are covered in Chapter 12.
3. A consequence of the technique is that no table will ever have a composite key.
4. More indexes will generally be required; in addition to the index on the generated primary key, indexes will usually be necessary for the other candidate keys previously used as the primary keys, such as Program Number, Project Code, etc., in the above example. If for no other reason, these additional indexes would be desirable to ensure uniqueness of these values in new rows of the table.
5. All foreign key columns will contain numerical values matching the generated primary key values. In the case of Microsoft Access, the generated keys are long integer (32-bit) values and hence the foreign key columns must use a long integer datatype.

Multi-valued attributes

The Programmer table of the example in the previous section has one column representing the 'language' attribute. If the programmer were conversant in more than one language, it would notionally require a set of values (per row) in the language column; this is not possible with conventional relational database tables. In terms of ER diagrams, the Programmer–Language situation might be drawn as shown in Figure 4.4, using only a sample number of attributes.

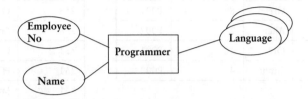

Figure 4.4   Multi-valued attribute.

To represent the multiple values within one column, one might be tempted to hold several values concatenated together into one string, e.g., 'Java, HTML, C++'. In some circumstances, this could be acceptable but the main limitation of this technique is that it complicates searching (using say, SQL) for values embedded in the middle of the string. An index created for the language column, for instance, would see only the whole string value (Java, HTML, C++) and not the individual components.

Another alternative would be to have several language columns; this again might be OK for a limited situation with a predictable small number of values. The main problems here are:

1.   A fixed upper limit has to be set on the number of such columns; we could allow for, say, three languages to be recorded. If a fourth was required – too bad!
2.   It complicates querying on the language values since every language column would need to be tested for a particular value.
3.   Essentially, it is not in the spirit of relational databases.

The recommended procedure for multi-valued attributes is to create a new table to hold the values. The ER diagram would then be as shown in Figure 4.5.

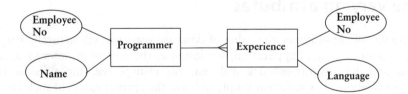

Figure 4.5   Multi-valued attribute.

The new table would have a primary key composed of the primary key of the original table (programmer's Employee Number) together with a qualifying value (since there will typically be more than one row per programmer), often simply the attribute value itself. For the programmer-language example, we would modify the programmer table and create a new Experience table.

Programmer

Employee Number	Name	Years Experience	Project Number
127	Jones	4	P001
258	Green	8	P001
361	Allen	2	P002
677	Orr	10	P001
780	Grant	4	P002

Experience

Employee Number	Language
127	Oracle
258	Oracle
258	Access
361	C++
361	HTML
361	Java
677	HTML
677	Java
780	Oracle

It is also possible that an entity class could have a group of repeating attributes. This would be handled in exactly the same way, namely, by using a new entity class with several attributes. For example, a company Employee entity could require attributes Child Name, Sex and Date of Birth. In table terms, this would be represented by a new table 'Dependent' with the format shown below:

Employee Number	Child Name	Child Sex	Child DOB

The primary key is the Employee Number (the primary key of the Employee table) and the Child Name.

? **4.5** Think of other applications where multi-valued attributes appear.

Time varying attributes

In virtually all applications, the value of database contents will naturally vary over time. In a stock control application, for instance, the cost of an item in stock can change and the quantity-in-stock will generally change even more frequently. In many applications, it is sufficient simply to know the current values of such variables; the previous history of changes is of no consequence. In a stock control system, if the quantity-in-stock changes from 120 to 100, it probably not necessary to record that it was previously 120.

However, in some applications it is necessary to record a history of value changes. An investment management system, for instance, would typically monitor the prices of stock market shares which vary from day to day, with a view to predicting future price movement. Hence, for one table attribute, say share price, we need to record a series of prices and date values. As we have already seen, we must handle this in relational database terms by forming a new table to hold the multiple values: see Figure 4.6.

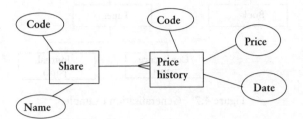

Figure 4.6 Time-varying attributes.

Typical data from this model might look like this:

Share

Code	Name
BT	British Telecom
MS	Marks & Spencer
SP	Scottish Power

Price history

Code	Price	Date
BT	3.34	12/10/96
BT	3.36	17/10/96
BT	3.41	24/10/96
MS	5.12	12/10/96
MS	5.22	17/10/96
MS	5.37	24/10/96

4.6 Think of other applications where a time series of values might be used.

Even in applications where no specific requirements for historical data exist, it may still be necessary to allow for changes in values over a period of time. For instance, if we work to a rule that says 'one Engineer will only work on one Project' and design the tables accordingly, the tables can only show the Engineer–Project assignment at one point in time. When an engineer moves to a new project, the tables cannot represent a temporary situation where the engineer is working on both projects. It is often advisable to make such relationships one-to-many to provide more flexibility in this respect.

Generalisation

Generalisation (opposite: specialisation) is the process of grouping similar entities under more general or 'higher order' types to indicate commonality in certain properties. A type hierarchy can then be formed, as shown in Figure 4.7.

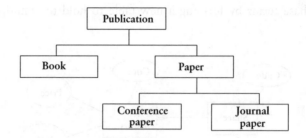

Figure 4.7   Generalisation example.

In Figure 4.7, the most general type is publication; this can 'sub-typed' or specialised into book and paper and so on. All entities share certain common properties, defined by publication while each sub-type has its own special properties. This situation is illustrated below:

TYPE	PROPERTIES
Publication	Publ_code, Title, Authors, Keywords
Book	As for publication plus: Publisher, ISBN, Year, Edition
Paper	As for publication plus:
Conference Paper	Name of Conference, Date, Proceedings Publisher
Journal Paper	Journal, Date, Vol, Number

This concept is an essential part of the object model where it is implemented as an inheritance structure, e.g., the Book class inherits the characteristics of the parent class 'Publication'. We can also say that the structure represents 'IS-A' relationships; i.e., a book 'is-a' Publication.

In the relational model, the representation of this situation is cumbersome; if we put all data pertaining to any publication in one table (e.g., Publication_Table), then it would require to have columns for all the data items given above. However, for a particular reference, say a book, the columns not relevant to a book (such as Journal Name) would have to be null. Alternatively, we would require three separate tables which would make general queries over all the data rather awkward. This topic is discussed in more detail in Chapter 12 where the limitations of the relational model are discussed.

Summary

1. Entity Relationship (ER) diagrams are used to assist in the design of relational database tables.
2. An ER diagram representing a database application can be converted to a set of tables that can be employed in the application.
3. In general, an ER diagram entity converts to a relational table.
4. Relationships between entities can be represented either by foreign key additions to entity tables or by additional tables, depending on the cardinality and optionality.

5. Foreign key values must match a primary key value in the related table or be null if the relationship is optional.
6. Multi-valued attributes and time-varying attributes can be represented by an additional table related to the base table in a one-to-many relationship.

Answers to in-text questions

4.1 This is a fundamental characteristic of relational tables; each table must have an attribute (or combination of attributes) that acts as a unique identifier for that row.

4.2 The Engineer table would become:

> Eng ID, Name

and the Project table would become:

> Proj Code, Title, Eng ID

4.3 Any row of the Project table could potentially refer to two or more engineers. For instance, project X99 has two engineers assigned to it. Multiple values cannot be represented within one row.

4.4 The 'language' attribute in the Programmer table is now multi-valued, i.e., it has two or more values for every row of the programmer table. A relational table cannot represent a set of values within one row and column so the language data has to be held in a separate table. The general way of tackling this kind of situation is described in the section following the question.

4.5 There are, of course, an indefinite number of examples of multi-valued attributes. Clearly defined examples include

- A Personnel table is required to hold information about the skills of employees. There will be several skill values per employee.
- In a Product table, a number of alternatives are recorded which can act as substitutes in the event of the main product being out of stock.

4.6 Possible examples include:

- In a Sales Ordering System it is necessary to record a series of price changes so that customers are charged the price prevailing at the time of their order.
- In systems that record Sports Results, a history of figures will be required for the results of each contest.

REVIEW QUESTIONS

Answers in Appendix C.

1 List the stages of the conversion process from ER diagrams to relational tables.

2 How do you represent a many-to-many relationship with relational tables?

3 Why is it often preferable to use two tables in a one-to-one relationship?

4 When is it permissible for a foreign key value to be null?

5 How do you represent multi-valued attributes in relational tables?

6 How do you represent time-varying attributes in relational tables?

EXERCISES

Answers to exercises flagged with an asterisk appear in Appendix D.

1 *Describe in detail the procedure for conversion of ER diagrams to relational tables.

2 *(a) The ER diagram shown in Figure 4.8 describes the situation in a college where each student is enrolled on one course, each of which is managed by one department. Each course consists of a set of modules and one module can be included in one or more courses. Construct an outline set of tables to represent this system.

(b) Suppose that each course can have a number of optional modules that each student can select. It is therefore necessary to record the module choice for each student. Extend the ER diagram to accommodate this change and show the changes to the tables.

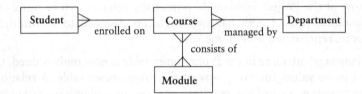

Figure 4.8   Exercise 2(a).

3 A university computer laboratory requires a booking system to enable students to book a specific lab computer at a specific time. The students must be enrolled on certain authorised courses. Some of the computers have special facilities and/or additional equipment such as large memory, scanner, speech input, etc.

Design an ER diagram to model this application and then derive a set of relational tables from the ER diagram, using appropriate choices for the table attributes. Indicate the foreign keys used and for each specify whether a null entry would be allowable.

5

Normalisation

Introduction

One of the principal objectives of relational databases is to ensure that each item of data is held only once within the database. For instance, if we hold customers' addresses, then the address of any one customer is represented only once throughout all the tables of the application.

The reasons for this are, first, simply, to minimise the amount of space required to hold the database, but also and more importantly to simplify maintenance of the data. If the same information is held in two or more places, then each time the data changes, each occurrence of the data must be located and amended. Also, having two 'copies' of the same data gives rise to the possibility of their being different.

In many cases, it is relatively easy to arrange the tables to meet this objective. There is, however, a more formal procedure called normalisation that can be followed to organise data into a standard format which avoids many processing difficulties. The process of normalising tables is described in this chapter.

Overview of normalisation process

In order to understand the process of normalisation, it is necessary to refer back to the concepts, mentioned earlier, of the 'ruling part' and 'dependent part' of the rows. The ruling part, also known as the key value of the table, is the column or columns that specify or identify the entity being described by the row. For instance, the key of the Project table is the Project code since this value uniquely specifies the project being described by the other columns of the row, the dependent columns.

The purpose of normalisation is

- to put data into a form that conforms to relational principles, e.g., single valued columns, each relation represents one entity
- to avoid redundancy by storing each 'fact' within the database only once
- to put the data into a form that is more able to accommodate change
- to avoid certain difficulties in updating (so-called anomalies, described later)
- to facilitate the enforcement of constraints on the data.

Normalisation involves checking that the tables conform to certain rules and, if not, re-organising the data. This will mean creating new tables containing data drawn from the original tables. Normalisation is a multi-stage process, the result of each of the stages being called a 'normal form'; successive stages produce a greater and greater degree of normalisation. There are a total of seven normal forms, called, in increasing degree and grouped for the convenience of description:

- first, second and third normal forms (abbreviated to 1NF, 2NF and 3NF)
- Boyce-Codd (BCNF)
- fourth normal form(4NF)
- fifth normal form (5NF) and domain-key normal form (DK/NF).

The normal forms 1NF, 2NF and 3NF are the most important and all practical database applications would be expected to conform to these. The likelihood of a set of tables requiring modification to comply with these is quite high.

The Boyce-Codd normal form is a more stringent form of 3NF and again should be applied to a practical system. There is less chance of this normal form affecting the structure of the tables.

The fourth and fifth normal forms are unlikely to be significant in a practical system that has been designed, say, using the ER approach.

The highest normal form, the domain-key, was devised by Fagin in 1981 (Fagin 1981). Fagin proved that this normal form was the 'last'; no higher form is possible or necessary since a relation in DK/NF can have no modification anomalies. However, this is mostly of theoretical interest since there is no known procedure for converting to this form.

The first three normal forms are the most significant and are usually sufficient for most applications. These will be described in some detail in the following section; the other normal forms will be covered in the subsequent sections in somewhat less detail.

Normal forms 1NF, 2NF and 3NF

The normalisation process assumes that you start with some informal description of all the data attributes that the database application appears to require; this is often called 'un-normalised data'. This set of attributes is then tested using criteria defined by each of the normalisation stages. If the data fails the criteria, there is a prescribed procedure for correcting the structure of the data; this inevitably involves the creation of additional tables.

The overall process of normalisation for the first three stages is summarised in Figure 5.1.

To understand what these steps imply, we can return again to the example initially introduced in Chapter 1 concerning a correspondence college. For convenience, the specification of this example is reproduced again below.

A small correspondence college offers courses in a range of topics. For each course, students complete a series of assignments which are sent to the college office; the assignments are gathered into batches, which are then dispatched by post to tutors for marking (i.e. complete batches of up to ten assignments are sent to tutors). Assume that there can be an indefinite number of tutors. The tutors mark the assignments, then return them, retaining them within the same batches A system is required that enables 'tracking' of the assignments, so that the college knows what assignments have been received, sent to tutors or marked. Also, the system should keep a running total of the number of assignments that have been marked by each tutor.

UN-NORMALISED DATA

├── Remove all repeating groups

FIRST NORMAL FORM

├── If the primary key has more than one field, ensure that all other fields are functionally dependent on the whole key

SECOND NORMAL FORM

├── Remove all transitive dependencies, i.e., fields dependent on non-key fields

THIRD NORMAL FORM

Figure 5.1

As we did in Chapter 1, we can represent the data diagrammatically as shown in Figure 5.1. We view this data design as a first attempt at forming a relational table to represent the application data. Naturally, we would prefer as few tables as possible so we have combined all the data into one tentative table design. The attribute Batch Number will be used as a provisional primary key.

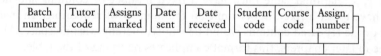

Figure 5.2   Correspondence college example.

In drawing Figure 5.2, we are not pretending that we have anything resembling a proper relational table at this stage; it is simply a trial combination of all relevant data items. Note, however, that the cardinality of the attributes is shown correctly: there is a group of attributes that have several values for each value of the others. If we were to attempt to organise this data into a table, it might look something like this:

Batch number	Tutor code	Assigns marked	Date sent	Date returned	Student code	Course code	Assign. number
23	JS	87	12/4/98	7/5/98	981230	PR007	3
					978001	AB003	1
					980239	PE009	7
24	GH	91	21/9/98	15/10/98	978001	AB003	4
					985100	GM201	3

As we have already noted in earlier chapters, we cannot have multiple attribute values in one row/column of a table. In other words, there is no way to create a relational table with this format. The purpose of 1NF is to produce a table with no such repeating attributes.

In the first chapter, we explored the possibility of duplicating the non-multiple attributes which would change the above table to that shown below.

Batch table

Batch number	Tutor code	Assigns marked	Date sent	Date returned	Student code	Course code	Assign. number
23	JS	87	12/4/98	7/5/98	981230	PR007	3
23	JS	87	12/4/98	7/5/98	978001	AB003	1
23	JS	87	12/4/98	7/5/98	980239	PE009	7
24	GH	91	21/9/98	15/10/98	978001	AB003	4
24	GH	91	21/9/98	15/10/98	985100	GM201	3

We now have a two-dimensional table and it could be represented in a relational database. However, this design was rejected on the basis that it required a substantial level of redundancy which is very undesirable.

Another possibility would be to repeat the columns horizontally to give, in outline, something like this:

Batch number		Student code	Course code	Assign. number	Student code	Course code	Assign. number	Student code	Course code	Assign. number

However, a relational table must have a fixed number of columns and hence you would have to set a fixed upper limit on the number of repetitions. In many rows, several of the repeated columns would be empty, thereby wasting space. Also, as we shall see in later chapters, this format complicates querying of the table.

This leads us to the conclusion that there is no 'one table' solution to this problem and that we need to split the table into two tables. The process of achieving this is described in the next section.

? **5.1** Does the normalisation process result in more or fewer tables?

First normal form

The first normal form is concerned with multi-valued attributes of the design. Figure 5.1 and the above tables show that the attributes Student Code, Course Code and Assignment Number repeat several times for each value of the other attributes such as Batch Number.

We require to remove the repeating items (i.e. StudentCode, CourseCode, AssignNumber) and to form a new table called Batch Items; this is the action needed to arrive at the first normal form (or 1NF). The steps involved in this are detailed below:

- remove the repeating items from the original table and form them into a new table:

Student code	Course number	Assign. number
981230	PR007	3
978001	AB003	1
980239	PR009	7
978001	AB003	4
985100	GM201	3

The original table is reduced to that shown below, with a primary key of Batch number:

Batch table

Batch number	Tutor code	Assigns marked	Date sent	Date returned
23	JS	87	12/4/98	7/5/98
24	GH	91	21/9/98	15/10/983

- create a new attribute of the new table which is the key value of the original table:

Batch items table version 1

Batch number	Student code	Course code	Assign. number
23	981230	PR007	3
23	978001	AB003	1
23	980239	PR009	7
24	972177	AB003	4
24	985100	GM201	3

- make the primary key of the new table this key value together with a qualifying value; this is usually one or more of the attributes of the new table or a sequence number. In our example we could possibly use the Student number (as shown underlined in the table above) as long as the resultant key yields unique values. In this example, this would mean that EACH batch could only contain one assignment from one student. Alternatively, a sequence number (counting within each batch) could be used as shown below:

Batch items table version 2

Batch number	Sequence number	Student code	Course code	Assign. number
23	1	981230	PR007	3
23	2	978001	AB003	1
23	3	980239	PR009	7
24	1	972177	AB003	4
24	2	985100	GM201	3

Note that the Batch number attribute acts as a foreign key to link the Batch items table to the original Batch table.

? **5.2** For Batch items table version 1, suppose that the same student number could appear more than once in one batch. Suggest and justify an alternative key attribute combination.

Second normal form

This form requires that *all non-key attributes are dependent on the whole primary key and not on a part of it*. The definition indicates that it is applicable only to relations that have primary keys consisting of two or more columns. In our example we see that Batch items (using version 1 above) has a compound key consisting of Batch number and Student code. Do any of the other dependent attributes depend on just one of the component key fields? This question is not immediately answerable; it depends on the Student–Course relationship. If each student is on one and only one course at any time, then the Course code depends solely on the Student code (i.e., knowing the student, we can determine the course). In this case, we should separate the Student–Course information into a separate table:

Batch items table

Batch number	Student code	Assign. number
23	981230	3
23	978001	1
23	980239	7
24	972177	4
24	985100	3

Student table

Student code	Course code
981230	PR007
978001	AB003
980239	PR009
972177	AB003
985100	GM201

Note that the new table consists of a primary key (the partial key component from the original table, namely, Student code) and the dependent column(s), in this case, Course code. The dependent columns are removed from the original table.

However, if it is possible to be dealing with a student working on two different courses, then the simple correspondence between student and course implied by the Student table above would not apply. Hence, it order to specify to which course the Assignment number refers in a particular batch, we need the Course code, as in the original version.

Third normal form

This form, 3NF, requires us to ensure that *no attributes are dependent on other non-key attributes*. We noted earlier that the Assignments marked attribute was a characteristic solely of the tutor and is unrelated (directly) to the Batch table key value. To comply with the 3NF requirements, we must separate the tutor information into a separate relation:

Batch

Batch number	Tutor code	Date sent	Date returned
23	JS	12/4/98	7/5/98
24	GH	21/9/98	15/10/98

Tutor

Tutor code	Assigns marked
JS	87
GH	91

Non-key dependency is also referred to as transitive dependency, because a transitive link exists between the key and the other attributes involved. That is,

Batch number   →   Tutor code   →   Assignments marked

          determines   determines

To summarise this example, the original data has been factored into four normalised tables, namely, Batch, Batch items, Student and Tutor. Thus we arrive at the design dictated by the normalisation process, which as you can see, corresponds to our intuitive design. The normalisation discipline helps us to understand more formally and clearly why we build the application relations in a particular way. The need to define the precise nature of the data in the application domain (e.g., can a student be on more than one course?) makes us study the situation more closely. In developing a practical application we must be careful to specify definitely what features of the data and its processing our design is intended to manage.

Anomalies

If we try to use tables in an application that do not conform to 1NF, 2NF or 3NF, we will encounter certain processing 'anomalies', i.e., inconvenient or error-prone situations arising when we process the tables. They can be classified as *update*, *delete* and *insertion* anomalies. The following table is used as an example.

Enrolment

Student number	Course number	Student name	Address	Course
S21	9201	Jones	Edinburgh	Accounts
S21	9267	Jones	Edinburgh	Maths
S24	9267	Smith	Glasgow	Maths
S30	9201	Richards	Manchester	Accounts
S30	9322	Richards	Manchester	Computing
S41	9267	Ferguson	London	Maths

This table is in 1NF but not 2NF. The key of the relation is shown underlined; we can see that Student name is dependent on one part of this key, namely, the Student number. That is, given a particular value of Student number, say S24, the value of Student name is predetermined, namely Smith. Similarly, Course is dependent on the Course number. Observe that every time the number 9267 apears in the Course number column, the course name Maths appears in the Course column. In general, there will be one row of this table for each Student–Course combination, hence these dependent items will be repeated with each occurrence of each value of either

Student number or Course number. It is important to note that this example assumes that a student can be on more than one course. This data is subject to three types of anomaly: update, deletion and insertion anomalies.

Update anomaly
Information about the address of students is repeated, once for each course they are on. If Jones moves to Aberdeen, every row in the table that refers to Jones would have to be amended. Failure to update all instances of Jones's address would result in two different versions of the address.

Delete anomaly
If the last student registered for a course withdraws from it, the details about the course are lost as well. The table only retains information on existing student-course combinations, not on courses independently. If student S21 leaves course 9201, no record remains of this course.

Insertion anomaly
This is the converse of the delete anomaly; we cannot record the existence of a new course without at least one student being assigned to it. If we introduce a new course on Physics, we cannot record any information about it until we enrol the first student. Note that we cannot use empty (null) columns; for instance, a row of the table such as that illustrated below is not allowed.

Student number	Course number	Student name	Address	Course
Null	9300	Null	Null	Physics

The use of nulls in the primary key of a relational table conflicts with the concept of entity integrity which was described in Chapter 2.

These anomalies can be avoided if the data is normalised to 2NF. For this example, the data would then also conform to 3NF. To comply with 2NF we must factor the table into additional tables where dependency on a partial key exists; this applies to Student name and Address dependent on Student number and Course dependent on Course number. This gives us a new table for students and for courses. These, and the residue of the original table, are shown below.

Student table

Student number	Student name	Address
S21	Jones	Edinburgh
S24	Smith	Glasgow
S30	Richards	Manchester
S41	Ferguson	London

Course table

Course number	Course
9201	Accounts
9267	Maths
9322	Computing

Enrolment

Student number	Course no.
S21	9201
S21	9267
S24	9267
S30	9201
S30	9322
S41	9267

The example illustrates the effect of anomalies arising from a design that does not conform to 2NF but anomalies can also arise from failure to comply with 3NF. An example of this is examined in the next question.

5.3 Consider the following table design. Assuming the usual interpretation of such data, why does it not comply with 3NF? What anomalies would it exhibit?

Order number	Order date	Customer number	Salesman number	Salesman name

Boyce-Codd normal form

This normal form was developed because of observed limitations of the third normal form that allowed redundancy and anomalies to arise under certain circumstances. It is sometimes referred to as 'strong' 3NF. Note also that some authors adopt the Boyce-Codd version as the third normal form. In practice, conditions necessitating Boyce-Codd normalisation are relatively rare.

The definition of BCNF is very compact:

'A relation is in BCNF if every determinant in the relation is a candidate key'

Revision

A determinant is the 'left-hand' attribute in a functional dependency, for instance, if we have the dependency OrderNumber → OrderDate, meaning OrderNumber determines OrderDate, then OrderNumber is the determinant. A candidate key is an attribute or combination of attributes that could serve as a primary key because its value will be unique for all rows or the relation. One candidate key is chosen to be the actual primary key.

To understand the implications of BCNF consider the following sample relation:

Student

Student number	Subject	Subject lecturer
10001	Accounting	Williams
10001	Maths	O'Connell
10022	Maths	Davis
10333	Economics	Edmonds
10333	Management	Fisher
14444	Accounting	Williams

The Student relation describes students, subjects that the students are studying and the Subject lecturers. The following rules apply to this application; the bracketed items indicate an example of each rule.

1. Each student can take one or more subjects (10001 takes Accounting and Maths).
2. Each lecturer teaches only one subject (Williams only teaches Accounting).
3. Each subject can be taught by one or more lecturers (Maths is taught by O'Connell and Davis).

Let us first look for candidate keys in this relation. The Student number cannot be a primary key since it is not unique. However, Student number and subject combined would provide a unique value as would Student number and Subject lecturer. Each of these candidate keys produces a functional dependency; in addition there is, by definition (rule 2 above), a functional dependency between Subject lecturer and Subject. Hence, we have three functional dependencies as follows:

1. Student number, Subject $\rightarrow$ Lecturer
2. Student number, Lecturer $\rightarrow$ Subject
3. Lecturer $\rightarrow$ Subject

Note that the relation is in 3NF. Regardless of whether we choose Student number, Subject or Student number, Lecturer above as the primary key, all non-key attributes are dependent on the whole key. For instance, if we choose a key of Student number, Subject then we have the dependency:

Student number, Subject $\rightarrow$ Subject lecturer

However, referring back to our definition of BCNF, we can see that functional dependency (3) conflicts with the requirements: Lecturer is a determinant but not a candidate key. Hence this relation is not in BCNF.

Non-BCNF relations can produce anomalies under certain circumstances. In the relation above if we delete the row for Student 10022 we lose the fact that Davis teaches Maths – this is a delete anomaly. If we want to introduce the fact that Peters teaches Management we must also find a student to enrol in the course – this is an insertion anomaly.

As always in normalisation, the solution is to divide the relation into new relations that comply with BCNF. The example relation above becomes:

Student	
Student number	**Subject lecturer**
10001	Williams
10001	O'Connell
10022	Davis
10333	Edmonds
10333	Fisher
14444	Williams

Lecturer	
Student Lecturer	**Subject**
Williams	Accounting
O'Connell	Maths
Davis	Maths
Edmonds	Economics
Fisher	Management

These relations each have only one candidate key and hence must be in BCNF. Anomalies arise in non-BCNF relations when:

- there is more than one candidate key
- the candidate keys are composite
- the attributes of the candidate keys overlap, i.e., they have an attribute in common.

Note that the BCNF definition does not mention earlier normal forms; it is evaluated purely on the basis of the definition given above. This means that in principle you could 'jump' directly to the BCNF stage without needing to examine for 2NF or 3NF; if the relation complies with BCNF, it must also comply with 2NF and 3NF. In practice, derivation of 2NF and 3NF is intuitively easier to understand and hence are more commonly used.

? **5.4** Using the above list of conditions for anomalies, show how the original Student relation given above satisfies these conditions.

4NF

The fourth normal form is concerned with a concept called a multi-valued dependency (MVD). The presence of MVDs in a relation leads to anomalies in the data. The unnormalised data shown below refers to personnel information about employees in respect of their dependents and their leisure-time activities. In general, each of these (dependents and activities) will be multi-valued.

Employee	Children	Activities
Andy Evans	Ann Martin	Golf Tennis Gardening
Gillian Walker	Eileen Mark Karen	Swimming Badminton

One possible way of organising this data into a table is shown below:

Employee	Children	Activities
Andy Evans	Ann	Golf
Andy Evans	Martin	Tennis
Andy Evans	*null*	Gardening
Gillian Walker	Eileen	Swimming
Gillian Walker	Mark	Badminton
Gillian Walker	Karen	*null*

An obvious feature of the data is that the two multi-valued attributes are independent. Accordingly, to organise the data as shown above is inappropriate since it seems to suggest some relationship between children and activities. In order to avoid this interpretation we need to replicate each occurrence of a child value with every value of activity producing the relation:

Employee	Children	Activities
Andy Evans	Ann	Golf
Andy Evans	Ann	Tennis
Andy Evans	Ann	Gardening
Andy Evans	Martin	Golf
Andy Evans	Martin	Tennis
Andy Evans	Martin	Gardening
Gillian Walker	Eileen	Swimming
Gillian Walker	Mark	Swimming
Gillian Walker	Karen	Swimming
Gillian Walker	Eileen	Badminton
Gillian Walker	Mark	Badminton
Gillian Walker	Karen	Badminton

This form of table exhibits multi-valued dependency. Since the primary key of this relation would need to be all three attributes it must be in BCNF, but there is still manifestly considerable redundancy in the data. The obvious solution to this is to decompose the relation into two separate relations:

Employee	Children
Andy Evans	Ann
Andy Evans	Martin
Gillian Walker	Eileen
Gillian Walker	Mark
Gillian Walker	Karen

Employee	Activities
Andy Evans	Tennis
Andy Evans	Gardening
Gillian Walker	Golf
Gillian Walker	Swimming
Gillian Walker	Badminton

The key of each of these relations consists of both attributes. As well as being in BCNF, these relations are also now in 4NF because the MVDs have been eliminated. The formal definition of 4NF is

> A relation is in fourth normal form if it is in BCNF and all dependencies are functional dependencies.

The solution arrived at above, of course, is that which would have been developed if using ER modelling or even an intuitive approach. However, there are more formal aspects to MVDs that we will not address in this text. Readers interested in further study of this topic should consult (Ullman 1997), (Date 1995) or (Kroenke 1992).

Higher forms: 5NF and DK/NF

The fifth normal form is concerned with the concept of join dependency. This is an assertion that, if a relation is subdivided into a number of projections, then the original relation can be reconstituted without loss of information by joins.

The Domain Key Normal Form was defined by Fagin (1981). The formal definition of DK/NF is

> A relation is in DK/NF is every constraint on the relation is a logical consequence of the definitions of keys and domains.

Fagin proved that this is the ultimate normal form: no other normal form is necessary or possible. Unfortunately, there is no known standard procedure for converting a relation to DK/NF.

Neither of these normal forms is used to any extent in normal practical database design and will not be pursued further in this text. For further details on these consult Date (1995) and Kroenke (1992). For a more formal approach consult (Ullman 1997).

Summary of normalisation

Normalisation is a formal procedure that can contribute to the design of relational tables and, using the notion of functional dependency, can allow you to verify that the designed tables do not contain any anomalies. It should be noted that the table designs emerging from normalisation show the natural usage of tables, i.e., each entity class in the application domain and (most) relationships between the entities are each represented by a separate table.

ER diagrams and normalisation

ER modelling and the techniques of normalisation are both used in the design of relational database systems. In this respect, the ER technique works in a top-down fashion, i.e., we proceed by identifying the large-scale objects in the application domain (such as programmers, projects, customers) and their relationships with one another, before analysing their component attributes in depth. This contrasts with the bottom-up normalisation approach where the entity descriptions emerge from an analysis of the component data attributes.

However, it must not be thought that the two methods are in competition or even alternatives. In general, both will be used in the design process for a new system. The ER approach is probably best in deriving the overall design, producing a set of relations; normalisation can then be applied to these tables to ensure that they conform to normalisation rules. Note that a design produced in this fashion is unlikely to need attention beyond the 3NF stage of normalisation.

Case study

In this section we present a fairly elaborate example based on the scenario of a staff employment agency. Job-seekers apply to the agency looking for employment and are asked to complete an application form. The data on the form must be captured by the agency's database system. Design a suitable set of relations to hold this data.

The data is divided into four categories, namely, Client details, Agency consultant, Qualifications and Previous employment. The latter two consist of a variable number of entries. The detail of each category is as follows:

Client Details   Registration no, Name, Address, Date of birth, Sex, Telephone.

Agency Consultant   Consultant ID, Name, Extension

Qualifications   Award, Awarding body, Level, Year

Previous Employment   Employer name, Address, Telephone, Job title, Reason for leaving, Date started, Date left, Final pay.

Table 5.1 shows the transformation of the unnormalised data through the successive normal forms. The keys of the tables are shown underlined. The numbers in parentheses refer to notes that are supplied below the table. The $\rightarrow$ symbol indicates that the referenced table is unchanged by that stage.

Case study notes

1. The Qualification and the Previous Employment data occurs several times for each client and hence must be factored into separate tables as shown. The RegNo must form part of the key of the new tables to form a foreign key link to the Client table. It is assumed that the Award entry is sufficient to make the combined key unique.
2. The requirements for the primary key of the Employment table are somewhat complex. RegNo is required as already mentioned. The addition of Employer

Table 5.1

Un-normalised	First normal form	Second normal form	Third normal form
Client Data	**Client Table**	→	**Client Table**
RegNo	RegNo		RegNo
Name	Name		Name
Address	Address		Address
DOB	DOB		DOB
Sex	Sex		Sex
Phone	Phone		Phone
Consultant	Consultant ID		
Consultant ID	Name		**Consultant Table (4)**
Name	Extension		Consultant ID
Extension			Name
Qualifications			Extension
Award			
Awarding Body	**Qualifications Table**	→	→
Level	RegNo (1)		
Year	Award		
Prev Employment	Awarding Body		
Employer Name	Level		
Address	Year		
Telephone			
Job Title	**Employment Table**	**Employment Table**	→
Reason for leaving	RegNo (1,2)	RegNo	
Date Started	Employer Name	Employer Name	
Date Left	Date Started	Job Title	
Final Pay	Job Title	Date Started	
	Address	Reason for leaving	
	Telephone	Date Left	
	Reason for leaving	Final pay	
	Date Left		
	Final Pay	**Employer Table**	→
		Employer Name (3)	
		Address	
		Telephone	

name is probably not sufficient since one could be employed by a company on more than one occasion. If the key is qualified by appending the Date of Starting, this would presumably give a unique key value.

3. The 2NF conversion required arises because, in the initial Employment table design, the employer address and telephone are dependent on only part of the key (Employer Name).

4. The 3NF conversion arises because of the functional dependency:

    Consultant ID → Name, Extension where Consultant ID is not a key.

Summary

1. Normalisation is a set of procedures that aid in analysing the design of a database.
2. Normalisation removes unnecessary redundancy from a database.
3. Normalisation can identify potential anomalies in the structure of the database tables.
4. An anomaly is a difficulty or inconvenience in the processing of the tables.
5. Normalisation is a multi-stage process where the product of each stage is referred to as a 'normal form'.
6. Normal forms 1NF, 2NF, 3NF and Boyce-Codd are the most significant from the point of view of practical design.
7. Other normal forms are, 4NF, 5NF and DK/NF.
8. Normalisation is used as part of the database table design process and complements ER diagram design techniques.

Answers to in-text questions

5.1 All the normalisation conversions inevitably produce more tables.

5.2 Batch Number/Student Code/Assign Number would be OK assuming that each student was on one course and one student could not submit two versions of the same assignment. No other combination would suffice. The essential requirement is that the attribute combination chosen as the key must have unique values per row.

5.3 The Salesman Name is dependent on the non-key field Salesman Number and hence the table is not in 3NF. If the Salesman's name was changed, multiple rows would need to be updated; this is an update anomaly.

5.4 There are two candidate keys (Student Number, Subject) and (Student Number, Lecturer). The candidate keys each have two attributes. Both candidate keys include Student Number, hence they overlap.

REVIEW QUESTIONS

Answers in Appendix C.

1   Define the term 'normalisation'.

2   What are the benefits of normalisation?

3   Outline the process of converting from unnormalised through the first, second and third normal forms.

4   Define the Boyce-Codd normal form.

5   What is the significance of the Domain Key Normal Form?

6   List the types of anomaly that can arise if database tables do not conform to 2NF and/or 3NF.

EXERCISES

Answers to exercises flagged with an asterisk appear in Appendix D.

1 *Normalise the data shown below, showing the development of your design through the forms 1NF, 2NF and 3NF.

Ordno	Date	Custno	Name	Address	Prodno	Desc	Price	Qty
1	5/1/96	22	Smith	London	A95	Jacket	55	4
					G17	Coat	120	8
					K10	Suit	90	5
2	19/1/96	47	Jones	Paris	G17	Coat	120	9
					D77	Shirt	35	20
3	27/3/96	25	West	Glasgow	E30	Tie	5	25
					D77	Shirt	35	4

2 Outline the kinds of anomalies that can arise in a relational database system by using unnormalised tables, using the following table as a means of illustration.

Student number	Student name	Address	Course code	Course name	Course start date	Exam result
9300111	Smith	Glasgow	BS002	Accounting	5/10/92	Pass
9300123	Anderson	Edinburgh	BS004	Maths	12/10/92	Pass
9300123	Anderson	Edinburgh	BS016	Economics	12/10/92	Fail
9300789	Jones	Dundee	BS002	Accounting	5/10/92	Pass

Show how the above data could be reorganised into separate tables to avoid these anomalies.

3 A financial consultancy company provides consultants to work on clients' projects. Each consultant works on only one project at a time, but a project may employ more than one consultant. The following (unnormalised) table provides an extract of data pertaining to the current assignments.

Consultant ID	Project no.	Hours	Project name	Consultant name	Project location	Fee rate
21	A92	450	Apollo	Gray	Glasgow	100.00
25	Z50	90	Zeus	Brown	Edinburgh	90.00
33	Z50	20	Zeus	White	Edinburgh	95.00
37	M75	135	Mercury	Green	Aberdeen	150.00

The Hours value is the total hours worked on the project so far, per consultant. The Fee rate value depends on the combination of the consultant involved and the project.

(a) Design a set of normalised tables derived from this data. The primary keys must be identified.
(b) Explain what changes would be required in the table's design if the consultants were allowed to work on more than one project at a time.

4 *Explain how, in a relational database application, anomalies can arise from the use of unnormalised data, using the following table as a means of illustration.

Project number	Project name	Employee number	Employee name	Department	Hours spent
1	Apollo	1001	Smith	Engineering	127
1	Apollo	1003	Jones	Accounts	45
2	Mercury	1002	Stewart	Marketing	70
3	Venus	1001	Smith	Engineering	21
3	Venus	1006	Brown	Engineering	124

Design a set of relational tables that would avoid the anomalies arising from the above table design, identifying the primary key in each table.

5 The following table has been designed by an unskilled database user to hold data on student exam results. Convert the table to a more efficient format.

Student number	Subject	Student name	Lecturer	Lecturer dept	Assess-ment 1	Assess-ment 1	Assess-ment 1
991010	Maths	Stewart	Mackay	MAT	45	23	69
991010	Stats	Stewart	Mackay	MAT	31	31	57
992001	Accounts	Ridley	Robinson	FIN	77	77	80
992001	Economics	Ridley	Ford	BUS	41	41	43
...							

6 Examine the following table that describes the working experience of a group of programmers in languages and database systems. What normal form is the table in? Convert the tables to 4NF.

Programmer name	Language	Database
David	COBOL	Oracle
David	COBOL	Access
David	C++	Oracle
David	C++	Access
William	Smalltalk	Informix
William	Smalltalk	Oracle

6

Physical design

Introduction

In earlier work we have described the activities involved in developing a conceptual model of the database that is required to support the target application. The conceptual design should include ER diagrams and the structure of each of the tables derived from the component relations and relationships.

The nature of the conceptual design is such that it should be independent of an actual database product, i.e., it should be possible to take the design and implement it on a range of different products. It is quite likely in practice that you have a particular database in mind or that you have no choice, for instance, you may work for a company committed, by virtue of many previously implemented systems, to a particular package. Nevertheless, it is desirable that the design should progress through an implementation-independent phase so that the requirements of the application system are not confused with the limitations of the database product. The current chapter and a major part of the rest of this book is concerned with a range of techniques that contribute to the production of the final database system and the factors that have to be considered in this design process. An overview of this work is provided below.

- Chapter 7 deals with the nature and facilities provided by database management systems (DBMS). The capabilities of the DBMS is a significant factor in how the database system will be implemented and indeed what it is capable of.
- Chapter 8 covers the topic of programming and programmability in database systems, which again, will have a considerable bearing on ones approach in developing the database solution.
- Chapter 9 deals with aspects of security and integrity that must be designed into the database.
- Chapter 10 deals with the topic of concurrency, i.e., the problems inherent in designing and operating a database with several on-line users.

The current chapter covers a number of additional topics not covered elsewhere including the following:

- choosing a database product
- aspects of table design
- aspects of form and report design
- indexing
- controlled redundancy.

93

Choice of database

As mentioned above, in many cases we have no choice in the selection of a database product but where a 'green-field' situation exists, there are a number of factors to be considered. In assessing the wide range of database products that are currently available, it is helpful to identify some major distinguishing features to simplify the process of selection. A number of such features are given below.

Scale
This term refers to the maximum number of users and the maximum disk space supported by the database. These parameters can also be limited by the host computer system; the system overall must be able to cope with the expected loading.

Performance
The number of transactions per hour that can be handled. This of course is also heavily dependent on the computer system used but it is important that the database and the computer are matched in power.

Support for data types
For example, you may require support for storing multimedia data. For specialised applications you may require to hold high precision floating-point values or 'long' integer values.

Connectivity
Support for the accessing of other databases or file systems. There may be a need, for instance, to access some 'legacy' system that uses an older database package. Also, your database may need to communicate with some other system in another office. This is an area of considerable activity in the database market at present fuelled by the current interest in promoting commerce via national and international networks. Several standard technologies have arisen from this.

Open database connectivity (ODBC)   ODBC is an application programmer interface (API) that facilitates communication, in client-server mode, between different database products using the Windows operating system. It consists of a set of dynamic link libraries that support a number of functions callable from various languages such as Microsoft Access Basic, C++ and Visual Basic. The underlying principle of ODBC is to provide a layer of software that reconciles the differences between the client and the server such that a client program written using ODBC will be able to communicate unchanged with any ODBC-compliant server.

Object technology   A number of technologies and products have appeared recently that take an object-oriented view of the interconnection and interoperation of processes and data on machines connected by networks. These include Microsoft's COM and DCOM and OMG's Corba specification.

World wide web   This is not a single technology but an environment embodying many new techniques. Some of these techniques facilitate communication between different systems in a platform-independent manner.

These topics are covered in more detail in Chapter 11.

Processing complexity

Many modern database products, particularly those addressing the PC market, provide extensive interactive facilities that can be used by end-users (as opposed to professional systems developers). Some, indeed, provide only for such usage. If the interactive facilities cannot cope with your proposed application, then you need to look for products that have some degree of additional programmability. It may be that your application requires some computation that is best handled by a conventional programming language. In this event, database access via embedded SQL or ODBC commands may be required.

Design of tables

The major decisions regarding the design of tables are generally tackled during the conceptual design of the system; the subdivision of the data in respective tables and the design of relationship tables should have been worked out. However, there remain a few factors worthy of your attention, dealt with in the subsections below. Some of the points covered overlap with topics studied elsewhere but are provided here for completeness.

Data types

Choosing the data type

The conceptual data design should establish the domains of the data items to be represented in the database tables. Factors such as the maximum admissible length of text attributes and maximum values and required precision for numerical items need to be determined. From this knowledge, appropriate data types can be chosen for the table columns. Note that the data type determines the storage mode, the behaviour of the data item on input and output and the permissible processing operations on the data. A summary of the main categories of data types generally provided by database systems is given below.

Text	character data, letters, numerical digits, special symbols, etc., based on standard character sets such as ASCII or Unicode.
Numeric	numerical values, either integer or real (floating point) numbers, with varying size and precision.
Counter	system-generated serial sequence of numbers, often used to create primary key values.
Date/Time	date and time values.
Boolean	logical value which can be interpreted as any pair of values, e.g., true/false, 1/0, Yes/No.
Binary	Set of binary data, held as unstructured item. Often used to store multimedia data.
Object	Binary data in standard object-based format such as OLE or COM.

The following sections provide some additional information about some of these data types.

Text

In general, the defined size of a text column is governed by the users' expectations of the data to be encountered in the application. Choosing an appropriate length in this respect involves a trade-off between coping with the data and the disk space required to hold the data; an extra 10 bytes per row in a table of 10,000 rows adds 100,000 bytes to the size of the table. Some systems support variable length text fields, which do not store trailing spaces and hence optimise storage requirements. An example of this is the VARCHAR2 type in Oracle. Many systems now provide a facility for storing text of indefinite length; examples are the 'memo' type in Microsoft Access which can hold text of up to 64,000 bytes and the Oracle 'LONG' which has a theoretical storage limit of two gigabytes. Such fields are limited in functionality. Typical restrictions are that they cannot be used in SQL Select lists, they cannot be indexed and there can be only one such item per table. In other words, they are used simply for the recording of textual information that cannot be conveniently accommodated in conventional text fields.

Numbers

For numerical items, there is a major split between integer and fixed-point and floating-point values. If the data is purely a whole number (e.g., a quantity in stock value), some integer representation is best; again, knowledge of the application domain should indicate the maximum value of the item. Most systems provide for more than one integer types; the SQL standard specifies INTEGER and SMALLINT. The actual size of these (in bits) is implementation dependent, subject to the former being larger than the latter, but possible values are 16 bits for SMALLINT and 32 for INTEGER. Microsoft Access provides Byte (8 bit), Integer (16 bit) and Long (32 bit).

A fixed-point representation provides a fixed number of total digits, which includes a fixed number of decimal places. Standard SQL has a datatype NUMERIC(n, p) where the total number of digits is $n+p$ and p is the number of decimal places. A fixed-point format would be used for currency amounts in the absence of a specific currency type (e.g., Microsoft Access). A floating-point value is represented in standard SQL using the FLOAT data type.

As an example of numeric data type provision, Table 6.1 summarises the types available in Microsoft Access.

Table 6.1

Data type name	Range of values	Storage
Byte	0 to 255, integer	One byte
Integer	−32,768 to +32,767, integer	Two bytes
Long integer	±2billion, approx, integer	Four bytes
Single	$\pm 3.4 \times 10^{\pm 38}$, approx, floating point, six digit precision	Four bytes
Double	$\pm 1.8 \times 10^{\pm 308}$, approx, floating point, ten digits precision	Eight bytes

It is important to distinguish carefully between integer and floating point representations: integers are inherently exact but ultimately limited in maximum value; floating point values are never 'exact' but can represent astronomically large and small values with a defined precision.

A point to note when deciding on a data type is that numerical types should be used only for actual numeric values. Some data items consist entirely of numerical digits although they are not a numerical quantity; identification codes such as product numbers fall into this category. In general, such items should be defined as a text field. As well as defining how the data item is stored, the data type defines the behaviour of the data on input and output. For instance, if a field is defined as text, rather than numeric, it will be left-justified in printed output and report generators will not try to generate automatic totals of the field.

Attribute domains

The data type cannot generally fix the data values within the precise domain dictated by the application. For instance, a numeric attribute may have a range of value from 1 to 500, but the nearest representation available is, say, a 16-bit integer with potential range of $-32,768$ to $32,767$. Ideally, it would be desirable to set the domain of an attribute to the exact values that exist in the application; this facility is not widely available but some current developments are moving in this direction. For instance, in the SQL 92 standard, there is a CREATE DOMAIN command defined (albeit with limited functionality) and several products now offer 'extended relational' facilities that include user-defined attribute types. These topics are covered in Chapter 12.

In the absence of data types that precisely define the attribute domain, suitable validation must be applied to prevent erroneous data from being entered into the database. The general principle is that no data that is outwith the domains of the table attributes should be allowed into the database. If this principle is to be imposed by validation it places the onus for its implementation on the database developer.

? **6.1** What data type would be the best choice for

(a)   an amount of money

(b)   quantity of televisions in stock

(c)   the dimensions of molecules.

Data redundancy

In earlier studies, the benefits of normalisation were described, namely, the removal of redundancies and avoidance of anomalies. It may come as a surprise then that it may be acceptable to tolerate data redundancy in the interests of convenience and/or performance. A common example is very widespread – the use of a post-code within an address. If we have an address consisting of a street, town and district then inclusion of a post-code is actually redundant and breaks third normal form because the address is functionally dependent on the post-code; given a post-code the city and street name is pre-determined. The alternative here is not too attractive; it theoretically requires a separate table mapping the post-code to the city and street address. Normally one would not implement this since the problems created by the redundancy are far outweighed by the convenience.

Another example is also very common and relates to applications having a one-to-many relationship such as Order to Order items. The main order information is held in the Order table (customer, date, etc.), with details of each item ordered (product code, quantity, etc.) stored in the Order detail table. This is illustrated in Figure 6.1. Additionally, it is likely that the item price may be held in a third table, say Products.

Order table

OrderNo	CustNo	Date	Salesman	Total

Order detail table

OrderNo	Product No	Quantity

OrderNo	Product No	Quantity

OrderNo	Product No	Quantity

Figure 6.1   Derived attribute example.

Now the total order value can be computed by querying the Order items and Products tables and totalling the individual amounts. However, if a large number of items are involved this causes a fair amount of accessing. Although it is clearly redundant, it would be possible to hold the total order value in the Order table, thereby having this value readily accessible without further querying. A table attribute that can be calculated from other database data is often called a derived attribute. It is clearly essential that the correspondence between the redundant total and the component Order item values is maintained continuously; any change to the Order item or Product tables must be reflected immediately in the Order table. This can be reliably achieved by using a transaction to update the Order and Order item tables together, guaranteeing that the two tables will always be 'in line'. Transactions are a database mechanism that allows database operations to be 'bracketed' together to ensure that all the operations therein are carried out as a unit. Transactions are covered in Chapter 9.

The examples described above could be viewed as relatively trivial and deciding to use them should not require any serious heart-searching. In circumstances where the database system and/or host computer are under considerable performance pressures, it may be necessary to de-normalise in more substantial measure. What this implies is that we deliberately design relations that are not in 1NF, 2NF or 3NF. The next sections discuss briefly the prospects and implications inherent in de-normalising at the various NF stages.

First normal form

Strictly speaking, it is not possible to represent data not in first normal form within a relational database because it implies the storage of more than one value in one table 'cell'. However, we can create an implicit non-1NF format by repeating a column definition. For instance, if we look again at an example shown in an earlier chapter, the difficulty here can be identified.

In this example, representing a video hire application, the videos currently on hire to a customer are held in a set of three identically defined column called Film Title 1, 2 and 3. Unused Film Title 'slots' are filled with null.

Customer table

Customer number	Name	Address	Balance owing	Film title 1	Film title 2	Film title 3
5567	Jones	Cross Road	2.50	Forbidden Planet	...	...
2913	Anderson	River Lane	0.00	Titanic	Shane	Casablanca
4890	Murray	West Street	1.50	Casablanca	Titanic	...
1622	Richards	Mill Lane	3.00	Schindler's List	...	...

The problems introduced by non-1NF relations are:

- Rows must be of a fixed number of columns, so there can be only a fixed number of repeated attributes.
- Typically, many of the attribute columns will be unfilled, representing wasted space.
- There is added complexity in querying. Since values of the same attribute are held in one row, querying these values involves multiple references to the attribute.

Using the above table, if we wanted to issue a query to find the occurrence of a particular film name in the Film title columns, it would require an SQL query like

SELECT CustomerNumber, Name FROM Customer WHERE FilmTitle1 = 'Titanic'
                                         OR   FilmTitle2 = 'Titanic'
                                         OR   FilmTitle3 = 'Titanic'

This would be very inconvenient for more than a few columns.

It is perhaps worth noting that 1NF differs in nature from 2NF and 3NF in the context of redundancy. If we have a relation not in 1NF it does not introduce any redundancy or anomalies. Indeed, it could actually economise in storage space. Failure to conform to 2NF or 3NF introduces redundancy and anomalies, the implications of which must be clearly identified and managed within the system design.

? **6.2** Reviewing the above discussion, can you suggest conditions within which a limited de-normalisation might be acceptable.

Second and third normal forms

If we choose to relax the 2NF or 3NF rules, the consequences are relatively obvious; we are introducing redundancy and the potential for anomalies for the possible advantage of increased performance. In effect, we are hoping to improve querying times by avoiding a join to another table. As an example, consider the example of post codes mentioned above. The conventional format for a name and address application is shown below:

Customer number	Customer name	Address	City	Postcode
B1717	Smith	30 Moon Street	Sunville	SV12 9TR
C2346	Jones	20 Moon Street	Sunville	SV12 9TR

In fact, given the postcode, the street name and the City can be determined as indicated in the (somewhat contrived) example. Customers Smith and Jones are near neighbours and hence have the same postcode. This format conflicts with 3NF since the Address and City columns are functionally dependent on the non-key column Postcode. The 'ideal' representation of this data would be

Customer number	Customer name	Street number
B1717	Smith	30
C2346	Jones	20

Postcode	Address	City
SV12 9TR	Moon Street	Sunville
SV12 9TR	Moon street	Sunville

In most applications involving addresses, it is unlikely that the properly normalised design would be used; the normalised version is not likely to save much space and other than adherence to the principles of normalisation has little advantage.

The circumstances that might indicate potential benefits in terms of using non-2NF or non-3NF tables are

- large tables that would take some time to join
- relatively limited duplication of data inherent in the de-normalisation
- relatively static data such as the postcode–address relationship.

As we pointed out above, it is generally possible to avoid anomalies by employing a transaction to guarantee that the duplicate updating is done correctly. So, for example, if an item of data is stored in several different rows of a table, a transaction would be used to amend all occurrences at the same time, ensuring that they all maintain the same value. Provided the above conditions are satisfied, the duplication of data is probably more of an inconvenience in the development and maintenance of the system.

Forms and report design

Overview

A form is a screen display that is used for data entry and querying of database data. Essentially a form provides a 'window' into the database, showing the data in a convenient user-friendly format. It is an alternative to the table-based interfaces that most DBMSs provide. Forms are primarily an end-user facility; their principal role is to facilitate the operation of the database application by clerical and administrative staff that are not familiar with the internal design of the database. To a considerable extent, the set of forms supporting a database application 'is' the database for such end-users.

Forms have been used in most database systems except those using a purely SQL-based command interface. The recent advances in graphical user interfaces (GUIs) have considerably enhanced the potential and facilities of forms. In this section, we highlight some of the main features of forms that would typically be found in a modern GUI-based database system and indicate some of the design issues of forms. Further reference to forms can be found in Chapter 7 where the facilities provided by database management systems are described.

A report is a printed output of information from the database system. The production of reports is necessary in order to communicate with other people such as clients, suppliers, employees, etc., that do not have access to the database computer. While there has been considerable progress towards 'paper-less' commerce in recent years, in the form of email, EDI and similar technologies, the need still exists to have the facility to produce printed reports such as invoices, delivery notes, management summaries, order forms etc. In this section we look briefly at the general nature of report production.

Elements of forms

A form provides a means of viewing and maintaining data held within a database. The simplest situation is where the form shows one row of data on screen at a time; this is illustrated in Figure 6.2.

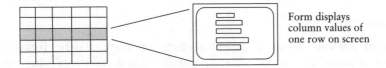

Figure 6.2   Simple one-row form.

However, there are several more elaborate possibilities, detailed below.

1. The form may be based, not on a physical table, but on the output from a query. A relational query by its nature produces a result that is also a relation and hence can be used as the source data of a form. When the form is used, the query may have to be executed to bring the data up to date, but this will be transparent to the user. Also, depending on the query, there may be restrictions on the updating of the data.

2. The form may display several rows of the table/query. This facility is used mainly in browsing-type operations where the user scans manually through a range of table rows to locate some specific item.

3. The screen display may hold two (or more) forms interconnected in some fashion. The most common mode of working in this respect is the use of a form/subform arrangement. This is used to display two tables having a one-to-many relationship such as Order and Order item tables in a Sales order application. The main form displays the 'one' side of the relationship (the Order data) while a subform typically shows several lines of the 'many' table (the Order items). An example of this is shown in Figure 6.3.

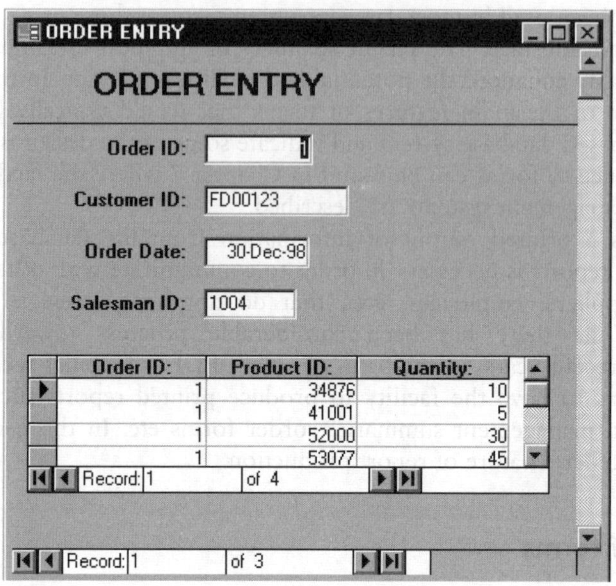

Figure 6.3   Order form.

Form controls

In current systems using a graphical user interface (GUI), forms can be constructed using the visual objects, usually called 'controls', that the GUI supports. For the purposes of a database form, the most important of these is the text box that is used to display data from the database columns. A text box can be 'bound' or 'unbound'. Bound means that the box is linked to a column of the table underlying the form; changes made to data displayed in the text box are reflected in changes to the table. Unbound means that the text box is not linked to a table column. Unbound columns are used to hold intermediate or temporary values.

Buttons are used to initiate some specified action, such as closing the form or moving the form display to the next row of the table. They are also used to construct menu systems using unbound forms.

List boxes are used to enable selection of a data value from a list of alternatives. The list can be directly entered by the designer or be derived from a reference table.

A combo box is a combination of a text box and a list box. It presents data in a list format but also permits entry of new values.

6.3 It was stated earlier that to end-users the set of forms supporting a database application 'is' the database. Explain what is meant by this statement.

Form applications

Forms are used for three main purposes within an application database system.

1. General table maintenance, i.e., adding, amending and deleting rows from tables.
2. Application transactions, i.e., performing the essential processing operations of the application such as entering a new order, issuing an invoice, recording stock received, etc. Such operations frequently utilise two or more tables.
3. Menu construction; in order to navigate through the various options within the database application, a system of menus constructed from form buttons is often used. This is an alternative to conventional 'drop-down' menus.

Form design considerations

The design of a form is partly an aesthetic matter and as such individual tastes will vary, for instance, some people will prefer many colours, others only grey, white and black. However, there are a number of factors of 'good practice' which ought to be taken into account. These, and some general design techniques, are described below.

1. **Use consistent conventions on all forms** so that the user does not have to become familiar with every form independently, e.g.,
   - use of header and footer
   - button placements and icons
   - placement and style of text and label boxes.
   Note that it is possibly useful to have some variation in colouring or format to provide visual cues for users.
2. **Use a comfortable font size and style.** Small font sizes can make reading difficult. If the form space permits, use larger font sizes to aid readability.
3. **Establish the correct tab sequence.** The tab sequence is the route the focus will take through the form controls when tab (or return) is pressed. The default tab sequence is simply the order of creation of the controls on the form. This is not necessarily appropriate.
   - The tab sequence is usually defined by a property of the controls. Check that the automatically generated sequence follows a natural path.
   - A control can be excluded from the sequence. By default, all controls will be included (by the form generator) in the tab sequence. In many cases this serves no purpose. For instance, buttons used to navigate through the table should be excluded.
4. **Divide the form into different functional areas.** For example, the form header could show a main title and a company logo, the form footer could hold control buttons and the central area would show the form details.
5. **Customise the system for end-users**
   - Modify menu and toolbars, disable design mode, remove irrelevant options.
   - Use an automatic start-up form to prevent access to database design windows.

6. **Ensure that the form has a convenient size**
   - It is generally advisable that the form covers all or most of the screen, to avoid visible 'clutter' from the rest of the screen and accidental switching to an underlying application.
   - If the form is to be displayed on a number of different computers, care must be taken that the form will be clearly visible on the range of screen sizes and resolutions likely to be encountered.

7. **Apply validation to data.** As a fundamental rule, it should be impossible for data to get into the database which is inconsistent with other data or which is not meaningful to the application. The input validation should form a barrier to such erroneous data.

8. **Use control buttons to facilitate user interaction.** Clearly labelled buttons should be added to the form that provide the user with the necessary actions for that form, such as adding a new row, deleting a row, exiting from the form, etc. In particular, it is desirable to have buttons to cancel the current transaction and to save/confirm the current transaction.

?

6.4 Why is it advantageous that each form within an application system has a consistent appearance and uses similar functionality?

Report design

Reports produced from a database application system are normally used as a means of communication, often with people outwith the company. It is important then that the report is well designed and conveys the information correctly and clearly. Fortunately, most database systems provide extensive facilities for the automatic production of reports so that the work involved for the database developer is dramatically reduced. Typical facilities offered by database packages in this respect are examined in Chapter 7; in this section we look at some general aspects of report design.

Note that reports can be generated from tables and from queries. In general, the more complex reports will require data obtained from more than one table and this is simply achieved by means of a query that joins the tables appropriately and selects the necessary data from the query output.

Report structure

In some respects, a report can be viewed as a printed form so that many of the principles of good form design (font sizes, consistent layout, etc.), described in an earlier section of this chapter, also apply to reports. There is of course, an indefinite number of ways of formatting a printed report, but we can identify a number of common features.

1. We can make the broad distinction between simple listing reports and reports that subtotal and/or summarise the data. This has a bearing on the 'zoning' of the report. The listing report in effect will simply consist of a set of columns of data drawn from the input table/query. A totalling report will have subtotals and grand totals interspersed with the row data.

2. A number of zones of the printout can be identified:
    • report heading; generally fixed heading giving a report name, date source, etc.
    • page heading; usually also shows report name and date and column headings
    • detail; shows the 'per row' detailed data from the report source
    • page footing; possibly, page numbers, page totals, etc.

The typical format of a group total report is shown in Figure 6.4. This report shows the sales of a product range, subtotalled by sales branch code.

Page No 1 10/09/98	Product Sales Report		
Product Code	Branch Code	Sales Quantity	Sales Value
B342	North	25	150.00
	South	31	186.00
	West	43	258.00
B342 Total			594.00
C100	North	102	1018.98
	South	55	549.45
	West	79	789.21
C100 Total			2357.64
E501	North	12	479.40
	South	5	199.75
	West	9	359.55
E501 Total			1038.70
Grand Total			3990.34

Figure 6.4

Figure 6.4 shows only one level of grouping; it is possible to have many more levels. For instance, the report might be required to show the sales figures broken down into the individual salespersons at each of the branches. With increasing levels of grouping, the report becomes progressively more difficult to interpret and it is even more important to use a clear and unambiguous layout.

Indexing

Principles

Indexes are used to speed up the retrieval of data from databases. They are an implementation requirement of practical systems rather than a theoretical feature. Somewhat surprisingly, it is the availability of very efficient indexing systems that primarily accounts for the success of relational databases. In the immediate period after the invention of the relational database idea, it was thought by many that it would not be feasible as a practical system because of the processing and accessing overheads implied. The databases current at that time were so-called 'navigational' systems, i.e., the records of the database were linked by explicit pointers in the data, although various indexing systems were also used. This reduced the need to search for data based on key values, as is the case for the relational database. The development of the B-Tree indexing system dramatically improved the management of large indexes and made key-based accessing feasible. In addition, the B-Tree index facilitates browsing forwards and backwards in key sequence and searching with partial key values. In effect, an index holds all the values of a specified column or columns of a table, together with the corresponding disk addresses of records with those values. For the purposes of this explanation, refer to the 'fragment' of a table as shown below.

Record number	Customer number	Customer name	Town
1	CD1234	Jones	Glasgow
2	AB3344	Smith	London
3	ZZ8811	Anderson	Belfast
4	RT0189	Campbell	London
5	FN2178	Harper	London
6	EC0012	Collins	Belfast

Note that the Record no. shown above indicates where the row is stored in the database; this value is not part of the row data.

It is possible to build indexes for one or more fields of the file enabling fast access to the data based on a known value of the chosen field. Fields used as indexes are often referred to as index keys. For example, a Customer no. key would conceptually look as shown below:

Customer number	Record number
AB3344	2
CD1234	1
EC0012	6
FN2178	5
RT0189	4
ZZ8811	3

An index based on the Customer name would look like this:

Customer name	Record number
Anderson	3
Campbell	4
Collins	6
Harper	5
Jones	1
Smith	2

Note that we have used a different box convention here to avoid confusion with a relational table; indexes are not held in relational tables and have an internal structure that is hidden from the database users.

It is possible for the index keys to have duplicate values. An index based on the Town attribute shows this effect.

Town	Record number
Belfast	3, 6
Glasgow	1
London	2, 4, 5

It is usually possible to specify whether duplicate key values are allowed; primary key indexes, of course, must be unique but other indexes often need to allow duplicate values.

The rationale for using indexes is that the index table would typically be much smaller than the data table, could be held substantially in main memory and hence can be searched more quickly. In the absence of an index, a search for a particular column value would necessitate a serial read of the entire data table. In fact, in practice, the index is structured in such a way as to further reduce the time to find a particular value.

From the above description, you may see that there are two separate ways in which an index helps:

1. searching rapidly for a single value

2. presenting the table in a different order.

To follow the second point, if for example, we used the Customer name index, and viewed the table using a database facility, the table records would appear to be in Customer name sequence. Typically, the data is actually held unordered, and the indexes used to present the data in the required sequence. The nature of B-tree indexes make this operation particularly easy. For an explanation of the internal working of a B-tree, see Appendix A.

Note that the user would never 'see' the index data, nor are they required to do anything to service the indexes other than to specify which columns require indexing. The database engine automatically maintains and uses the indexes and they are entirely transparent to the user.

An index may consist of one or more columns. This enables us to use any arbitrary sorting sequence of the data. For instance we could sort the above data tables into Town-Customer Name sequence. This would order the data firstly into Town sequence; since there will typically be more than one customer in each town, the records pertaining to each town will then be sorted in Customer name sequence. Note that there is no point in joining index fields in this way if the first field has unique values. For instance, consider the first table shown on page 106.

An index key of Customer number-Town makes no sense since the first field (Customer number, presumably unique values) determines the sequence; the Town value would not affect the overall data sequence.

Choosing indexes

In general, the primary key of a table would be indexed; other fields might be indexed if a fast search on that field value were desirable. The database engine would use an index if one were available; otherwise a serial search of all rows would take place. To help to clarify this point, consider a query on a Customer table that is required to list all customers with the name 'Smith'. In SQL this query would be expressed as

> SELECT Name, CustomerNo FROM Customer
> WHERE Name = 'Smith'

In the absence of an index on the Name attribute, this query would be evaluated by reading every row of the table; there is no alternative since any row could have the Name equal to 'Smith'. If an index existed for the Name attribute, then the index would effectively provide the SQL interpreter with a list of the rows that contain 'Smith'. The benefit of this increases as the number of rows increases.

Query interpreters, in working out how best to resolve a query, will take account of what indexes are available and utilise these if it will speed up the query execution. Systems will generally construct an index for the primary key column of each table; it is up to the application developer to create additional indexes for columns that feature in frequent and/or 'heavy' queries. Specifically, an index should normally be created for

- the primary key
- foreign keys used in joins
- columns used in GROUP BY and/or ORDER BY clauses
- columns referred to in selection criteria of commonly-used queries.

Conversely, creation of indexes is not indicated in the following cases:

- Very small relations: the time taken to search the whole relation will be quite small and probably less than the overheads of indexing.
- Where the index is used only in an infrequently used query. Again, the overheads associated with the indexing would outweigh the benefits.

Indexing overheads

Note, however, that indexes have to be kept constantly up to date, so that amendments to the data may require modification of the indexes. For instance, the addition of a new row to the table will necessitate the update of every index for that table. This can constitute a considerable overhead during updating. A balance has to be found between the necessary speed of access and the updating overheads. In some situations, for example in periodic reports or updates run, say, once a month, it is better to 'drop' the index during normal operations then re-build the index specially for the monthly job. For an example, refer back to the Sales application tables illustrated in Figure 6.1. The Salesman attribute identifies the salesperson responsible for the sale. If we assume that a report is required summarising the total sales per salesperson for the month then an index based on the Saleman attribute would be desirable. However, this index would need constant updating during the month as new rows were added and amended. A better procedure might be to drop the index after one month's report and rebuild it again before the next report is produced.

Indexes also require disk storage space which can be substantial. For every index defined, the index will contain the index key value and a disk address, plus some additional space required by the B-tree structure. If an index key is a substantial part of the row, then that index could be larger than the data storage space. In most cases, the index space will not be a cause for concern but it is a factor that ought to be considered during the database physical design.

It is worth noting that most of the work involved in indexes is transparent to the user. For instance, updating and searching of indexes are carried out automatically by the database engine. When issuing an SQL query, the SQL interpreter decides which indexes to use. Chapter 7 contains more details about the facilities provided by the DBMS for the creation and maintenance of indexes.

?   **6.5** What is meant by saying that indexes are an 'implementation feature' and not a theoretical feature of relational databases?

Multi-field indexes

An index can be based on two or more columns combined. Typically, this can be done without regard for the column types, e.g., an index can be formed from a concatenation of a text value and a date. Multi-field indexes are necessary for compound primary key values and to speed up queries using GROUP BY and/or ORDER BY operations on multiple columns. Examples of these cases are given below.

Compound primary key
In many applications, compound primary keys arise in tables representing a 'relationship' between two other tables, e.g.,

> Orders Table: OrderNo CustomerNo Date
> Products Table: ProductNo Description Cost BinNo
> Order Detail Table: OrderNo ProductNo Quantity

The underlined items are primary keys.

Order by
In the above tables, we may want to list all Order table data in customer number order and, for each customer, in date order. Using SQL, this would look like:

> SELECT OrderNo, CustomerNo, Date
>   FROM Orders ORDER BY CustomerNo, Date

Order by and Group by operations can sometimes extend to more than two columns. For instance, in Chapter 5 we described an example based on a staff employment agency. To generate a unique primary key for the previous employment table, a combination of the attributes RegNo, Employer name, Job title and Date started was required. This combination would need to be specified in the Order By clause to display the data in this sequence.

Note that an index for compounded columns can also serve as an index for 'left-hand' subsets of these columns. In general, a compound index consisting of columns c1, c2, c3 . . . can also serve as an index for c1 and c1-c2 and c1-c2-c3, etc. This effect arises from the nature of the ordering process itself and the fact that index systems can search using only a left-hand portion of the search value. In the case of the SELECT example above, if an index was built on the Customer no.–Date combination, this index is OK as a Customer no. index alone, since it is in the appropriate sequence. The following list shows customer data sorted by Date within Customer no. Note that the customer numbers are in sequence; hence this index could be used, for example, to display the data in customer number sequence:

Customer number	Date
10	12/1/98
10	27/2/98
10	4/4/98
20	15/12/98
30	10/11/98
30	6/5/99

The same is not true of the 'right-hand' subsets, since these are in separate sequences grouped within the major key. For instance, the aforementioned Customer no.–Date index cannot serve as a date index and a separate index would need to be built if required.

The practical consequence of the 'left-hand' subset effect is that if you have an index for say columns c1-c2 then you do not need to build an index explicitly for c1 alone.

Note that there is no point in forming an index based on compound fields if the first field has unique values. For instance, the index key of Customer no.–Town makes no sense since the first field (Customer no., presumably unique values) determines the sequence; the Town value would not affect the overall data sequence.

Summary

This chapter has covered a number of factors to be considered within the process of physical database design. Additional topics in this area are covered in later chapters. The topics covered here are summarised below.

Choice of database
Factors to be considered are the scale and required performance of the application, required data types, connectivity and processing complexity.

Table design
The most important table design considerations are choice of data types, application domains, introducing redundancy and de-normalised relations.

Form design
- Forms are the users' window onto the database.
- Forms are generally used to process the routine transactions of the database application.
- Attention should be paid to the design of the form to maximise its usability.

Indexing
Indexing is a practical rather than a theoretical requirement of relational databases. It provides two main benefits: faster access to individual rows and accessing of rows in a prescribed sequence.

Answers to in-text questions

6.1 (a) If the database provides a Money or Currency datatype then this is the obvious choice. Failing this, it is best to use a long integer (holding the value in pence or cents, etc.) rather than a floating point value because of the finite accuracy of the latter.

(b) A quantity of televisions (or similar) will always be a whole number, so an integer type would be required. The size would depend on the maximum number required; a two-byte integer would provide a maximum of 32,767 which would suffice for most applications.

(c) The dimensions of molecules are microscopically small, so the only convenient representation would be a floating point type, either single or double, depending on the precision required.

6.2 To avoid wasted space, a situation where a definite small fixed number of attribute instances occurs is necessary. An example might be a Product file that stores two or three alternatives to the row item, in the event of a stock shortage. Also, a small number of occurrences will make the querying less awkward.

6.3 In general, many end-users (clerical and administrative staff) do not have (or need) any insight into the internal structure of the database, in terms of tables, queries, etc. Their view of the database is defined by the interface presented by the forms. The fact that, for example, the data presented by an Order form is derived from three separate tables is irrelevant; they see the Order information.

6.4 If consistent conventions are used on each form it makes the system easier to understand by new users and reduces the likelihood of errors.

6.5 Indexes and the use of indexes do not form part of the relational model. The practical difficulties of accessing the database with acceptable speed is not addressed by the theoretical model. As it turns out, relational databases depend to a great extent on the use of indexes to provide satisfactory performance.

REVIEW QUESTIONS

Answers in Appendix C.

1 Summarise the main factors to be considered in choosing a database system.

2 Outline the main data types generally provided by a database system.

3 What are the main benefits provided by indexing?

4 What advantages could be derived from introducing redundancy in table designs?

5 What are the main functions performed by forms?

6 Describe the format of a report using group totals.

EXERCISES

Answers to exercises flagged with an asterisk appear in Appendix D.

1 *In a Sales Order processing system, information on orders received is entered into a database using principally two tables, namely, the Order table and an Order item table. There is one row per order in the Order table and the Order item table has several rows per order, i.e., one row per product within the order. Within the Order Item rows, the Product description and Product price (obtained from the Product table) is stored in each row. This facilitates the production of invoices without reference to the Product table. The format of these tables is shown below:

Order table

Order number	Customer number	Order date	Total order value

Order item table

Order number	Product number	Product description	Product price	Quantity

Within this scenario, indicate where and how the tables do not conform to rules of normalisation. For each such case, discuss the merits of the case in terms of potential benefits compared with the disadvantages.

2 (a) In what respects is the use of validation less satisfactory than datatypes as a means of preventing the input of invalid data?

(b) Using the example datatype descriptions given in the chapter, we can see that a long integer datatype and the single precision floating point datatype both use 4 bytes. Compare the range of values and contrast the applications of the two types

3 Describe the factors to be considered in the design of forms.

4 Using the table shown below, show the order of the rows of the table indicated by the following indexes: (*a) Product Code, Branch, (b) Branch, Product Code, (c) Branch, Sales Value.

Product code	Branch	Total sales
B342	North	350
C100	South	100
C100	North	250
E501	North	400
B342	South	300
E501	South	150

Why would it be inefficient to create two indexes for this table of Product code and Product code, branch?

7

Database management systems

Introduction

Database packages, more correctly called Database management systems or DBMSs, such as Oracle and Microsoft Access provide us with all the facilities necessary to design and use an application database. In this chapter we will examine the components of a typical DBMS to show how the DBMS supports the user in these tasks.

A DBMS can be viewed as having three components:

1. The user interface is the software that 'talks' with the user in creating and accessing the database. There are several aspects to the interface including the generation and use of tables, forms and reports.

2. The database engine: this is the software that manages the storage and accessing of the physical data stored on disk.

3. The data dictionary: a repository of information about the application database.

We will look at each of these elements in the following sections.

User interface

Introduction

The user interface to a database provides the means by which the user and the system developer can interact with the DBMS in providing the required services. Reference to the 'user' and the 'system developer' immediately indicates two distinct aspects of the interface, namely, the design of a facility or service and the use of same. For example, we need a facility to specify the structure of a new table to the system and subsequently we need to be able to enter data into the table and to perform any necessary processing of the data. This dichotomy, therefore, should be taken into account in the descriptions of the components of the user interface.

The major elements of the user interface in a typical database system are

- schema manager; i.e., design and usage of tables.
- forms generator; a form is a 'full screen' view of data (typically one row) extracted from a table or tables. Forms are used to improve the interface to the data for end-user access.
- query processor; a query is a definition of conditions used to extract specific required information from the database.
- report generator; reports are formatted presentations of information usually destined for printed output and typically derived from the results of a query.
- programming interfaces; some applications cannot be achieved solely by the interactive facilities of the interface. Resort then has to be made to various forms of programmed specification.

These elements are described in more detail in the following sections.

Schema Manager

A schema is a definition of the structure of a database. The schema definitions are stored somewhere accessible by the database software and application programs, usually in a data dictionary (see later section in this chapter).

A schema could be created using a Data definition command in a database language such as SQL. The SQL language is covered in some detail in Chapter 13 but for the purposes of illustration at this point a typical table creation command in SQL is shown below:

```
CREATE TABLE Schools
(
    Schcode   NUMBER(3) NOT NULL,
    Name      CHAR(20),
    Town      CHAR(15)
)
```

The important aspect of such a command is that symbolic names (such as Schcode, Name and Town) are defined for the table columns and are preserved by the system (as a schema) for later reference by the DBMS or application programs. In Chapter 1, we indicated that one of the essential properties of a database was that it was 'self-describing'; this means that descriptions of the database tables (attribute composition and datatypes) are stored within, or at least accessible to, the database software.

A more common technique for specifying a table design in current database packages is by means of a tabular screen form. An example of such a form, as found in Microsoft Access, showing a partially completed table definition, is given in Figure 7.1.

When the table format has been specified and saved, the user can then invoke the table in 'use' mode to enter data; see Figure 7.2.

7.1 Distinguish the purposes of the interface screens shown in Figures 7.1 and 7.2.

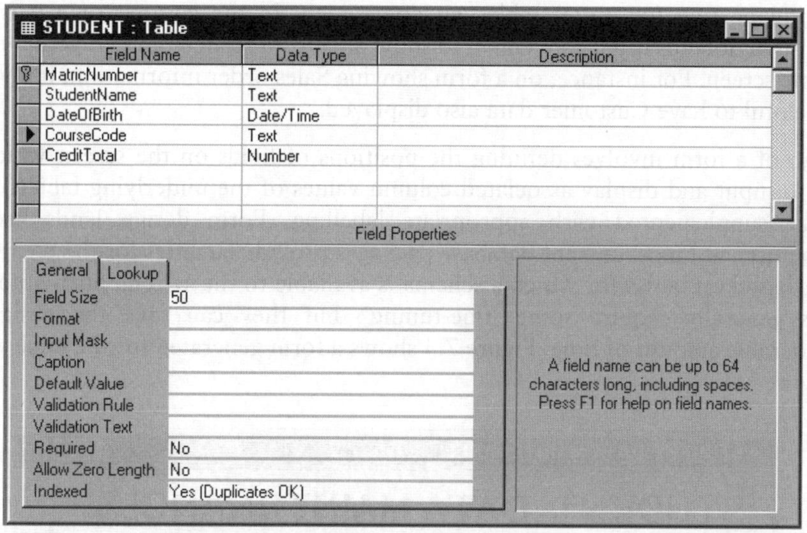

STUDENT : Table

Field Name	Data Type	Description
MatricNumber	Text	
StudentName	Text	
DateOfBirth	Date/Time	
CourseCode	Text	
CreditTotal	Number	

Field Properties

General | Lookup

Field Size	50
Format	
Input Mask	
Caption	
Default Value	
Validation Rule	
Validation Text	
Required	No
Allow Zero Length	No
Indexed	Yes (Duplicates OK)

A field name can be up to 64 characters long, including spaces. Press F1 for help on field names.

Figure 7.1   Table definition screen.

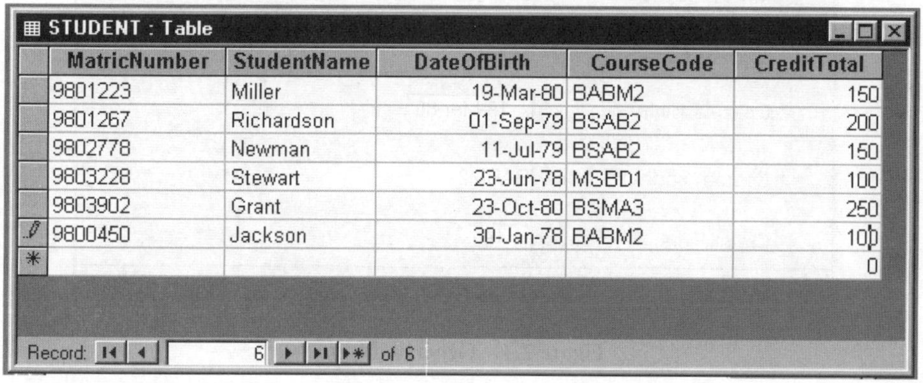

STUDENT : Table

MatricNumber	StudentName	DateOfBirth	CourseCode	CreditTotal
9801223	Miller	19-Mar-80	BABM2	150
9801267	Richardson	01-Sep-79	BSAB2	200
9802778	Newman	11-Jul-79	BSAB2	150
9803228	Stewart	23-Jun-78	MSBD1	100
9803902	Grant	23-Oct-80	BSMA3	250
9800450	Jackson	30-Jan-78	BABM2	100
				0

Record: 6 of 6

Figure 7.2   Table data screen.

Forms generator

The presentation of data using a full screen form has been the standard method of user interaction ever since addressable computer screens first appeared. Within an information processing application system forms are used as the focus for the management of transactions. For instance, the various transactions within a sales order processing system, such as entry of a new customer, entry of a sales order, issue of an invoice, etc., are each handled by a different form available to the sales clerk.

The simplest form of presentation shows one row of one table over the screen extent, but some variations and extensions of this basic style are often employed. Typical variations are

- using more than one 'screenful' per row; this is often necessary simply to accommodate the amount of data involved.

- showing two (or more) tables on one screen. In the context of a particular transaction it is often convenient to show data from related tables together on the one screen. For instance, on a form showing Sales order information, it might be helpful to have Customer data also displayed.

Design of a form involves defining the positions of fields on the screen which are used to input and display associated column values of the underlying table(s). This can be supplemented with appropriate labelling. Form design lends itself to automation and most current database packages provide facilities for the creation of forms based on tables for which a schema is available to the system. Such automatic forms generally require some 'fine-tuning', but they can save the designer a considerable amount of time. Figure 7.3 shows a form generated for the table shown in Figure 7.2.

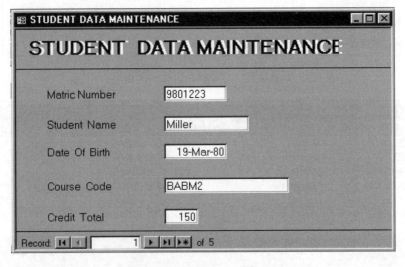

Figure 7.3   Generated form.

Query processor

This term covers any mechanism (language or other) that enables the user to extract required information from the database. This, of course, is the whole point of using a database and it is perhaps nor surprising that a large proportion of the research and development work that has been done in the database field is concerned with querying.

In order to obtain the information that is required, the user has to specify, in some fashion, the conditions to which the desired data must conform. If we want to extract data from the Student table pertaining to a particular course, then a necessary condition might be

CourseCode = "BSAB2".

If, in addition, we wanted to refer to students on this course born after a specific date, we might then use

CourseCode = "BSAB2" AND DateOfBirth > "01/09/79".

In practice, such conditions have to be expressed within the context of some query language or other query system. By far, the most important database query systems are the structured query language or SQL and a table-based method called 'Query by example' or QBE.

SQL is an industry standard language that provides commands allowing full control of databases and not, as the name implies, simply a query facility. Its significance is that, being (relatively) standardised it can be used as a common interface language, enabling communication between different database types. It also facilitates portability of applications between different software and hardware platforms.

SQL is covered in some detail in Chapter 13 but the following example illustrates how the conditional expressions would appear in an SQL statement:

Select * From Students

Where CourseCode = "BSAB2" And DateOfBirth > "01/10/79"

SQL is a declarative language (as opposed to a procedural language such as Pascal or C). This means that the commands define what result is wanted by the programmer, but not the detail of how to obtain the result. For instance, the SQL command makes no reference to searching the rows of the table, although this would need to be done to solve the query. It is generally thought that declarative languages are easier to use than procedural languages.

The term 'QBE' does not refer to a standardised system but to a generic type of table-based, language-free, querying technique that is available in various forms in many database packages.

The original QBE was developed as a research project by Zloof (1977) on IBM mainframe systems. The first PC implementation of a QBE interface appeared in the Paradox package, now marketed by Borland. Microsoft Access also offers a QBE-type interface. A QBE tableau corresponding to the above SQL statement is shown in Figure 7.4.

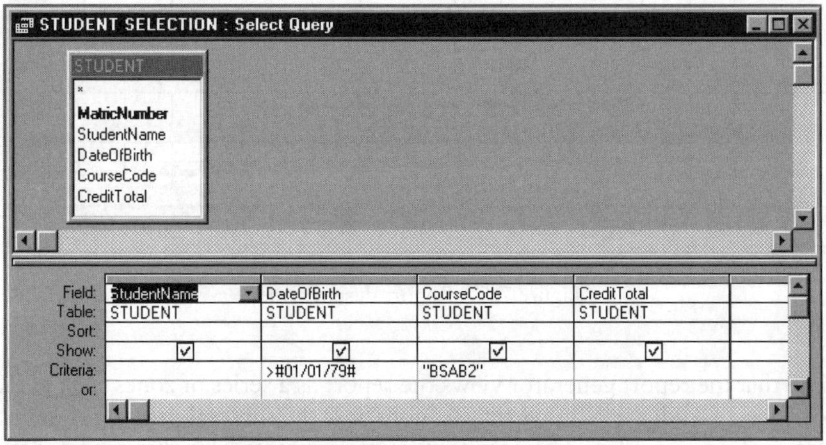

Figure 7.4   Query by example screen.

The names at the top of the grid columns are names of fields from a database table; the selection criteria are expressed in the grid row labelled 'Criteria'; the crossed boxes indicate those fields to be included in the query output.

SQL and QBE are theoretically equivalent. Microsoft Access demonstrates this by enabling conversions between SQL and QBE query definitions.

Report generator

In addition to extracting information from the database, it is necessary to display or print the information in a format convenient and understandable to the recipient. It was realised by software designers many years ago that the production of printed reports was an activity that could be readily automated. Report generators, therefore, have a long tradition in information processing systems.

The simplest kind of report is a non-selective columnar listing of all columns of a table, using table field names as column headings. Typically, however, we need to achieve rather more than this simple effort. For instance, many reports will be selective, reporting only table rows conforming to some conditions. To achieve this, the report would be based on the output of a query. It is also frequently necessary to show totals and sub-totals over specified groupings of the data. For example, in the Student table shown earlier, we may wish to provide a report that totals the credits gained by students within each course. The design of an automatically generated report for this purpose is shown in Figure 7.5.

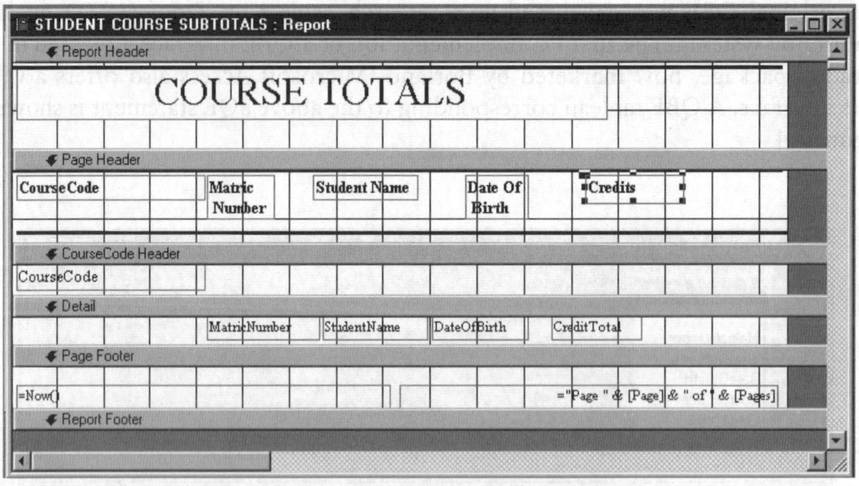

Figure 7.5   Report design screen.

Note that the report generator views the report as a series of zones such as Report Header, Page Header, etc. In particular, note how the subtotal printing is defined by the CourseCode Header. The resultant printout created by this report design is shown in Figure 7.6.

COURSE TOTALS

Course Code	Matric Number	Student Name	Date Of Birth	Credits
BABM2				
	9800450	Jackson	30-Jan-78	100
	9801223	Miller	19-Mar-80	150
BSAB2				
	9801267	Richardson	01-Sep-79	200
	9802778	Newman		150
BSMA3			23-Oct-80	
	9803902	Grant		250
MSBD1				
	9803228	Stewart	23-Jun-78	100

Figure 7.6   Report output.

Programming interface

The capabilities of the 'interactive' facilities of a database system can only achieve so much. More complex applications, or even some special requirements within a simpler application, can sometimes only be implemented by resorting to some form of programming. Typically, the database system will have a programming facility 'below' the interactive interface. For instance, in Microsoft Access, it is possible to use program modules written in Access Basic. This is a fairly extensive topic and is discussed in more detail in Chapter 8.

7.2 List the components of the user interface.

Database engine

The database engine is the part of the DBMS that does the actual work of storing and accessing application oriented data (i.e., tables, rows, etc.) from physical storage. As implied by the name, the engine is the operational heart of the database system.

The database itself may be stored in a number of separate files or it may be contained entirely in one physical file. The role of the engine is to maintain this data and to enable it to be accessed in terms of the application. For instance, we may wish to examine the contents of a Personnel table; the engine has information available on the structure of this table (from the data dictionary) and how it can be retrieved from the database file(s). In effect, the engine provides the user with an abstraction layer that deals with tables and rows and columns, while the engine converts these concepts into physical disk locations and blocks.

The engine has other responsibilities in addition to those indicated above; the list below summarises all its roles. For completeness all its roles are documented at this point but note that many of the topics mentioned are the subject of later chapters and hence the description here is brief.

- Physical data management and accessing including
  - Index management: indexes are special tables created and maintained by the engine which speed up retrieval of data from the database. Indexes are described later in this chapter.
  - View management: a view is essentially a 'virtual table' generated from a query on normal tables. The view query can be stored in the system as if it were a conventional table. The principles of views were described in Chapter 2.
- Accessing of data dictionary.
- Concurrency control. Most commercial databases are accessed by multiple on-line users; this requires special handling to avoid corruption of data and/or loss of updates.
- Security: access rights.
- Integrity: validation, referential integrity, transactions, recovery.

In effect, the engine is the heart of the database; it is the mechanism that deals directly with the data and through which all other functions must operate.

Indexes

The principles of database indexes were described in Chapter 6. To recap, indexes are used to speed up access to the rows of database tables and to enable the table rows to be read in a specific sequence. In this section we look briefly at the typical facilities provided by DBMSs for the creation, use and management of indexes. Microsoft Access and Oracle SQL are used as exemplars for this purpose.

Indexing in Microsoft Access

In Microsoft Access, indexing is specified as part of the table design process. Figure 7.1 earlier in the chapter shows a typical table design screen. The column CourseCode is currently being designed and has been specified as an indexed column by setting the INDEXED property to 'Yes(Duplicates OK)'. The primary key is specified by clicking on a key button on the screen toolbar when the appropriate column is selected. Note that the MatricNumber column has been defined as the primary key; this is indicated by the key icon in the selector box to the left of the column name.

If a multi-field index is required, an additional dialogue box is used, invoked by using the View-Indexes menu option. An example of the index design dialogue screen is shown in Figure 7.7. The index design screen shows that the table has three indexes: MatricNumber (Primary Key), CourseCode and the composite key CreditTotal-MatricNumber.

Indexing in Oracle SQL

The SQL92 standard does not include any commands to create or remove indexes, however, most SQL implementations including Oracle provide such commands which have been accepted as *de facto* standards.

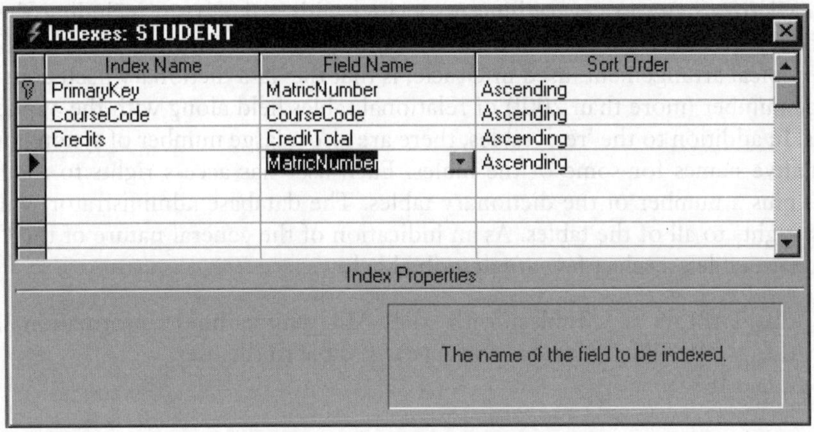

Figure 7.7   Index definition box.

To create an index in SQL, we use the CREATE INDEX command, an example of which is shown below. The example creates an index on columns CustID and OrderDate of the SalesOrder table:

CREATE INDEX index1 ON Students CourseCode, StudentName

To remove a previously created index, the DROP command is used:

DROP INDEX index1

7.3 Identify two distinct ways of specifying table indexes.

Data dictionary

A Data dictionary is a centralised repository used to record all information about a database including the names of all tables, the schemas for each table, the location of tables, view definitions, details about indexes, access rights, etc. In other words, it is a database about a database. In most systems, the data dictionary system tables that hold the user definitions are also accessible to database users (such as system developers); access to this data would normally be in read-only mode, to avoid any risk of corruption.

We can distinguish between active and passive dictionaries. In a passive system, the information held is purely documentary to be referenced by database developers and administrators. In an active dictionary the data is used by the database software as a repository of name references to database 'objects' such as tables, attributes, forms, etc.

Note
Not all DB systems have a Data dictionary. In such systems, the responsibility for locating a file, associating indexes with files, etc., lies with the user. In dBase IV, for example, the schema for each table is physically stored at the start of the table file.

In Microsoft Access, everything associated with a database, including the data dictionary and the data itself is held in one physical file with a .mdb extension. A more typical arrangement, used in Oracle, is that the data dictionary itself consists of a large number (more than 200!) of relational tables held along with the application tables. In addition to the 'real' tables, there are also a large number of synonyms, i.e., alternative names for some of the tables. Each user has access rights to their own tables plus a number of the dictionary tables. The database administrator will have access rights to all of the tables. As an indication of the general nature of the Oracle dictionary tables, a select few are described below:

ALL_TABLES ALL_INDEXES ALL_VIEWS	Tables with the ALL_prefix hold information about database objects accessible to the user.
DBA_USERS DBA_VIEWS	Tables with the DBA_prefix hold information accessible only to the Database Administrator.
USER_TABLES USER_TAB_COLUMNS	Tables with the USER_prefix hold information created by or directly applicable to the user. USER_TABLES holds a list of all the tables created by the user. USER_TAB_COLUMNS contains a list of all the columns of all the tables created by the user.
TABS COLS	The system holds a number of synonyms, i.e., alternative names for system objects. TABS is a synonym for USER_TABLES. COLS is a synonym for USER_TAB_COLUMNS

It is worth noting the fact that these data dictionary tables are themselves relational tables within the same database; for instance, we can view the tables simply by using suitable SQL commands:

SELECT * FROM TABS   would list all tables created by the user.

SELECT * FROM USER_INDEXES   would list all the user's indexes.

Summary

The following list summarises the principal elements of a database management system.

Data dictionary
A repository for all information about the database, including the table schemas.

Schema manager
Enables creation and modification of table structures. May be part of a more comprehensive data dictionary system.

Database engine
The database engine is the 'core' of the data storing and accessing system. It is invoked by the other database components but is otherwise hidden from normal user view. One of its most important roles is to maintain and utilise the indexes that have been created for the tables.

Forms generator
Design of screen based input/output facility. Forms can be used to enter, edit and query database tables.

Query system
For example, languages such as SQL, or 'form driven' (QBE, Query by Example) systems. Extracts data from table(s) defined by selection criteria.

Report generator
Facilitates production of printed or displayed reports including headings, footings, totals, sub-totals.

Menu generator
Enables a 'front-end' to be created which links the application together. There are many different kinds of menu mechanisms; in Windows, drop-down menus are common but a system of push-button selectors is also possible.

Procedural language facility
For example, Access Basic, dBase language, Oracle PL/SQL, Paradox PAL. For complex applications, it is often necessary to be able to execute arbitrary procedures expressed in a high-level language. For instance, in Microsoft Access, many applications can be done using the visual interactive facilities. If necessary, to implement a more unusual operation in a system, Access provides a Basic programming language which can be used to write user-defined procedures and functions.

Answers to in-text questions

7.1 Figure 7.1 shows a screen provided by the schema manager that provides facilities for the design of tables. Figure 7.2 shows the screen which enables the table data to be viewed and edited.

7.2 The main elements of the user interface are schema manager, forms generator, query processor, report generator, programming interface.

7.3 Two methods of specifying indexes are by use of an interactive dialogue box such as that provided by Access or by use of the SQL CREATE INDEX command.

REVIEW QUESTIONS

Answers in Appendix C.

1 List the components of the user interface that would be provided by a DBMS.

2 What support for indexing would you expect to find in a DBMS?

3 Outline the role of the database engine.

4 Distinguish between an active and a passive data dictionary.

EXERCISES

Answers to exercises flagged with an asterisk appear in Appendix D.

1 *Explain what is meant by a Database Management System (DBMS) and outline the main functions that a DBMS performs.

2 Describe the facilities you would expect to find in a DBMS for the production of forms, reports and indexes.

8

Database programming

Introduction

This chapter describes various aspects of the use of programming languages in database application development. In many modern systems such as Microsoft Access, Borland Paradox and Oracle, databases can be constructed and used interactively (using GUI techniques), without requiring any programming. Table design is specified using a 'form-filling' and point-and-click approach and forms and reports can be automatically derived from the table specification. Chapter 7 described some of the facilities of this type provided by DBMS software.

A non-programming interactive approach is clearly more suitable for 'end-user' development, where the database designer may have limited programming knowledge. However, it does ultimately limit the potential of the software in producing a system exactly to the user's requirements. Professional database system developers typically have to stretch the software to meet the needs of the client and this often necessitates the use of programming. Even within systems offering effective interactive facilities, implementations can often be improved by the use of programming.

Programming languages are used by programmers to direct the computer to perform desired tasks. Conventional languages such as Pascal, COBOL, C++, etc., are general-purpose languages designed to carry out almost any task within a fairly broad application domain. Languages are also available that provide more specialised facilities for certain application areas, for example, Prolog for artificial intelligence, ECSL for simulation, etc. The facilities available in such 'application oriented' languages are specialised to make the design of systems in that area more convenient for the programmer and to exploit the machine and operating system services available. In particular, the domain of database applications is served by a number of languages, designed to facilitate the development of database systems. Such languages generally interface to a specific database management system or may in fact be part of the DBMS itself.

Database languages come in a number of different 'flavours'; some are general purpose, while others are designed for specific tasks within the database area. A number of these are described briefly, under the categories below. Specific examples of these are described in later sections.

- Data Definition, Manipulation and Control language categories (DDL, DML, DCL)
- query languages, including SQL.

- SQL in other language systems: call-level inteface and embedded SQL.
- fourth generation languages (4GL)
- interactive and event handling development environments.

Data definition language – DDL

The term 'Data definition language' refers to a category of language, not an actual language or product. It refers to facilities in a language, or a subset of commands within a language, that allow the data structures of a database to be specified and consequently constructed. In relational database terms, this means defining the table structure and attributes of the database relations. A typical example of a DDL command is the SQL CREATE instruction that specifies the attributes, attribute types and other features of a relation.

Data manipulation language – DML

The term 'Data manipulation language' again refers to a category of language; the category refers to facilities in a language, or a subset of a language, that can be used to access, add to and modify the data within a database. Typical DML commands are the SQL SELECT and UPDATE instructions.

Data control language – DCL

This is again a language category; it refers to language commands that are used to provide certain control facilities, usually in the area of database security. For instance, the assignment of access rights of users to database tables is the role of the DCL commands. Examples are the SQL GRANT and REVOKE commands.

Query language

In general terms, a query language is a language used to extract information from a database. Since the principal purpose of a database is to record data that can be referred to later, the extraction of information from the database is of course quite fundamental to the whole database philosophy. Note that we refer to the storage of 'data' and the extraction of 'information'. This is to emphasise that database applications in general do not simply regurgitate raw data, but reorganise, select and interpret relevant facts from the database. Although the term 'query', strictly interpreted, only implies reading of the database, in practice query languages (and other querying systems) can also typically update the database.

The subject of database querying is dominated by the SQL language. Programming in SQL is covered in some detail in Chapter 13 and it is referred to in various contexts in other chapters. In this section we will provide a brief history and some introductory notes.

History of SQL

The history of relational databases effectively began with the publication of Codd's (1970) seminal paper while working in IBM's Research Laboratory in San Jose. In 1974, another researcher at the same laboratory designed a language called Structured Query Language or SEQUEL. The design objective of SEQUEL was to provide a language that implemented the operations of the relational algebra in a programming context. Later versions of this language were renamed SQL because the acronym SEQUEL was found to be owned by someone else. 'SQL' is still pronounced 'see-quel' by many people although ANSI (American National Standards Institute) who are responsible for standardisation of the language have defined the offical pronunciation as 'ess-q-ell'.

In 1979, the company now known as Oracle announced the first commercial SQL-type product. Other products appeared in the early 1980s from INGRES and IBM. Standardisation of the language began in 1982 by ANSI who were joined in these efforts by ISO in 1983. The first ISO standard appeared in 1987. A revised definition, known as SQL2 or SQL-92, appeared in 1992 (ISO 1992). Most current implementations are based on this standard. In effect, the standard defines a minimum set of features that any implementation should support but an implementation can include many extensions peculiar to one vendor. In general, one is likely to learn the SQL dialect of a particular vendor, such as IBM or Oracle, that one is involved with, rather than the pure standard. Another SQL standard, SQL3, is currently being developed and will include object-oriented features.

Important features of SQL

SQL can be viewed partly as a programming language implementation of the relational algebra described in Chapter 2. In addition to the algebraic operations such as Restrict, Project and Join, SQL provides commands for a wide range of other database related tasks such as the creation and deletion of tables, views, indexes, etc. SQL can be classified as a declarative language; this implies that SQL commands are concerned with the 'what' of an answer rather than the 'how'. SQL commands therefore do not use any of the usual constructs found in conventional procedural languages such as IF statements, loops and input-output commands.

SQL is executed by means of an interpreter. The interpreter has the responsibility of resolving the command by converting the declarative specification contained in the user's query into a series of physical table accesses that obtain the data implied or defined by the request.

As we shall see in this chapter, SQL can be used in a number of different ways within a range of programming environments. Additionally, we will find in Chapter 11 that SQL is also used in client-server situations where a database request from a client computer is expressed in SQL and sent to a server computer that interprets the request and returns the answer as a relation.

?   **8.1** What is meant by the expression 'SQL is a programming language implementation of the relational algebra?'

SQL in other language systems

Although SQL is very powerful in terms of querying, it is not in itself a full programming language. Database applications will typically need to add some further processing capability beyond that provided by SQL. Accordingly, it makes sense to try to integrate SQL with other language systems; a number of methods to this end are described in this section.

Application programming interface

An application programming interface (API) is a software layer that provides access to a computer resource by means of functions called from application programs. It could also be referred to as a 'call-level' interface. In the context of SQL and databases, an API consists of a set of functions that communicate with an SQL system and simulate SQL commands. A number of such APIs exist, notably, Microsoft's ODBC and Javasoft's JDBC. These topics are covered in more detail in Chapter 11 in the context of networked databases.

Embedded SQL in 3GLs

In some systems where the main development is in a third-generation high-level language such as COBOL, PL/1 or C, it is possible to 'embed' SQL statements within the 3GL code. The HLL compiler cannot directly understand this code and hence it has to be converted into equivalent subroutine calls by means of a pre-processor. To help the pre-processor delineate the SQL commands from the normal program code, sections of SQL are introduced by the words EXEC SQL. The pre-processor creates an intermediate source program which is then compiled by the language compiler in the normal way. For example, we could create a table as follows:

```
EXEC SQL
CREATE  TABLE  Product
    ( ProdCode    CHAR(4),
      ProdDesc    CHAR(20),
      ... etc.
    )
EXEC SQL  COMMIT
```

When a SELECT statement is executed, it notionally produces a result table. This is effectively assigned to an internal array structure which can be 'scanned' by an internal pointer called a cursor (not to be confused with the arrow thing on a Windows screen!). The cursor can be used to reference successive elements of the result array. In this way, the program can use SQL to select some subset of the table data and then process this subset using conventional programming instructions. An example is given below:

```
EXEC SQL DECLARE  K  CURSOR FOR
    SELECT  ProdCode, ProdDesc, ProdQty
        WHERE  ProdQty > 100      ... etc.
```

The above statement creates a cursor called K then executes the given SELECT command, producing a result table. This table can then be accessed using K as a row pointer or subscript. Rows can be obtained from the cursor using

> EXEC SQL FETCH K
>> INTO Pcode, Pdesc, Pqty

where Pcode, Pdesc and Pqty are local program variables. The FETCH command transfers data items from the cursor to local variables. The database can subsequently be updated using an embedded SQL UPDATE command.

SQL in 4GLs

Fourth generation languages (4GLs) are discussed in more detail in the next section and in particular the Oracle PL/SQL system is described that implements SQL embedded commands. The principal difference presented by 4GLs compared with 3GLs is that in the former the integration of SQL with the procedural coding is closer. This is because the system has been designed as an integration of SQL and procedural code rather than as two separate language systems.

SQL in Microsoft Visual Basic

SQL can be used in VBA (Visual Basic for Applications, the basic language underlying several Microsoft products including Access). We will return to this topic later when Event Handling languages are described.

?   **8.2** Why is it found useful to embed SQL statements in other language systems?

Fourth-generation language – 4GL

Overview

Many database packages, such as dBASE IV, Oracle and Informix, include general-purpose languages that are similar in many respects to conventional languages such as Pascal. Like Pascal, they provide structured (while, if, etc.) and modular (procedures and functions) programming facilities. However, they also include higher-level instructions and additional constructs designed to facilitate close interaction with a DBMS. For instance, the dBASE language provides high-level commands such as LIST that produces a listing of a database table. More significantly, such languages will include commands that interface directly with the database. Such languages are often called 4GLs for fourth-generation languages (Pascal, etc. being 3GLs). Note that, in common with much computer-related terminology, there are differing interpretations placed on the term '4GL'. There is also an additional concept of 'fourth-generation environment' to provide further confusion. These alternative approaches tend to focus on certain integrated environments providing high-level and integrated database facilities. For our purposes here, we will adhere to the definition given above.

The principal advantage of these languages is that they combine general-purpose programming facilities with close links to the database engine. In contrast to general-purpose programming languages that would require to use function libraries for database access, commands to create, access and manage database tables form part of the language vocabulary. They will also provide facilities to assist in the development of applications based on a database; these would include data entry forms and reports generators. Another significant feature is that many of the language commands can be used both interactively (i.e., by using a command interpreter supplied as part of the DBMS) and by program, embedding the command within the source code of a program. This arrangement facilitates program development and debugging.

In this section we look briefly at two 4GL systems, namely, dBASE and Oracle PL/SQL. The treatment here is necessarily brief and is intended only to indicate the general nature of these systems.

dBASE

A well-known 4GL language system is that derived from the original dBASE product. This has evolved over the years into a number of separate dialects (e.g. dBase III and IV, Clipper and Foxpro) and in current versions has become object-oriented. An extract from a Clipper program is shown below.

```
@ 18, 18 CLEAR TO 18, 70          && Enq number display
      entering = .T.
      DO WHILE entering
         mconfirm = " "
         SET ESCAPE ON
         SET COLOR TO w+/b, w+/rb
         @   7,  6   SAY "Title"
         @   7, 18   GET  mtitle  PICTURE "@!" VALID
            Zval_Title(mtitle)
         @   7, 25   SAY "Initials"
         @   7, 34   GET  minits      PICTURE "@!"
         @   7, 40   SAY "Surname"
         @   7, 50   GET  msurname PICTURE "@K"  VALID
            znotblank(msurname)
         @  11,  6   SAY "Address"
         @  11, 18   GET  madd1
         @  12, 18   GET  madd2
         @  13, 18   GET  madd3
         @  14,  6   SAY "PostCode"
         @  14, 18   GET  mpost       PICTURE "@!"
         @  16,  6   SAY "Course Code"
         @  16, 18   GET  mcourse PICTURE "@!" VALID
            Val_Course1(mcourse)
         @  16, 23   SAY "Media Code"
         @  16, 35   GET  mmedia  PICTURE "@!"  VALID
            Val_Medcode(mmedia)
         @  20, 18   SAY "Enter Y  to confirm this data "
         @  20, 49   GET mconfirm
         READ
         k = lastkey()
```

```
        IF UPPER(mconfirm) = "Y"
            entering = .f.
        ENDIF
        IF k = 27
            entering = .f.
        ENDIF
    ENDDO      && while entering
```

The SAY and GET commands are used for inputting and outputting data from a screen form. The data is collected in memory variables such as madd1 and mpost. After suitable processing, the data can be written to a database row using commands such as

```
    REPLACE enqsurname WITH msurname
    REPLACE enqnumber WITH menqno
    REPLACE enqtitle WITH mtitle
    REPLACE enqinitial WITH minits
    REPLACE enqaddr1 WITH madd1
    REPLACE enqaddr2 WITH madd2
    REPLACE enqaddr3 WITH madd3
    REPLACE enqpostcd WITH mpost
    REPLACE enqdate WITH date()
    REPLACE enqmedcode WITH mmedia
    REPLACE enqcourse WITH mcourse
```

where enqsurname, enqnumber, etc., are database table column names. Note the ability of the language to refer directly to database schema names; this is not possible in 3GL type languages.

In spite of being a higher-level language in terms of the integration with the database and the expressive power of many of its commands, this style of programming language is essentially relatively low-level compared with newer systems. For example, in the coding above, we see the need to explicitly code the format of a form and to allocate local variables for temporary storage of form field values. Most current systems using such languages will also have facilities for form, query and report production that generate the detailed coding automatically.

8.3 What are the most significant features of a 4GL language?

Oracle PL/SQL

In its PL/SQL system, Oracle has extended the capabilities of its SQL language by adding procedural language facilities. The resultant combination of declarative SQL commands and a closely integrated procedural language is a very powerful database development tool.

The procedural language provides all the facilities one would find in conventional procedural languages: block-structure, procedures, functions, control instructions, range of datatypes, etc. In addition there are a number of facilities to provide the integration with SQL commands and the database. A PL/SQL program consists of a number of program blocks, each of which can contain nested blocks. A block has the following basic structure:

[DECLARE
    data declarations]

BEGIN
    instructions
[EXCEPTION
    exception handlers]

The items in square brackets are optional and need not appear in a particular block. The data declarations define variables used within the block; these are not database table references. A full range of datatypes are available including character, number (various representations), Boolean, etc.

The instructions available are similar in effect to those provided by languages such as Pascal and C. In particular, module support is provided by functions and procedures. There are one or two notable exceptions to this, however. Firstly, PL/SQL provides facilities for integrating its instructions with SQL commands. Also, it provides no I/O instructions; it is assumed that all interaction is with the database tables.

Exception handlers are used to trap and process errors that occur during the execution of the program. Run-time errors can arise from a variety of sources including programming errors and hardware failures. Normally such error would cause termination of the program and a return to the control of the operating system. The exception handling in PL/SQL enables error to be trapped; this provides the opportunity of dealing with the problem within the program code and perhaps continuing normally or at least failing gracefully under control of the program.

The following sample program illustrates some of points made above. The program is trivial and is given for purposes of illustration only. A table Employee is accessed using a cursor and new rows are added to a second table called Temp using selected columns of the Employee table.

```
 1   DECLARE
 2       CURSOR c1 is
 3           SELECT emp_id, name, salary FROM Employee;
 4       my_id      CHAR(4);
 5       my_name    CHAR(15);
 6       my_salary  NUMBER(7,2);
 7   BEGIN
 8       OPEN c1;
 9       LOOP
10           FETCH c1 INTO my_id, my_name, my_salary;
11           EXIT WHEN c1%NOTFOUND;
12           INSERT INTO Temp VALUES (my_id, my_name, my_salary);
13       END LOOP;
14       CLOSE c1;
15       COMMIT;
16   EXCEPTION
17       WHEN NO_DATA_FOUND THEN CLOSE c1;
18*  END;
```

The following notes will help in understanding this example.

Lines 2–3   Defines a cursor (the concept of a cursor was covered in the section 'SQL in 3GLs' earlier in this chapter) called c1 that is used to accept the output from a Select query.

Lines 4-6   Defines a number of local variables used in the subsequent code.

Lines 8-15   Constitutes the body of the procedure code.

Line 8   Opens, i.e., makes available, the c1 cursor. At this point it will contain the result of the Select query on line 3.

Line 9   Activates a continuous loop. The program will continue in this loop until the end of the cursor is reached. At this point the Exit command on line 11 will cause termination of the loop.

Line 10   The Fetch command extracts data from the current row of the cursor and stores the data in the local variables listed. The cursor pointer will then be moved on to the next row of the cursor.

Line 12   This is an SQL statement. It inserts a new row in the table Temp, using as values the data held in the local variables.

Line 17   Illustrates the use of an exception definition.

The important concepts to be learned from this example are the way in which the language system integrates SQL and procedural commands and in particular how cursors are used in this context.

8.4 Why is a combination of SQL and a procedural language considered to be a powerful database development tool?

Event handling language

In most interactive-style databases, additional power can be derived from the software by employing a language that operates 'behind' the interactive facade. An example of this is the language VBA (Visual Basic for Applications) that underlies Microsoft's Office Suite of programs including Access and the Visual Basic development system. This language can also be viewed as a 4GL, since it provides a procedural language interacting directly with the database system. In the context of Windows-based software, the programs operate in an 'event driven' fashion, i.e., the coding is based on providing a response to user interface events, such as depressing screen buttons, entering text, etc. In effect, each such event has an associated module of code that is executed when the event occurs.

As an example of how the VBA language system works, consider a form that inputs sales order information. Let us assume that the coding of Customer codes in use in the company has been recently modified and we wish to 'trap' entry of old

codes which begin with the letters AB or AC. The sales order data is entered through
a form called Order Entry.

The procedure used to enter an event handling procedure into the form is as
follows:

- In the form design window, the Customer ID field is selected. Each 'object' on
  the form (and the form itself), such as input fields, list boxes, etc. has an
  associated list of properties. The property list for an object defines its static
  characteristics such as colour, font style and size, etc. In addition, the property
  list details the events that can be trapped for that object. The database developer
  can write an event handler (in VBA) for each event that the applications needs to
  deal with.
- From the menus, View - Properties is selected which will cause display of the
  property list for the Customer ID field of the form; the picture shown in
  Figure 8.1 shows part of the property list, including the event types such as 'On
  Exit'; i.e., action to be taken when the field is exited.

Text Box: CustomerID	✕

Format	Data	Event	Other	All

Border Width	Hairline
Fore Color	0
Font Name	MS Sans Serif
Font Size	8
Font Weight	Normal
Font Italic	No
Font Underline	No
Text Align	General
Shortcut Menu Bar .	
ControlTip Text . . .	
Help Context Id . . .	0
Tag	
Before Update	
After Update	
On Change	
On Enter	
On Exit	[Event Procedure]
On Got Focus	
On Lost Focus	
On Click	
On Dbl Click	
On Mouse Down . .	
On Mouse Move . .	
On Mouse Up	
On Key Down	

Figure 8.1   Text field properties list.

- By clicking on the button labelled ... , the code for the event is shown:

```
Private Sub CustomerID_Exit(Cancel As Integer)
    prefix = Left$(Forms![Order Entry]![CustomerID], 2)
    If prefix = "AB" Or prefix = "AC" Then
        MsgBox "Obsolete Customer Id used: " + prefix, 48, "Customer Id Error"
        DoCmd.GoToControl "CustomerID"
    End If
End Sub
```

The line

```
    prefix = Left$(Forms![Order Entry]![CustomerID], 2)
```

extracts the leftmost two characters from the Customer ID as entered on the form.
  The string

```
Forms![Order Entry]![CustomerID]
```

is an object-oriented reference to the Customer ID text field value within the Order entry form object. The Customer ID is checked to see if it starts with AB or AC and, if so, displays an error message box (see Figure 8.2).

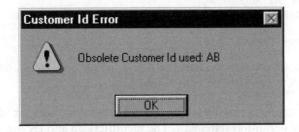

Figure 8.2   Error message box.

For each screen object, such as a data field or a button, there will be a number of different events which can be handled; in the case of the Customer ID example above, the events can be seen in the Properties list box. For purposes of illustration, a few of these are defined below.

On Change   Executes when the content of the field changes. This would occur each time a character was entered, not simply at the end of a sequence of entered characters.

On Got Focus   Executes when 'the focus' goes to that field. An object is said to have the focus when it is able to receive input from keyboard or mouse actions. On a displayed form only one object will have focus at any one time.

On Click   Executes when the mouse button is clicked once while the object has the focus. This event is more applicable to screen interface buttons.

On KeyDown   Executes when a keyboard key is pressed down when the field has the focus. Note that the system can distinguish between the key being depressed and being released.

Note that one user action can produce a series of more than one 'event'. Entering a character from the keyboard, for instance, will generate KeyDown, KeyUp and Change events. The designer may have to take account of the sequence of the events.

Using SQL in VBA

SQL can also be employed in Microsoft's VBA. This is more likely to be of value in Visual Basic or Excel rather than Access but the method employed is common to all these.

The approach taken in VBA is based on the concept of a 'recordset', which not unexpectedly, is a set of records. The set of records can be all the rows of a database table or the result of a query applied to one or more tables. A recordset based on a query can be created by a series of VBA instructions as illustrated below:

```
1. Dim db As Database
2. Dim rec As Recordset
3. Dim strSQL As String

4. Set db = CurrentDb();

5. strSQL = "SELECT * FROM Employee WHERE salary > 20000.0"
6. Set rec = db.OpenRecordset(strSQL)
```

Lines 1 to 3 set up local variables. The 'Dim' keyword is short for 'dimension' and introduces a data definition statement. The identifiers db and rec are unusual in that they define system objects that represent, respectively, a database and a recordset. Line 4 assigns to db the current database, i.e., the database currently opened by the application program. Line 5 supplies an SQL command as a simple character string and assigns this string to strSQL.

Line 6 creates a recordset based on this SQL query and assigns the recordset to the object 'rec'. The row attributes of the query result can then be referenced by the convention recordset!attribute. For instance, the salary attribute would be referred to as rec!salary. Initially, the recordset would be positioned at the first row of the query output. Navigation through the rows is possible by commands associated with the recordset object. For instance, to move to the next row, the instruction rec.MoveNext would be used.

The purpose of these notes is only to show how SQL can be utilised in VBA code. In effect, a string containing the SQL command is formed which is sent to the SQL interpreter by the program run-time system. Although implemented in a different way, it has some similarities to SQL embedding described earlier; the essential requirements are a means of expressing SQL commands and a technique for referencing the query result within the context of the language system coding. For further information on VBA within Microsoft Access consult Smith (1997).

Summary

In this chapter we have tried to show the range of alternative approaches available to the database developer, from a purely interactive interface at one end of the spectrum to 4GL languages at the other. In particular, we have covered the following database language concepts and systems:

- Language categories: Data Definition, Manipulation and Control (DDL, DML, DCL).
- Query languages including SQL are designed primarily to facilitate extraction of required information from the database.
- Embedded SQL; SQL commands contained in programs written in conventional languages such as COBOL and C, and in 4GLs.
- Fourth-generation languages such as Oracle PL/SQL that provide an integration of conventional and database-oriented facilities.
- Event-driven systems that function within an interactive database environment.

Answers to in-text questions

8.1 The relational algebra is a set of mathematical operators that can be applied to 'relations' in the mathematical sense. It is not concerned with the computer-based representation of relations. SQL performs the same operations as the algebra but on physical database relations.

8.2 SQL provides a standardised effective approach to extracting data from a database. Other language systems have their own qualities that make them suitable for their intended purpose. Combining the two can provide an ideal solution to designing applications that require access to a database.

8.3 Significant features of a 4GL are

- high-level language constructs that reduce the amount of coding required.
- close integration with database access facilities
- specialised user-interface facilities to simplify database form design, etc.

8.4 While SQL excels at database querying, it is not a complete programming language. A combination of SQL and a procedural language as in PL/SQL provides an environment that can perform any computational task as well as having effective access to database information.

REVIEW QUESTIONS

Answers in Appendix C.

1 Explain the meaning of the terms DDL, DML and DCL.

2 What is meant by the term 'query language'?

3 What is the most significant query language in current use?

4   What is meant by 'embedding' of SQL commands?

5   Explain what is meant by the term 4GL.

6   How is an event-handling language used in conjunction with an interactive development
    database environment?

EXERCISES

Answers to exercises flagged with an asterisk appear in Appendix D.

1   *Discuss the significance of SQL in modern database development. Outline the ways in which SQL
    can be used in various programming environments.

2   Describe the nature of 4GL systems and explain how 4GLs provide a powerful tool for database
    development.

3   Discuss the ranges of approaches that can be adopted for the programing of a database
    application indicating the suitability of each approach for different classes of developer.

9

Integrity and security

Introduction

This chapter gathers together a range of topics under the general umbrella of 'integrity and security'. We are concerned here with studying techniques that ensure that the data held on a database is correct, consistent and secure. There are a number of issues and topics involved here and a general overview will probably be found helpful.

The purpose of a database is to model some system in the real world; the system being modelled is often referred to as the universe of discourse, which sounds rather pompous, or by the friendlier label, application domain. When a database holds data that says Mr Jones of 12 Acacia Avenue, Smalltown owes the Acme Equipment Company £200, then we would hope that this is an accurate representation of the facts. When the facts change, for instance when Mr Jones pays his debt, again we expect that the database will be changed to reflect this change in the application domain.

Regrettably, these kinds of expectations of computer databases in the real world are sometimes not realised. Some errors can be viewed as trivial; if Acacia was misspelled as Accacia, no-one would view this as a serious misrepresentation. However, it would viewed somewhat more seriously if the amount was recorded as £2000.

A major objective of database design must be to ensure that the database is protected from anything that might affect its accuracy. At the logical design phase, the term constraints is used to refer to a set of rules and restrictions that define the admissible content of the database. Some constraints are based on the domain of the data values and other natural limitations; for instance, it is readily seen that an employee's name cannot be a numeric value or their age a negative value. Some constraints, on the other hand, are determined by the application system designers as being rules and restrictions to which the application system and the database must conform. Such constraints are often called business or enterprise rules. Business rules, by their nature can be quite arbitrary; for instance a company may make the rule that no customer should have more than £2000 credit or a university cannot enrol more than 30 students on a course.

In addition to our expectations about the accuracy of the data, we would also hope that the database is safe against software and hardware failure and that it cannot be accessed by anyone not properly authorised. These aspects of database integrity and security are also described in this chapter.

139

Threats to the database

As this chapter is discussing the subject of maintaining the integrity and security of databases it is perhaps worth while to reflect briefly on things that can threaten these.

User errors   The database users can accidentally (or otherwise) enter erroneous values, amend data incorrectly or delete valid data. Errors may also be generated by mistakes occurring in the data collection process prior to data entry into the computer.

Software errors   Programming errors in the database or in the application system software can introduce errors into the database.

Hardware failure   Breakdown of computer equipment, physical damage such as flooding, loss of power, etc., can result in the database being left in an inconsistent state or in the storage medium being rendered unusable.

Malicious damage   For their own motives, a database could be corrupted by authorised or unauthorised users.

Breach of confidentiality   Unauthorised persons may get access to the database. While this does not corrupt the data *per se*, it may have a serious influence on the owner of the information and indeed the future commercial or political value of the information.

Concurrency errors   When a database is accessed by two or more users simultaneously, errors can arise due to specific kinds of interference between the actions of the users. This subject is covered in some detail in Chapter 10.

This array of threats to the database requires a corresponding array of defences to be marshalled at all stages of the database design, construction and operation. The following sections covers a range of relevant topics, which are summarised below. Not covered herein are some topics related to this area of study but which are outwith the scope of this text; these include specific physical protections that might be applied in a computer installation (access controls, fire protection, etc.) and manual procedures such as batch controls.

To summarise, this chapter covers the following topics:

1.   threats to the database; a look at what can go wrong
2.   database constraints and techniques for supporting them including
     - data validation
     - assertions and triggers
     - transactions
3.   backups, checkpoints and transaction logs
4.   database access controls.

Database integrity

The term integrity in the context of databases refers to the correctness and consistency of the data stored in the database. The meaning of these terms can be further detailed.

'Consistency' implies that the data held in the various tables of the database is consistent with the concept of the relational model. Consistency is expressed in terms of two characteristics:

1. Entity integrity is concerned with ensuring that each row of a table has a unique and non-null primary key value; this is the same as saying that each row in a table represents a single instance of the entity type modelled by the table.

2. Referential integrity is concerned with the relationships between the tables of a database, i.e., that the data of one table does not contradict the data of another table. Specifically, every foreign key value in a table must have a matching primary key value in the related table. For example, if a Sales Order table refers to a customer code AB1212, then that code must appear in the Customer table that defines such codes. This 'linking' of foreign key to primary key is fundamental to the way in which component tables are used to form an integrated database. Referential integrity was discussed in more detail in Chapter 2 in the context of the relational model.

'Data Integrity' or 'Correctness' implies that data captured for entry into the computer does in fact correctly represent the 'real-world' data that it is supposed to. This involves taking care with the capturing and handling of data at all stages prior to data entry to the database. Particular care has to be taken with data input; even if the correct data is established prior to data input, an error can still occur in the transference of data to the computer. Common forms of error are transposition of numerical digits, misspelling of names, repetition of characters, etc.

The primary defence against invalid data is data input validation, which is described in the next section. The major contribution that can be made by the database validation is to form a barrier between the outside world and the database ensuring that the data passing through this barrier conforms to company rules and other basic tests of reasonableness, e.g., preventing someone's age being entered as 250, or a clerk's salary as £200,000 a year.

? **9.1** How complete do you think such validation tests can be?

Data validation

In order to provide some defence against the introduction of erroneous data into the database, a database system will typically provide a range of facilities to check data as it is initially entered. As noted earlier, data errors can occur at any time in the data collection/data entry process. Regardless of the source and cause of the errors, the philosophy applied to input data validation is that the errors should go no further than the data entry phase of processing. Data validation should provide a filter such that all data passing through the filter is sensible and meaningful to the database application system, as far as this can be accomplished. The following sections describe a typical range of validation facilities one would expect in a modern DBMS.

Type checking

The most fundamental error checking mechanism in relational databases is the 'typing' of attributes (columns), i.e., each attribute has to be declared as being of a particular type such as numeric, text, date, etc. In effect, this specifies the domain of the data item, i.e., the pool of values from which the data item is drawn. This prevents gross errors such as trying to assign text values to a date column or trying to perform arithmetic on text fields. Also, the type dictates the maximum size and shape (e.g., in numeric fields, the number of decimal places) of a column. In effect, the type of an attribute determines its behaviour, i.e.,

- the range of acceptable values on input
- the admissible operations on the data (for instance, you can do arithmetic only on numerical or date columns)
- how it is handled on output (e.g., left or right justified on a printed report).

Data typing is used in almost all programming languages; 'strongly-typed' languages (e.g., Pascal) insist on maximum adherence to the rules of type behaviour, while 'weakly-typed' languages (e.g., C) allow the programmer to bend the rules to achieve some advantage in simplicity of coding or performance.

However, the domains of common types are very large, for instance, an integer (two byte representation) has a value range of $-32,768$ to $+32,767$ which will generally be much wider than any integer application value such as 'quantity ordered'. Ideally, types should constitute a classification system that enables us to identify database objects (such as table attributes) as representing corresponding classes of entities in the real world. Basic types such as 'NUMBER' and 'CHAR', however, are very general classifications and provide relatively little segregation of data.

It would be helpful if the database system allowed us to define our own types but this kind of facility is generally available only in general-purpose languages such as Pascal and C++. Simple examples are the Pascal sub-range type definition

Quantity : 1..999;

The above command defines a datatype (not to be confused with a data variable) so that 'Quantity' can now be used as a type in subsequent instructions, such as

OrderAmount : Quantity;

which defines the variable OrderAmount to be of type Quantity. This would mean that OrderAmount would be constrained to values between 1 and 999.

Another possible specification technique is the definition of composite data items. For instance, in Pascal we can define composite data items by means of the RECORD facility. The example shown below defines a composite item to represent a calendar date.

        Date = RECORD
        BEGIN
            Day, Month, Year: String[2];
        END

Most current popular relational databases do not allow you to define your own types in this way. However, some more recent software, referred to as 'extended-relational' or 'object-relational' databases, do provide such facilities. These systems are described in more detail in Chapter 12. It is perhaps worth noting that the SQL2 standard allows the definition of domains, using a CREATE DOMAIN command, by which the values in a table column can be defined as being within specified limits. However, it really only provides a constraint on the data and does not provide any functionality or, in object-oriented terms, 'behaviour'. This command is not widely implemented at present.

In the absence of built-in facilities for defining sub-range types, database packages generally allow the user to specify explicit input validation criteria; this topic is pursued in the next section.

9.2 Why is the CREATE DOMAIN command mentioned above deficient as a means of defining datatypes?

Validation techniques

Validation controls should be available within any DBMS facility that can enter or amend database data. This encompasses interactive facilities such as forms or a graphical representation of a database table, or programmed access such as SQL commands. Ideally, it should be possible to define the controls at the table level and to have these controls effective for any type of access, such as a form. Note, however, that forms are typically used to implement application procedures such as entering sales transactions, booking a hotel room, etc. It may be that the validation requirements will vary from form to form; hence, validation defined at the table level would need to be overridden by the specific requirements of the particular form.

We will describe here some techniques generally provided by a database management system to assist in maintaining data integrity. In particular, the facilities of Microsoft Access and SQL are described. (It should be noted that other techniques exist in the area of system controls applied to the general process of data entry, e.g., batch totals. These are not covered here.)

Microsoft Access

MS Access provides extensive facilities for validation of database data. Validation can be applied at a number of points, namely, within the column (field) definitions, and at the table and form levels. The field level validation is intended to check that the values within each field independently conform to specified criteria. At the table and form levels, checks can be made that reference two or more fields of the table, thereby enabling interdependence of fields values to be verified. For instance, we could check that DeliveryDate > OrderDate.

Validations applied at the field or table levels are also enforced when using a form based on the table; any form validations are applied *in addition* to the underlying validations.

- Input Mask prescribes a basic format for the data; e.g. an order number could have a format such as AB1234. This could be defined as a mask of AAnnnn.
- Validation Rule/Text defines a conditional expression which is used to test the input data. If it fails an error message appears using the supplied validation text. For instance, if a field has a maximum value of 100, the validation test would be < 100, and the text might be 'Please enter a value less than 100'.
- Required: In many applications, it is not allowable to omit certain data items. The most obvious example here is the primary key field of any table; this is enforced automatically by Access. In a sales order input application, omitting the customer number would be unacceptable. While such errors would soon be detected by later processing, it is advantageous to prevent them occurring at the earliest possible opportunity.

An example of a validation definition for a table attribute is shown in the table design screen shown in Figure 9.1.

These validation rules are known as field-level validation, being defined at the column level; the validation test can refer only to the current field. In Microsoft Access, if you wish to apply some validation that refers to two or more columns of the table, then the validation must be defined as a property of the table. The table properties list includes Validation Rule and Validation Text entries which can include tests to be applied across two or more columns of the table. Examples of validation dependent on two columns are

- A hotel is only bookable for a single night if there are more than two guests booked into the room.
- An order for more than £1000 will only be accepted if the credit rating of the customer is A or B.

Note that it is inherently difficult to define validation constraints at the table level because it implies that every software tool using the table has to comply with the defined constraints. Also, there could be potentially a large processing overhead in ensuring that every change to the database tables, down to individual field level, does not conflict with any recorded constraint.

SQL

In the latest SQL standard, it is possible to specify checks within the CREATE TABLE command. When a new row is added to the table, or a row is amended, the specified checks must be tested and verified or the proposed table update is rejected. For example,

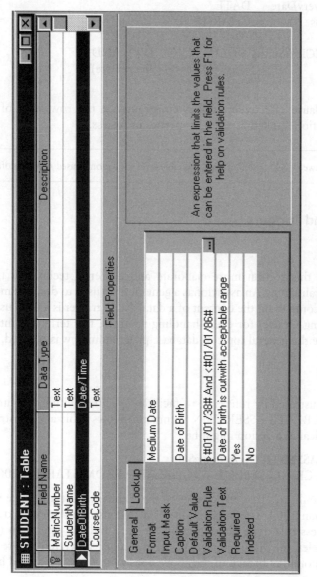

Figure 9.1 Attribute validation.

```
CREATE TABLE STOCK
(
        OrderNo         CHAR(6),
        CustNo          CHAR(7),
        OrderDate       DATE,
        DeliveryDate    DATE,
        Status          CHAR(1),
        . . .
        CHECK ((Status in ('A', 'B', 'C', 'D') ) AND
                        (OrderDate < DeliveryDate))
)
```

The CHECK clause effectively applies constraints at the row level of the table, similar to validation applied as table properties in Access.

9.3 Distinguish between field (column) level and table level validation as used in Microsoft Access.

Assertions and Triggers

Introduction

We consider in this section more elaborate and powerful techniques that can be applied to data validation. An assertion is a general term used to describe methods that impose general controls on the content of a database. A trigger is a term used in many systems (including Oracle) for event-handling routines; this term was introduced in Chapter 8 where the general topic of database programming was covered.

Assertions

These can be illustrated by reference to facilities specified within the current SQL2 standard. The CREATE ASSERTION command allows arbitrary constraints to be specified. A typical expression might be

```
CREATE ASSERTION  AverageSal
        CHECK   ( ( SELECT  AVG(SALARY) FROM STAFF) < 2000 )
```

This constraint indicates that any change to the database must not make the average salary greater than 2000. The implications of such constraints are considerable; they impose a 'business rule' type restriction on the data and any operation (data input, modification, deletion) that might break the rule must be vetted before execution. For instance, a potential breach in the above constraint could be caused by

- increasing the salary of one or more employees
- deleting a row or rows of the table
- inserting new rows into the table.

In effect, if any of the above operations is requested, the query defined in the CHECK clause above must be executed to verify the transaction.

With regard to all of the above SQL special clauses, it should be noted that while these are part of the SQL standard, products will vary in the degree to which these features are implemented.

Triggers

A trigger is a more general validation mechanism, it enables execution of units of code when certain related 'events' occur. Events in this context can be any operation that modifies a table or they can be simply some change at the user interface, for example, the cursor entering a form field, leaving a field, changing the value in a field, etc. When activated, the trigger will invoke some response that has to be programmed into the system by the system designer. (Note: In Microsoft Access, the term 'trigger' is not used, the term 'event-handler' being used in preference.) The response coding will generally be defined in some procedural programming language. In Oracle, for example, it would be written in PL/SQL, which is a procedural language system that can contain SQL statements. Oracle triggers can be specified at the table level, which are activated when any operation affects the table and at the form level which are activated whenever a specified user interface events occurs. In Microsoft Access, event-handling code is written as a macro or as an Access Basic procedure. Figure 9.2 shows the Event Property list belonging to a text field on a form. It shows a macro (Verify Date) has been specified for the After Update event and a procedure (Access Basic code) has been specified for the On Exit event.

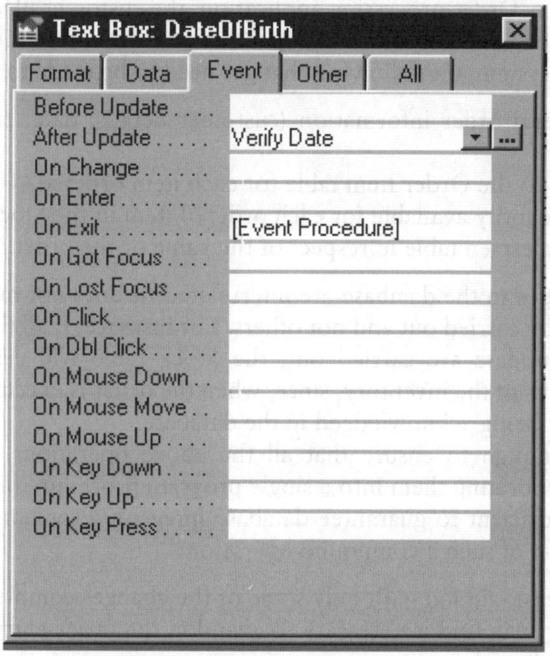

Figure 9.2   Event-handling details.

Triggers provide a lower-level facility that can achieve the same as the CHECK and ASSERTION techniques mentioned earlier in that they can validate the value of table data every time it is altered. The Oracle database provides extensive trigger facilities within its forms system.

Some dialects of SQL provide commands for trigger definition. In Oracle, CREATE TRIGGER is essentially a PL/SQL command since the trigger action is specified as a PL/SQL code block. Other SQL systems provide for the execution of SQL as the trigger action. Such commands have the basic format:

```
CREATE TRIGGER trigger_name
ON table_name
FOR update_modes
AS  SQL_statements
```

where update_mode is one or more of INSERT, UPDATE, DELETE.

Transactions

In general terminology, a transaction is some activity involving a transfer or exchange of goods, services or money. Used in the context of a database system, it has a related connotation but also a more specific meaning. It refers to a group of changes and/or queries to the database which, for the purposes of database integrity, must be performed as a single unit. An example will quickly clarify the above statement and illustrate the need for transactions.

In a typical Sales Order processing application, the customer places an order for a number of items of various products. When this order is entered into the computer order processing system, the following changes need to be made to record the order:

● Add the general order information (customer details, date, etc.) to the Order table.
● Add one row to the Order Item table for each item ordered.
● Update the quantity available for each ordered item in the Stock table.
● Update the Salesmen table in respect of the value of the order.

All of these changes to the database are interrelated; it does not make any sense for some of them to be carried out and not others. For instance, if all the changes except the Stock table update are carried out, the Stock table will cease accurately to represent the status of the inventory, since, when the order is executed, goods will be removed without being acknowledged in the database.

It is simple enough to ensure that all the above operations were carried out together by incorporating them into a single program procedure or procedure form, but this is not sufficient to guarantee database integrity. Problems like these could arise in the middle of such a compound operation:

● The computer could fail with only some of the changes completed.
● The operator may find it necessary to abandon the order entry due to lack of a crucial item of stock.
● A communication link used by the order entry system could fail.

Database transactions are designed to prevent the database being left in an inconsistent state regardless of the circumstances of the attempted update. A transaction can be defined as follows:

> A transaction is a group of database operations that is treated as an atomic unit, i.e. they are all completed or none of them is completed.

In effect, the DBMS must support this commitment regardless of the mode of failure of the transaction. For instance, if the sales order clerk is half-way through entering an order when a power failure occurs, they would expect to find on re-starting the computer, that no changes pertaining to the interrupted order had been carried out. Also, if the clerk wanted to abandon an order part way through data entry, this should not involve any complex backtracking, it should be a simple option provided by the data entry program. It is sufficient for the data entry software to signal to the DBMS that the transaction is to be aborted. This aspect of transaction management is provided by two generic system operations known as 'commit' and 'rollback', described next.

Commit and rollback

The commit and rollback operations are supported by the SQL language and by any system that implements transaction management. For simplicity, their effect is described by reference to the implementation in SQL. Similar facilities are found in other non-SQL systems.

- The Commit statement signals the successful end of a series of updates within one transaction. It tells the DBMS to save all the amended data and to terminate the current transaction.
- The Rollback statement aborts the current transaction. All updates, within the current transaction, are cancelled and the database reverts to its state before the start of the transaction.

Note that, under this model, a transaction is considered to start when the first database update command is issued after the end of the previous transaction.

Note

Some systems (e.g., Microsoft Access and Sybase) also provide a Start Transaction command, which defines a specific start point for a transaction. The implication of the presence of this command is that it is possible to perform database operations which are not governed by transaction 'bracketing'.

We can illustrate the Commit and Rollback commands by means of an example, based on the Order Input scenario given above. (For simplicity, the Salesman table update is ignored). We have used SQL commands but a similar logic would apply if some other input mechanism were used (e.g., a form in Microsoft Access).

In the first case given below, the data entry proceeds without any problems and is terminated with a Commit command. This causes all the preceding commands to be finally applied to the database.

Enter order data

```
Insert into Orders Values ('AB1024', '12-Oct-98', S016)
```

Enter order item data

```
Insert into OrderItems Values( 'AB1024', 1, 'P234', 25)
Insert into OrderItems Values( 'AB1024', 2, 'T877', 3)
. . .
```

Amend stock table

```
Update Stock
      Set Qty-in-Stock = Qty-in-Stock  - 25
      WHERE  ProductCode = 'P234'
Update Stock
      Set Qty-in-Stock = Qty-in-Stock  - 3
      WHERE  ProductCode = 'T877'
. . .
```

Complete the transaction

Commit

It should be clear that all these actions are part of the same 'package'; it would not be acceptable to execute some and not the others. We will suppose now, that part way through this sequence, a mistake in an earlier entry is noticed. The data entry operator can use the Rollback command to abort the commands entered up to that point, returning the database to its state prior to the start of the current transaction.

Enter order data

```
Insert into Orders Values ('AB1024', '12-Oct-98', S016)
```

Enter order item data

```
Insert into OrderItems Values( 'AB1024', 1, 'P234', 25)
Insert into OrderItems Values( 'AB1024', 2, 'T877', 33)
```

** error in previous line, 33 instead of 3 **

```
. . .
```

Amend stock table

```
Update Stock
      Set Qty-in-Stock = Qty-in-Stock  - 25
      WHERE  ProductCode = 'P234'
```

** error noticed **

Operator decides to abandon transaction

Rollback

Now the database is returned to the state prior to the start of the transaction, as if these commands had not been issued.

The other contingency that the system must cope with is some failure (hardware or software) occurring 'in the middle' of the transaction that prevents its proper completion and the user is not given the opportunity of issuing either commit or rollback. In this event, failure to reach the Commit command has the same effect as the Rollback – the transaction effectively disappears.

9.4 While serving as a useful illustration of the Rollback command, the above example is nevertheless somewhat unlikely to happen. Why?

Backups and recovery

The most fundamental technique for protecting against loss of database data is periodically to copy the data onto some other storage unit and place the copy in a secure location. This is known as 'backing up' the database. Backups are generally taken when the system is inactive; this avoids the problem of dealing with transactions that are only partly completed. If some mishap later befalls the database, it is then possible to recreate it, albeit using the older data held in the backup. Transactions that were processed between the backup and the system failure have to be re-entered, either manually or with the aid of a transaction log, which is explained below. The generality of this approach means that the backup gives protection against a wide range of events that affect the data, from corruption by faulty software to physical damage due to fire, etc.

The frequency of taking backups is dictated by a number of factors including

- the rate of transactions applied to the database
- the level of availability of service demanded by the application
- the balance of time required to perform the backup compared with the potential delay in recovering.

These factors would have to be considered by the system designers when developing a specific application.

Reverting to a backup version of the database can often imply considerable pre-processing of transactions; although this can be done automatically with the aid of a transaction log, it would be advantageous to be able to reduce the recovery time. This can be achieved by means of checkpointing. A checkpoint is a special record saved periodically in the transaction log that indicates the transactions that are currently executing at that time. Checkpoints are described in more detail below.

Transaction log

A transaction log or journal is used to record the effect of all changes made to the database by transactions generated by application systems. For instance, new rows

added to the database are recorded in the log; deleted rows are recorded as at the time of deletion; the values of amended rows are recorded before and after the update (called the before and after images). In the event of a system failure, it is possible to recover the database by restoring the most recent backup and then re-executing the transactions recorded in the transaction log. Databases that provide transaction logging will generally provide a utility or DBMS function that will process the transactions automatically, avoiding the need for manual re-entry of the data.

Checkpoints

Checkpoints are transaction status records taken at intervals during normal processing of transactions. Typically, a checkpoint would be taken at frequent intervals during the routine processing of the database. At the checkpoint time, the following actions take place:

- initiation of new transactions is temporarily suspended
- all memory buffers are flushed to disk. This ensures that all committed transactions have indeed been actioned on the physical database.
- all currently active transactions are noted and recorded in the transaction log.

In the event of a failure of the database system (for instance, a power failure or program crash) where the database is not damaged but is probably inconsistent, this information enables the database to be recovered more quickly. This is achieved because it is necessary to pre-process only transactions from the checkpoint rather than returning to the previous backup. Figure 9.3 illustrates the situation; in this figure, the arrowheads indicate the start and finish (commit) points of the transaction.

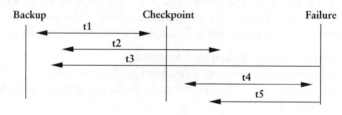

Figure 9.3   Checkpointing.

Figure 9.3 shows the possible conditions of transactions occurring from backup time, through a checkpoint, to the point of failure. Our purpose here is to show how, in the event of failure, the checkpoint technique handles each of the transaction types illustrated.

Transaction t1   begins and ends before the checkpoint (it will not appear on the checkpoint record) and hence will be correctly implemented on the database.

Transaction t2   started before the checkpoint and would be flagged as a current transaction by the checkpoint. Although the transaction log would show that it had committed, there would be an element of doubt about whether the in-memory buffers were written to disk. To be certain, the 'after-image' from the transaction log would be written to disk. A similar argument applies to t4.

Transactions t3 and t5 were incomplete at the time of failure and hence may be partially written to disk. To restore the database to a known consistent condition, the before images from the transaction log would be applied. These transactions would then need to be re-executed.

? **9.5** Some systems will preserve two or more copies of a database taken at different intervals. Can you think of a justification for this procedure?

Database privileges or permissions

In any enterprise running a multi-user database system, it is necessary to be able to control the data that is accessible and/or modifiable by each user and class of user. This is necessary to ensure that data can only be read or changed by users who are entitled to do so. Additionally, it is necessary to control who has system permissions such as the right to create, alter or drop a table, to grant privileges to others, etc. Rather than identify the access permissions of each individual user it is more convenient to classify users into workgroups and to assign rights to these groups. Systems will vary in the way access rights are specified and in the granularity of 'objects' that can be controlled. As an example, the security facilities in Microsoft Access are described below.

The security facilities of Microsoft Access effectively display a 'three-dimensional' organisation, the dimensions being group or user, object (table, form, etc.) and permissions. So, for instance, we could assign read permission to the table Clients for group Personnel. The database objects and the assignable permissions are described in Table 9.1.

Table 9.1

	Database	Table	Query	Form	Report	Macro	Module
Open/run	X			X	X	X	
Read design		X	X	X	X	X	X
Modify design		X	X	X	X-	X	X
Administer		X	X	X	X	X	X
Read data		X	X				
Update data		X	X				
Insert data		X	X				
Delete data		X	X				

Note that the 'Administer' permission allows the user or group to change the permissions of anyone's permissions. It is important therefore that this permission is bestowed only where absolutely necessary.

Facilities in SQL

Access rights are specified in SQL by the GRANT and REVOKE commands. The GRANT command shown below gives the users Joe and Mary the right to view and update data in the Orders table:

GRANT select, update ON Orders TO joe, mary

The following REVOKE command removes Joe's right to update the table:

REVOKE update ON Orders TO joe

More information on these SQL commands can be found in Chapter 13 where SQL is described in some detail.

Summary

The topics covered in this chapter are summarised in the following list.

- Database integrity
  Entity, referential and data integrity.

- Data validation
  Techniques used to ensure that data entering the database is correct. This covered the individual topics of type checking, validation techniques, assertions and triggers.

- Transactions
  Transactions define groups of database operations as atomic units that must be treated as a single database update. This is a very important concept that influences many other areas of work.

- Backups and recovery
  Describes methods used to ensure that the database system can survive failures and other threats. This includes backups, transaction logs and checkpoints.

- Database privileges or permissions
  Describes methods used to control users' access to the database.

Answers to in-text questions

9.1 There are definite limits to how comprehesive validation tests can be. The content of textual information for instance is difficult to validate. If tests are made too prescriptive, natural changes such as inflation of monetary amounts can often cause problems. Many coding systems have an arbitrary structure that cannot be readily checked.

9.2 As well as a range of values, a datatype definition should include a definition of the behaviour of the data such as its handling on input and output.

9.3 Field level validation applies only to one column of the table; checking for correspondence between two or more columns is not possible. Table level validation can refer to two or more columns within one validation criterion.

9.4 It is unlikely that a system would depend for its accuracy on manually entered values as suggested. The related updates of the OrderItems and Stock tables would more likely be done automatically to guarantee integrity.

9.5 There is the possibility that a backup version of the database itself contains errors. This can arise, for example, if a processing program contains an error that is corrupting the data. If such an error is not detected for some time, the most recent backup may be unusable. If older versions of the backup are retained (say, based on a weekly or monthly cycle) then they could be free of the error although being substantially out of date.

REVIEW QUESTIONS

Answers in Appendix C.

1 What is meant by a database constraint?

2 Identify some of the problems that can threaten the integrity of the database.

3 What is meant by data validation?

4 How do datatypes contribute to the accuracy of data?

5 Distinguish between an assertion and a trigger.

6 What is a database transaction?

7 What is a transaction log used for?

8 What are the SQL commands GRANT and REVOKE used for?

EXERCISES

Answers to exercises flagged with an asterisk appear in Appendix D.

1 *Explain what is meant by transactions in the context of a database system and why they are needed. Describe the facilities that a DBMS should provide for the support of transactions.

2 Discuss the techniques that can be employed in database systems to ensure that the information stored in the database is accurate.

3 Describe the techniques employed by database systems to ensure that the data can be recovered in the event of failure or damage to the database.

10

Concurrency

Overview

When a database is accessed simultaneously by two or more users, certain problems arise that do not exist for the single user. Why this should be the case is perhaps not immediately obvious; one would think that several users could read and write data to/from the database more or less independently without difficulty.

A closer inspection of what can happen during simultaneous updates reveals that serious corruption of the data can occur. These problems arise when two users attempt to update the same data simultaneously. Among other problems, the possibility exists that one of the updates will be 'lost', i.e., effectively overwritten by the other. In this chapter we will look at the nature of this problem and show how it is managed by a technique known as locking. In addition, we discover that locking in fact produces its own problem in the form of a situation known as deadlock.

Problems of concurrency

Lost update

An example is the best way to illustrate the problems that can arise during simultaneous updates. We shall assume that two clerks, Anne and Bill are updating a Customer accounts database. To appreciate the source of the difficulties, we must first examine the internal 'mechanics' of updating a row of the database.

When a database user accesses a row of data from the database with a view to amending the data (the data may be displayed on a screen form), the actual data is read from the database storage and held in a temporary buffer area in main memory. This situation is illustrated in Figure 10.1.

In effect, the form provides a 'window' into the memory so that the stored row can be viewed and modified. The most significant point about the above process is that a copy of the database row has been created and held temporarily in memory. The process of updating the database involved modifying the in-memory copy (via the form) then writing it back to the database storage on disk.

The above narrative shows the effect of one user updating the database; if we extend the picture to include two users, Anne and Bill, certain complications arise.

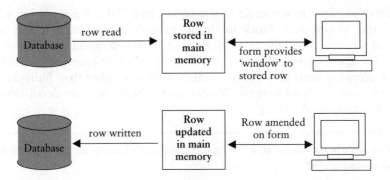

Figure 10.1 Data buffering.

First of all, it is probably clear that if Anne and Bill are accessing totally different parts of the database and/or working at disjoint time periods no interference between their efforts is likely to occur. However, if they both attempt to apply an update to the same row at the same time, things can go badly wrong. This is illustrated in Figure 10.2.

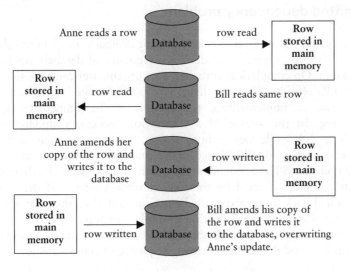

Figure 10.2 Concurrent updates.

The result of this sequence of operations is that Anne's update of the database has been lost – this is commonly known as the lost update syndrome. This effect happens due to the fact that copies of parts of the database are held in main memory for the purposes of the update process. While it is perhaps fairly unlikely, the possibility exists of two users holding and amending the same row at the same time. In this situation, it is inevitable that one of these updates will be lost. In spite of the low probability of such an event, it is generally not acceptable to ignore the possibility, since it results in an undetected corruption of the database.

Additional note
The situation in practice is actually worse than that indicated above. Data transfers to and from a database actually involve at least one physical disk block possibly holding

many database rows. In the example shown in Figure 10.2 Anne and Bill will each hold a copy of one such block in the in-memory buffer. Even if they are not amending the same row, Bill's re-writing of the block will cancel the effect of Anne's update. The consequence of this is that for a problem to arise the coincidence in database accessing need only apply to database blocks rather than individual rows. This is far more likely to happen. We discuss this topic in more detail later in the section 'Granularity of locking'.

?   **10.1** What would be the effect of (a) the row size and (b) disk block size on the problem indicated in the previous paragraph?

Other problems can occur as a result of interleaving of transactions; two of these, known as the uncommitted dependency problem and the inconsistent analysis problem are described below.

Uncommitted dependency problem

This effect occurs as a result of the Commit/Rollback mechanism described in Chapter 9. To recap, a transaction defines a sequence of database operations to be treated as a unit. On completion of the transaction, the user can choose to cancel the whole sequence (rollback) or to have it finally accepted (commit). The main technique used in implementing transactions is the immediate update with transaction log. In the course of a transaction, necessary updates are written immediately to disk while 'before images' (i.e., the previous value of the data) are written to a transaction log file. Hence, in the 'middle' of the transaction, some of the transaction updates will be actioned on the database and visible to other users, whose own updates may be affected by the uncommitted changes. If the transaction is eventually rolled back (by applying the before images), the other dependent changes are invalidated. Consider the following example which might occur in a bank. Mr Smith's account, with an initial balance of £1000, is being updated simultaneously by two transaction A and B and the following sequence of actions ensue:

1. Transaction A is a withdrawal for £600. The database is updated to show a balance of £400.
2. Transaction B reads the £400 from the database into an in-memory buffer and adds a deposit of £300, giving a balance of £700.
3. Transaction A now executes a rollback, returning the database to £1000.
4. Transaction B now writes its in-memory balance value of £700 to the database and commits the transaction.

At this point the database has been corrupted; the balance should be £1300 but is actually £700. This effect is similar to the lost update but differs in the timing of events. Note that the above example would not have caused a problem if the rollback had not occurred because transaction B read the balance after update by transaction A.

Inconsistent analysis problem

This effect again arises from interleaving of transaction operations and demonstrates how erroneous results can be obtained by a transaction which is only reading the database. In this instance, we assume that one transaction is reading the database to provide some analysis (say, computing a total balance value) while it is simultaneously being amended by another transaction. We assume for this example that Transaction A is reading a set of three accounts and summing the balances. Transaction B, over the same time interval, is transferring money from one of these accounts to another. We will assume that the accounts are called ACC1, ACC2 and ACC3 with starting balances of £100, £200 and £300 respectively.

1. Transaction A reads ACC1 and sets running total to £100.
2. Transaction A reads ACC2 and adds £200 to total giving £300.
3. Transaction B reads ACC2, withdraws £50 and deposits it in ACC3.
4. Transaction A reads ACC3, reads £350 and adds it to total giving final total of £650.

Note that the transfer of cash from one account to another should not have affected the overall total and hence it should still show 100+200+300 = £600. However, the summary report shows £650. In this example the database has not been corrupted but a database user has obtained a query result that is quite erroneous.

?   **10.2** What would be the effect of reversing steps 2 and 3 in the above example?

Serialisation of transactions

It is clear that the potential corruption and inconsistencies described in the foregoing sections cannot be allowed to occur. In the management of concurrent transactions it is essential that the DBMS prevents such unacceptable interference. In effect, each database user should be able to access and update the database without fear of these problems occurring. The objective of the DBMS in this respect can be expressed as the concept of 'serialisability of transactions', which can be stated as follows:

> When two or more transactions are executed concurrently on a database, their effect should be the same as if they had executed serially, with one completing before the other starts

Suppose we have three transactions TA, TB and TC that are executing at least partly at the same time. We can illustrate the relative timing of the transactions as shown in Figure 10.3(a). Note that some or all of the transactions overlap at various times. Figure 10.3(a) illustrates serial execution of the transactions, with one transaction finishing before another starts. The concept of serialisability states that the effect on the database for each of these two transaction sequences Figure 10.3(a) and (b) should be the same.

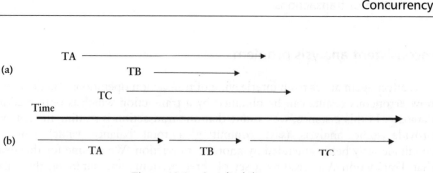

Figure 10.3 Serialisability.

To achieve serialisability, we need some method of allowing the transactions to proceed in parallel, while at the same time avoiding the interference problems described earlier. This can be accomplished by means of a technique known as locking, described next.

Locking

Locking is used by all commercial databases in implementing concurrency. If we examine the problems (such as lost update) that occur between concurrent transactions, we can see that they result from two or more transactions accessing the same data at the same time. The idea of locking is that interference between concurrent transactions can be controlled by enabling transactions to lock parts of the database data while that part is being amended, preventing other transactions from amending/reading the same data. When the amendment is complete, the lock is released enabling other transactions to continue. If we revisit the lost update problem illustrated in Figure 10.2 we can see how locking could avoid the problem. Note, however, that this example does not show the full picture – a further problem can occur. The nature and resolution of this additional problem is dealt with shortly.

1. Anne reads a database row into a memory buffer.

2. Anne's transaction locks the disk block holding the row.

3. Bill tries to read the same row but is prevented by the lock; his transaction enters a 'wait' state.

4. Anne writes the updated row to disk and releases the lock.

5. Bill's transaction now proceeds and reads the updated row.

6. Bill's transaction locks the block to prevent access by other users.

7. Bill updates the row and writes to disk, releasing the lock.

The two updates have been successfully carried without any corruption. The process has involved a delay in completing Bill's work but this is a small price to pay for maintaining the integrity of the database. However, the duration of the lock is obviously relevant; if Anne and Bill are on-line clerks dealing with, say a telephone ordering system, then lock delays could become significant.

Two-phase locking

In fact, the simple locking scheme described above does not actually guarantee complete protection from concurrency problems. The lost update and the other problems described above can still arise if multiple locks are applied during one transaction; although each individual update is protected, the fact that updates from two or more transactions can interleave in time can cause data corruption. As an example of how this can occur, consider the following sequence, based on the same scenario used above.

1. Anne starts a transaction and reads a row of a table after applying a lock.
2. Bill tries to access the same row but is prevented by the lock
3. Anne updates the row, writes it to disk and releases the lock.
4. Bill now succeeds in reading the row, locks it and updates it. Note that Bill's update was based on the data *after update by Anne*.
5. Bill now writes the row to disk and releases the lock.
6. Anne's transaction, for whatever reason, now fails and is rolled back, restoring the row to its state before Anne's update. Bill's update has now been lost.

The problem here is that a lock has been released too early, allowing for the possibility of interference from another transaction. A slightly more elaborate locking scheme, called two-phase locking avoids this situation. In the two-phase locking scheme every transaction has two phases, a growing phase when locks are acquired and a shrinking phase during which locks are released. In other words, within one transaction, *all lock operations must precede the first lock release*. In the above example, at step 3, the lock would *not* be released, thereby preventing Bill from proceeding as indicated in steps 4 and 5. When the rollback of Anne's transaction eventually occurs, Bill's update is not lost because it never took place.

? **10.3** As the number of on-line users of a database increases, how would you expect the frequency of lock conflicts to change?

The foregoing description of locking is rather simplified; there are a number of variants on this basic model and these are described in the following sections.

Granularity of locking

A lock can be applied in a variety of 'levels' of varying severity, in terms of the relative amount of data locked; this is often referred to as the 'granularity' of the locks. The most severe would be to lock the entire database, preventing all other activity. This is the simplest to implement but is very wasteful and would degrade the performance of the database dramatically. Total locking like this is used only when performing some global operation on the database such as compacting, re-indexing, etc.

A less severe lock is table-level locking, where each table required by a transaction is locked, leaving other tables free for access by other transactions. This does permit some degree of simultaneity but is still generally too restrictive. Many applications require access to several tables for one transaction; for instance, in a Sales Order Processing system, sales order entry would use tables Customer, Product Stock, Orders and Order Items simultaneously. Locking all these tables would bar access, for instance, to a transaction updating the Product Stock table, say, to record the arrival of a stock delivery. Again, table level locking would be applied only when a large-scale operation is being performed on the table, such as archiving or indexing.

Probably the most logical level is row(or record) level locking, which locks only one row of a table at a time, providing a high degree of simultaneity. In practice, it is technically quite difficult to maintain locks at the row level and often page level locking is used as a compromise. (Note however, that some systems do implement true row level locks.) Page locking applies locks in units of whole physical blocks or pages of the database storage medium such that the row being accessed is contained within the locked zone. If the size of the row is less than or equal to the page size, then a single page lock will suffice. If the row spans several pages all pages holding part of the row will be locked.

A drawback to page locking is that locked pages will often contain other rows not involved in the transaction. This is particularly significant for tables with a small row size, where several rows will be 'packed' into one physical page. For instance, a typical page size of 4096 could hold 100 rows of a table with a row length of 40 bytes. The implication of this effect is that a single row lock will actually be locking another 99 rows, preventing access to these rows by other users, for the duration of the lock. However, page level locking ties in with the practice in disk systems whereby the unit of transfer between disk and main memory is the physical block. Hence, the whole block will be re-written after update of any part of it.

In principle, locks could be extended to an even finer level of granularity – to the column level. This would certainly the reduce the likelihood of locks actually causing any conflict between transactions and hence would provide optimum performance. However, the technical difficulties exceed even those for row locks and no major system currently implements column locking.

Other locking variants

There are other variations on the theme of locking, in addition to the granularity of the locking. These are described in the sections below.

Optimistic and pessimistic locking

This term refers to the manner in which locks are applied relative to the reading, amending and writing activities. As the name implies, optimistic locking assumes that your transaction will not conflict with another and hence updating proceeds without a lock being applied. At the point of committing the transaction, a check is made to ascertain whether in fact any other transaction has accessed the same data. If so, the transactions are rolled back and must be restarted.

Pessimistic locking assumes that a conflict will occur and the data is locked at the start of the transaction. Once the data is locked, the transaction can run to completion without hindrance.

Contrasting the two approaches, optimistic locking tries to optimise the system performance by minimising the duration of a lock, while pessimistic locking imposes locks for much longer periods. On the other hand, a transaction controlled by optimistic locking may not immediately succeed and may require rerunning; this will not happen with pessimistic locking. Another advantage of pessimistic locking is that read accesses will always see the most up-to-date data; in optimistic locking, one could read a record that is currently being updated.

The choice between optimistic and pessimistic locking depends mostly on the loading of the system. If the application system is busy, with a large number of transactions being processed per hour, conflicts between transactions are therefore probable and pessimistic locking is preferable. If the loading is light, optimistic locking will generally produce a better overall performance.

Shared and exclusive locks

Another variation on the locking theme is to vary the level of 'exclusivity' of the lock. In this respect there are usually two forms of lock

> Shared or S lock : A shared lock is applied when one requires only to read the data.
> Exclusive or X lock: An exclusive lock is applied when data is to be updated.

These are sometimes referred to as locking modes. Several transactions can apply an S lock simultaneously, enabling each user to read the database. At the same time, no transaction can apply an X lock until all the S locks terminate. If an X lock is applied to a unit of data, no other locks can be applied. In other words, at any instant, there can be no locks, one or more S locks or one X lock (for one unit of data).

? **10.4** Distinguish between an exclusive lock and a full database lock.

Deadlock

Introduction

While solving the problems inherent in concurrent access to a database, locking produces a problem of its own, known as deadlocking. A deadlock can occur when on-line users are able to apply two or more locks at the same time. This can result in a circular wait situation that brings the activity of both users to a halt. An example will clarify this concept.

Suppose we have an airline seat reservation system using concurrent access to a database. At some instant, two customers Anne and Bill are being served by the on-line operators. Both Anne and Bill intend to book a seat on flight AB123 and a later flight AB456. Anne's sales assistant first of all accesses the AB123 flight information, thereby placing a lock on it. At the same time, Bill's assistant accesses flight AB456 and similarly locks it. Before committing the first flight booking, each assistant now tries to access the other flight but of course finds that it is locked. Never mind, they think, it will be unlocked soon. However, the two booking operations are now deadlocked; Anne is waiting to book AB456 while holding AB123, while Bill is waiting for AB123 while holding AB456. We can summarise this sequence of events as follows:

> Anne locks AB123
> Bill locks AB456
> Anne requests AB456 . . . waits!
> Bill requests AB456 . . . waits!

A circular wait situation now exists and will persist until one user rolls back their transaction. It is important to appreciate that deadlocks occur as a result of the locking mechanism. Locking is used to avoid corruption of the database arising from concurrent accesses but unfortunately it is itself marred by its potential for causing deadlocks.

Dealing with deadlocks

A number of techniques have been devised to deal with deadlocks. The most significant of these are prevention and detection.

Prevention

In the above example, each user applied two locks with a time gap between. A deadlock can be avoided if all exclusive locks are applied at the same time. Failure to lock all required records at the start of the transaction causes an immediate release of all locks already made thereby preventing the circular wait situation. The difficulties with this approach are, firstly, that a number of locks may be applied for a considerable period of time, thereby limiting access by other users. Secondly, in many applications it is not possible to predict what records will need locking until later in the processing. The only way to manage this would be to release all current locks when a new lock is required, then applying all locks again; the principle applied here is that all locks are applied or none are applied.

Detection

It is possible for the DBMS to detect the presence of a deadlock by checking for circular waits within the locks and lock requests. When detected, the deadlock can be resolved by rolling back one of the member transactions. This will have the effect of removing all locks held by the transaction and hence breaking the deadlock. The on-line user responsible for the aborted transaction would need to be informed that the transaction did not succeed and must be re-started.

The DBMS can use a matrix technique to detect circular waits in the current resource locking situation. A resource in this context refers to the unit of data that can be locked by transactions; as indicated earlier when dealing with granularity of locking, this will generally be one or more disk blocks. The current pattern of transaction requests and resource locks can be represented by a matrix as shown in the examples below:

Example A

Transactions	Resource A	Resource B	Resource C
1	Locked		Wait
2		Wait	
3		Locked	Locked

Example B

Transactions	Resource A	Resource B	Resource C
1	Locked		Wait
2		Wait	
3	Wait	Locked	Locked

In example A, each of transactions 1 and 2 are waiting on resources B and C respectively, which are both held by transaction 3. Transaction 3 is not waiting on any resource and hence will presumably eventually release B and C so, at this time no deadlock exists. However, example B shows that transaction 3 has now requested resource A which is locked by transaction 1. This now creates a circular wait.

Summary

This chapter has dealt with the problems inherent in concurrent users accessing the same database. We have seen that corruption of the database and/or invalid results can arise if proper safeguards are not employed. It should be noted that problems encountered can occur as a result of overlapping of disk to memory data transfers and also as a result of interleaving in time of separate transactions. Locking is used to avoid these problems and in particular it was shown that two-phase locking is necessary to ensure proper protection against concurrency problems. Deadlock is an unfortunate by-product of the locking mechanism and must itself be managed with suitable techniques.

The topics covered in this chapter are

1. Problems of concurrency: lost update, uncommitted dependency, inconsistent analysis.
2. Serialisation of transactions.
3. Locking: general principles, two phase locking, granularity of locking, shared/exclusive, pessimistic/optimistic locking.
4. Deadlocks: causes, dealing with deadlocks.

Answers to in-text questions

10.1 (a) Larger block sizes would accommodate more rows per block and hence would tend to aggravate the problem. (b) Larger row sizes would mean fewer rows per block and hence would reduce the effect.

10.2 The following table shows the effect on the three account balances and the running total after each step.

	ACC1	ACC2	ACC3	Total	
1.	100	200	300	100	
2.	100	150	350	100	previously step 3
3.	100	150	350	250	previously step 2
4.	100	150	350	600	

The final running total is £600 which is correct. This shows that the result critically depends on the specific sequence of events.

10.3 One might expect that the occurrence of lock conflicts would increase with increasing numbers of users; however, a mitigating factor in this respect is that the larger the number of users, generally, the larger the database.

10.4 An exclusive lock means that only one transaction has access to the locked data which typically will be a single disk block. A database lock refers to the granularity of the lock, i.e., the amount of the database locked by one lock.

REVIEW QUESTIONS

Answers in Appendix C.

1 Why does concurrent access to a database give rise to potential problems?

2 What is meant by the terms lost update, uncommitted dependency problem and inconsistent analysis problem?

3 What is meant by serialisation of transactions?

4 Explain the concept of locking and why it is used.

5 What is meant by two-phase locking?

6 Explain the term 'granularity of locking'.

7 What is a deadlock and how is it caused?

8 What methods are used to manage deadlocks?

EXERCISES

Answers to exercises flagged with an asterisk appear in Appendix D.

1 *In a database system within a banking application, transaction A is transferring £1000 from account ACC1 to account ACC2. At the same time, transaction B is processing every account record and adding interest payments by increasing each balance by 1.5%. Initially, ACC1 has a balance of £4000 and ACC2 £5000. The following sequence of operations take place:

Transaction A	**Transaction B**
Read ACC1 record and lock	
Reduce balance by 1000	
Write balance	
Release lock	
	Read account ACC1 and lock
	Update balance by 1.5%
	Write ACC1 and release lock
	Read account ACC2 and lock
	Update balance by 1.5%
	Write ACC2 and release lock
Read ACC2 record and lock	
Increase balance by 1000	
Write balance	
Release lock	

What should be the final balance values if the transactions were performed serially? What are the actual final values ensuing from the above sequence? How can this error be avoided?

2 Explain the purpose of locking in database processing and distinguish between shared and exclusive locks and between optimistic and pessimistic locking. By means of a suitable example, show how the use of locking in a database application can cause deadlocks.

3 The following matrix maintained by a DBMS shows the current transaction-resource situation for the database. It indicates, for instance, that transaction 1 has locked resource B and C and is waiting for D.

Transactions	Resource A	Resource B	Resource C	Resource D
1		Locked	Locked	Wait
2	Locked		Wait	
3	Wait			Locked

Does a deadlock exist in this situation?

11

Networked and distributed systems

Introduction

In this chapter, we cover a number of topics with the common theme of networking. Using a number of computers interconnected by a network introduces a number of new opportunities and problems. We start by discussing the client-server technique that is used extensively in multi-computer environments, identifying its strengths and weaknesses. This leads us to the concept of distributed databases where the data is stored in a number of physically separate computers (connected by a network) each having its own database files. The benefits and drawbacks of a range of different distribution techniques are explored.

Also covered within the chapter are techniques currently in use to facilitate platform-independent communication with and between databases. These techniques include Microsoft's ODBC and Sunsoft's JDBC.

Finally, we take a brief look at database systems on the World Wide Web in terms of how databases can be used and implemented in this new environment.

Client-server systems

The philosophy of server systems arose within Local area network technology. LANs enable multiple personal computers to share common resources such as file stores, printers, electronic mail, etc. To facilitate this sharing process, it was found convenient to place each resource under the control of one dedicated computer within the network. These dedicated computers are referred to as resource servers, hence we have printer servers, disk servers, email servers, etc. For instance, if an application program wants to produce printed output, it sends the data to the printer server, which services the request. Another common mode of working is to provide disk storage on a large server computer that can be used as general storage space for other computers on the same LAN. To the user, this space is identical in nature and functionality to 'local' storage; in MS/DOS/Windows systems, for instance, server disk volumes can be assigned conventional drive letters such as E:, F:, etc., and directories and files within this disk space can be addressed using normal pathnames. This mode of working whereby application programs run on some computers and servers on others became known as client-server, reflecting the fact that some computers (the clients) send requests to a provider of services (the server) which attempts to comply with the requests.

Client-server is a rapidly growing architecture for data management, particularly for personal computers within a local area network. In effect the functions of the DBMS are split into two parts. The client or 'front-end' interfaces to the user; it is where application programs execute and it provides facilities such as interactive querying, report generation, transaction forms, etc. The server or 'back-end' provides the database engine that manages the physical data and responds to queries sent from the client. In modern systems SQL plays a major role; SQL is used as the communication language that enables the client to define the queries that are sent to the server for execution. It is important to distinguish between an SQL-based client-server system and file server systems. In a file server, the user's computer has its own DBMS but accesses database files held on the server. Application programs request data via the local DBMS, which transmits the request to the server. The server resolves the query and returns data blocks to the application program. This is illustrated in Figure 11.1. In an SQL server environment, the client application sends SQL queries to the server which responds with the query 'answer', in the form of rows of data. Figure 11.2 illustrates an SQL client-server system.

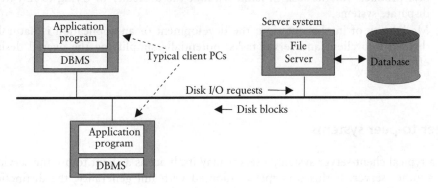

Figure 11.1   Disk server system.

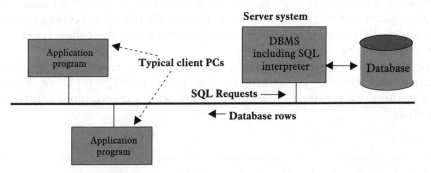

Figure 11.2   SQL client-server system.

Advantages of client-server approach

The client-server approach provides many benefits, the more important of which are listed below. In this respect, the approach is being compared with the use of a centralised database facility or a network system using only file servers.

- Scalability; it is easier to extend the size of a system. This can be done 'horizontally', i.e., by adding more client and/or server machines or 'vertically', by making the server machines larger, perhaps moving to a new platform such as UNIX or a mainframe.
- The computers used in the system can be optimised for the role they play. The client machines can be PC workstations that can provide very effective user interfaces at a low cost. The server machines can be configured with large memory and a fast disk system to cope with their role as data providers.
- This approach divides the processing burden between client and server; much of the processing is performed locally, i.e., on the client system, near to where the data is produced and required. This consequently minimises network activity needed to service the application.
- 'Open systems' facilitation; it encourages the use of a mixture of different hardware and software systems. This enables the system designer to choose the best products for the task in hand without the difficulty of trying to integrate disparate systems.
- Modularity of implementation; the development of an application is naturally divided into client and server tasks, potentially simplifying the overall design effort.

Peer-to-peer systems

In a typical client-server system, a server may itself act as a client to use the services of another server. If this principle is adopted with full generality, the distinction between client and server computers would disappear; any machine could act as a server and any as a client. In effect, 'client' and 'server' would be *roles* adopted by the computers as required by application systems. Such an arrangement is called a peer-to-peer system and forms the basis of an ultimate distributed processing model. In this model, all networked computers can offer services to, and use the services of, the rest of the network.

At this point we are digressing somewhat into the realms of general open systems architecture. To return to the more specific topic of database architectures, we continue in the next section with a description of distributed databases.

?   11.1 Distinguish between roles of the 'client' and 'server' in a client-server system.

Distributed databases

Overview

In a distributed database, the data comprising the database is held in a number of physically separate locations, connected by a network, which can be accessed by users independently of their location. There are a number of ways in which distribution of a database may be desirable; the principal motivation is to minimise network traffic, improve access times (for locally stored data) and hence improve overall system performance by placing data near to where it is most commonly accessed.

In the following sections we cover a number of topics which are summarised below.

- Types of distribution: a look at a number of techniques used in splitting the data across a number of sites. In this respect we cover homogeneous and heterogeneous systems, partitioned, horizontal and vertical distribution and replication.
- Distributed schemas: how a distributed system manages multiple schemas.
- Query processing: the problems involved in executing queries when the data is stored in several different sites.
- Concurrency.
- Date's objectives: idealised requirements for a distributed database system.
- Advantages and disadvantages of distributed databases.

Homogeneous and heterogeneous

Each node within a distributed database must have a local DBMS. A homogeneous distributed database has the same (or related) DBMS at each node, while a heterogeneous one does not. For instance, a system consisting of several networked computers each running the Oracle DBMS is a homogeneous system. A system with one or more computers running Oracle and others running IBMs DB2 and/or Microsoft's Access is heterogeneous.

A heterogeneous system is technically more difficult, especially to implement in a general way (i.e. to allow an arbitrary mixture of disparate systems) than a homogeneous one and hence the latter are much more common and more advanced in practice. Full realisation of general heterogeneous systems will need the development of some standardised approach, possibly via distributed object technology such as CORBA. CORBA is a generalised architecture developed by the Object Management Group (OMG) that allows applications running on different computers to communicate with one another no matter where they are located or what software platforms they are based on. The OMG is an association of about 800 software vendors, developers and end-users. For more information on this topic, consult Siegel (1997) and the OMG Web site at www.omg.org.

Partitioned, horizontal and vertical

These terms refer to the way in which the database is 'chopped-up' between the sites that host portions of the database.

Partitioned

By far the simplest and most common form of distribution is to partition the tables of the database into separate sites; hence, one site may have the Customer, Order, OrderItems and Product tables while another site may have the Sales and Purchase Ledger tables. This form of fragmentation is well supported in current products. The principal justification for this arrangement is that tables can be held close to where they are mainly used, thereby minimising network traffic and increasing access times, while at the same time still providing global access to all the data. It also is a useful technique where interconnection of previously separate systems is required.

Horizontal fragmentation

Horizontal fragmentation refers to the splitting of tables such that groups of rows are held at different sites. To give a crude example, rows 1 to 1000 could be stored at site A, rows 2001 to 4000 at site B, etc. It is less clear why this might be desirable; in fact, this example using numerical subdivision is pretty well useless! However, consider the following example.

A chain of estate agents, with geographically dispersed offices, use a database of properties under their management. Typically, each office would normally cater only for properties within their geographical area, but occasionally they may have to respond to a client's request for properties in some other area. In these circumstances, it might be convenient to have a 'global' property database horizontally distributed on the basis of the office. That is, database rows pertaining to properties under the jurisdiction of office A would be held in office A, properties of B at office B, and so on.

Figure 11.3 illustrates this principle. Note that the subdivision would be based on a key value of the table, not on physical row numbers as the figure might suggest. This would provide rapid access for local enquiries while retaining the option of an enquiry over the whole (or selected parts) of the full database. Additionally, network traffic would be minimised due to the relative rarity of global enquiries. Note that in such a scenario, users at any one office can notionally 'see' the full database at any time. It is simply that their local enquiries will not require the system to search outwith the local portion of the database. Horizontal fragmentation will normally be based on some such selection of rows related to the nature of the table data.

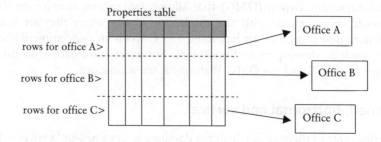

Figure 11.3   Horizontal fragmentation.

? 11.2 In the estate agent example described above, the Properties table uses a primary key called Property Code that identifies each property being handled. Suggest a way in which the Property Code could be constructed to facilitate horizontal fragmentation.

Vertical fragmentation

Vertical fragmentation refers to the splitting of tables such that the columns of the table are distributed over two or more sites. Again, it is perhaps not immediately obvious why this might be advantageous. If we return to the estate agent example, we can see that details about clients might be vertically fragmented, with local information about the client (name, address, phone, etc.) being held in the regional offices while columns related to billing and accounting details (amount owing, invoice date, etc.) are held on a main office database. This arrangement would serve the same purpose as in the horizontal example: it optimises access times and minimises network traffic. Vertical fragmentation is illustrated in Figure 11.4.

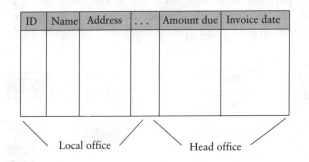

Figure 11.4   Vertical fragmentation.

Figure 11.4 implies that each column is allocated exclusively to one fragment; a problem with this, however, is the need to preserve the primary key in each fragment so that the table data can be accessed by the key and can be rejoined for querying. As an alternative to replicating the natural primary key, a 'row number' can be assigned uniquely to each row and recorded in all fragments of the table. This can then be used as the join key when it is necessary to query over combined fragments.

Note:
You may notice that this notion of subdivision of columns on the basis of information usage is reminiscent of the way in which the view mechanism is often used. Views are often used to present users with a subset of the columns of a real table, these being the columns that they require to 'see' in the execution of their job. Vertical fragmentation reflects this mode of working in a physical separation of the data..

11.3 What would be involved (in general terms) in adding a row to:
    (a) a horizontally fragmented table? (b) A vertically fragmented table?

Replication

In the examples described above, the database is fragmented for reasons of efficiency; some data is stored local to where it produced and used and less frequently used data is held remotely. There are many situations, however, where data produced at one location is frequently required at other locations. If the remote sites are required to access such data via a network, the network traffic will be high and the overall performance of the system in terms of access time could be poor.

An alternative approach in such circumstances is data replication; as the title suggests, data replication involves storing copies of data produced by one site at some or all of the other network sites, thereby avoiding cross network accesses. A database can be fully or partially replicated, i.e., the whole database is copied or just a fragment of it. Be careful to distinguish between a fragmented database and replicated fragments of a database. This is illustrated by Figure 11.5.

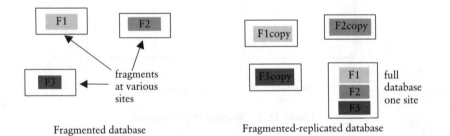

Fragmented database   Fragmented-replicated database

Figure 11.5   Replication.

In the fragmented case, the 'whole' database does not exist at one site but is dispersed between the sites. In the replicated-fragmented case, the whole database exists at one site but copies of fragments exist at other sites.

While avoiding the problems of network performance, replication creates its own problems, the principal of these being the management of the copying activity and maintenance of data consistency. These problems are discussed in a later section.

In view of the problems described above, replication is particularly suitable for databases which are essentially maintained at a central location and required principally for reference only at other sites. An example might be distribution of engineering change information from a manufacturing or software company.

Note that replication is also used as a means of data security; duplicate copies of the database are maintained continuously so that, in the event of loss of one machine, the system can continue to operate using the other.

Transparency

It is a major objective of a fully fledged distributed database that the underlying mechanisms such as fragmentation are not apparent to the user. Certainly, it is very desirable that the user need take no special action related to the location and fragmentation of the data. This objective is referred to as data transparency. There are three 'flavours' of transparency that need to be considered, namely, location, fragmentation and replication transparencies.

1. *Location transparency.* The database user should not be concerned about the storage location of the data beng accessed. In particular, it should not be necessary explicitly to address a query to a specific location.

2. *Fragmentation transparency.* The database user should not be concerned with how the data is fragmented over the network.

3. *Replication transparency.* The database user should not be concerned about whether the data being accessed is the source version or a copy thereof. Problems regarding the consistency of the data are the responsibility of the DBMS software and not the individual users.

? **11.4** Why is it considered desirable that distributed database systems exhibit transparency?

Schema management

Within a database system, a schema describes the information held in the database. This will include the design of tables and views, indexes, constraint definitions, etc., as well as location information indicating to the DBMS where a particular item is stored. The schema enables the DBMS to translate names (tables, attributes, etc.) used by the application programs into physical disk addresses. In conventional single-site databases, the schema would naturally be stored in the database itself or at least within the same disk system. In a distributed system, the situation is somewhat more complex. The problems presented are

- location information more complex; network site addresses as well as disk addresses are required
- the schema information is required at all the sites
- the schema requires additional information about how each table is fragmented and/or replicated.

Query processing

It is perhaps not difficult to see that processing a query in a distributed database system is more complicated than in a single database. Since the data is distributed over several physical locations, responding to a query in general will involve accessing several network sites and dealing with the implications of the query. We should note here, however, that these are problems for the DBMS to resolve; the concept of transparency implies that the database user should not be concerned with such matters.

If we use the word 'query' in a general sense to include both reading and updating of the database then the problems inherent in query processing can be summarised as listed below.

Fragmentation of the query
In order to issue the query to the respective sites, it must be split into sub-queries applicable to the data fragment at that site. For example, if a query is addressed to a table that is horizontally fragmented over three sites, then the same query must be sent to each site for execution.

Distribution of updated and inserted data
If the query involves an update or insert operation, then the data must be written to the various sites as demanded by the distribution scheme. For example, if a new row is added to a table that is vertically fragmented over two sites, then it must be re-expressed as an insertion of two projections of the original row into the respective sites.

Collation of results
When individual sites respond to the sub-queries, the requesting client site must collate these into one unified answer. For instance, a select type query addressed to a table that is vertically fragmented over two sites will result in two result relations that must be joined.

Optimisation of queries
To resolve a query will typically involve movement of data between sites. In general, there will be several strategies available for resolving a query, involving different movements of data between the sites. The efficiency of this operation critically depends on the method chosen. For instance, suppose a table of 10,000 rows at site A is to be joined to a table of 10 rows at site B. To get the data together, it is clearly more efficient to send the 10 rows at site B to site A and to perform the join there. Typically, the optimisation process will consist of two levels: the global optimiser will decide how to move data across the network to best resolve the query; the local optimiser will then deal with the data at the target site in efficiently implementing the query.

Concurrency control

Management of concurrent transactions in a distributed environment is similar in general nature to that in a single database environment. It is still necessary to protect against loss or corruption of data arising from simultaneous access to the same data and deadlocks can still occur. However, the dispersion of the data means that a transaction may also be dispersed, i.e., it may be necessary to execute transaction code at several sites to complete the overall transaction task. In principle, if a transaction T requires separate execution of dispersed component transactions T1, T2, etc., then successful execution of the transaction requires a commit of each of the transactions T1, T2, etc. Conversely, a rollback of any of the component transactions would necessitate a rollback of all of the component transactions. Management of this kind of operation requires that one site acts as a co-ordinator for the whole system. When a site completes its part of the transaction, it will send a message to the co-ordinator indicating that it is ready to commit or to rollback as the case may be. If and when the co-ordinator receives a 'ready to commit' from every site, it will send a commit to all the sites which are then forced to commit. If any site fails to provide a 'ready to commit' then the whole transaction is rolled back at all sites.

Date's 12 objectives

The well-known authority on database matters, C.J. Date (1995) presented a set of objectives that a fully fledged distributed database system should aspire to. While no currently available database conforms to all these objectives, they form a useful reference standard and a target for future developments. Many of the points covered have already been discussed earlier in this chapter so the list also forms a useful summary of the chapter.

1. Local autonomy. All sites should be independent of other sites, i.e., it should not be necessary to refer to another site before initiating a transaction.

2. No master site. There should be no site that performs special services for the rest of the sites. In particular, tasks such as transaction management should not be vested in one site.

3. Continuous operation. Making changes to one site, such as upgrading the hardware or software, should not involve closing down the whole system.

4. Location transparency.

5. Fragmentation transparency.

6. Replication transparency. These transparencies were described in the previous section.

7. Distributed query processing. Queries involving multiple sites should be resolved as efficiently as possible, taking into account the distribution/replication of the data and the effect of transmission delays.

8. Distributed transaction management. Management of transactions should not be vested in one site. In order to manage the commit or rollback of a transaction, it is necessary that one site acts as a co-ordinator, but objective 8 says that any site should be capable of undertaking this role.

9. Hardware independent.

10. Operating system independent.

11. Network independent. A distributed database should be capable of working on any network consisting of a mix of different computer types, e.g., PCs, minicomputers and mainframes using a variety of operating systems. Conformance to the network criterion is less of a problem; most vendors software can operate using a variety of networking architectures.

12. DBMS independent. This is possibly the hardest objective to meet. It implies that a distributed DBMS product from one vendor (say, IBM) be capable of 'talking' to a variety of local DBMS products from other vendors. This can only be achieved by the establishment of industry standards such as SQL.

?   **11.5** Why is it considered advantageous to have 'DBMS independence'?

Advantages and disadvantages of distributed databases

In considering the advantages and disadvantages, we are effectively comparing distributed databases with the alternative of a centralised database. In such a system, all remote sites would need to communicate over a network to a single large database.

Advantages

1. Improves system efficiency due to reduced network traffic and faster access to local data. This is probably the main factor favouring distributed databases.
2. Enables each site to retain control of their local data.
3. Improves availability; if one site fails the rest of the system can continue operating (at least to the extent that the services of the failed site are not required).
4. By subdividing the work, the system capacity is improved.

Disadvantages

The principal arguments against distribution are concerned with the additional complexity in several areas which are listed below.

1. Query processing; data may have to be gleaned from several sites requiring additional work in resolving and optimising the query.
2. Concurrency; there is additional complexity in managing synchronised commits and rollbacks.
3. Schema management; it requires additional levels of schema to specify location and fragmentation of relations.
4. Update of replicated data; it is necessary to ensure that replicated data is kept synchronised with the original.
5. Database design; database developers have a more complex task in deciding how to distribute the data and how to administer the overall system.

Summary

The overall case for distributed databases could be summarised as 'worth while but complicated'. It provides very real practical benefits but the design and operational complexities are daunting.

Other network technologies

Overview

In this section, a number of other technologies of relevance to networked and distributed databases are briefly described. These include Microsoft's ODBC and Sunsoft's JDBC. The section also includes a look at factors arising from the integration of databases into the World Wide Web. In view of the complexity and rapid change in this area, these notes are necessarily an introduction. A good source of useful additional information on these topics is the Web. Some useful Web references are given in this section.

ODBC

Microsoft's Open Database Connectivity (ODBC) specification was created with a view to making it easier for an application developer to write systems involving communication with different types of databases. The objective was to make it possible to develop an application system that would work unchanged with a variety of different databases. Although it was originally designed by Microsoft, it is now supported by all major database vendors and is subject to international standardisation.

ODBC consists of an API (Application Programmer's Interface; a standard set of functions that interface with some other software layer) and a set of drivers that provide communication between the API and the database. This arrangement is illustrated in Figure 11.6.

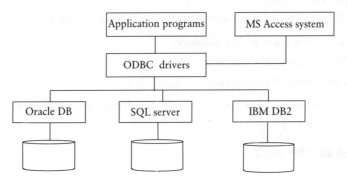

Figure 11.6   ODBC architecture.

The application programs use the set of functions defined by the ODBC API (the API is defined as C language functions). These communicate with drivers (implemented as dynamic link libraries) that are specific to the database being accessed. The Access package itself can communicate with the ODBC drivers, either using Access Basic or by using built-in GUI procedures.

Using ODBC enables communication with one or more different database types within one application system. This is particularly convenient when attempting to build upon an older application system by integrating it with newer database technology; the old and the new can operate side by side prior to a phased removal of the older system.

When used with Microsoft Access, it provides two main facilities; attached tables and pass-through queries, which operate in quite different modes. Access allows database tables belonging to other systems to be attached to an Access database. This means that Access treats these tables as if they were conventional Access tables; they can be queried, joined, updated, etc., in the same way as native Access tables. Using the pass-through facility, queries (in SQL) are sent directly to a database server. No attachment of tables takes place.

JDBC

JDBC is a Java API for communicating with relational databases using SQL commands. It consists of a set of classes and interfaces written in the Java programming language. JDBC performs a similar role to ODBC; it provides a platform independent interface that enables a single version of an application system to access any compliant database. Like ODBC, it does require the availability of a software driver for each type of database to be accessed. A JDBC-ODBC bridge is also available; this enables JDBC to work with any database for which an ODBC driver is available.

The Java language has become popular recently because of its use within World Wide Web browsers; it is used to write applets which are programs that execute within the context of a web browser interface. However, it is also a general-purpose programming language that provides a convenient object-oriented vehicle for developing general applications. JDBC enables Java to be used for applications requiring database access.

Using JDBC the programmer can perform three basic functions:

- establish a connection with a database
- send SQL queries to the database
- process the result of the queries.

For further information about JDBC, consult Hamilton (1997) and Sunsoft's Web site.

Databases on the Web

Overview

Since its inception in 1993, the World Wide Web has enjoyed phenomenal growth. Its popularity is very broad-based and includes the general public, commerce and academia. Web sites hold information organised into 'pages' that are formatted using a textual notation called HTML – Hypertext Markup Language. HTML documents utilise a combination of hypertext data links combined with multimedia objects (graphics, photographs, sound, etc.)

The Web works essentially in client-server mode; server sites host information that is accessed by client computers. Whatever the motivation for hosting a site, a common factor is that each site is a source of information. In many cases, all the site information is held within the Web pages that can be downloaded by the client and displayed using a browser such as Netscape. However, it is quite likely that the site host would wish to have available a greater volume of data than can be held in Web pages; it is possible that they would wish to provide access to a current database. This is especially true for companies wishing to use the Web for commerce, particularly sales and marketing. A number of techniques have appeared to meet this requirement and the area is one of considerable activity. It should be noted that there is no such thing as a Web database; the databases used in Web applications are simply conventional systems such as Microsoft Access and Oracle. Some use is also made of object-oriented databases. The topic of interest in this area is the interconnection of Web systems with these established database technologies. The following sections describe some of the factors to be considered in Web-database development and some of the techniques currently in use in this area.

Web protocol

The World Wide Web communication is primarily based on a protocol called Hypertext Transport Protocol (HTTP) which is a text-based messaging system. A major problem that exists in respect of using HTTP for access of a database at the server Web is that Web connections are 'stateless'. In effect, this means that after the server has responded to a client's query it retains no 'state' information about the query or the client. If the client makes a follow-up query (for example, requesting another related server page) it is treated as a new query. This differs from more conventional communication protocols that establish a 'session' during which the client and server are engaged in an ongoing dialogue until one of the parties terminates the session. The difficulty that statelessness creates for database access is that the client cannot retain direct access to the database, for example, to browse through a series of rows. Continuous re-opening of the database for a client query also has serious implications for system performance.

A technique that has been developed to overcome the statelessness problem is called 'cookies'. A cookie (in Web terminology) is a small data structure that is sent from the server and held on the client computer. It contains state information about the previous communication with the server. In appropriate circumstances, the cookie is returned to the server to assist in servicing a new query. A couple of examples may help in understanding how cookies can assist in servicing client interaction with a Web site.

Example 1
Many sites now allow users to browse through a product catalogue and deposit items in a 'shopping basket' metaphor prior to formally ordering them. As each item is picked, a record is sent in a cookie to the client computer. When the final ordering takes place, the accumulated ordered item list is returned to the server. Such a system is in use by Amazon, an American on-line booksellers (http://www.amazon.com).

Example 2
Some sites allow temporary access to stored information by clients by issuing a 'guest' username and password. When a client is provided with these, they are also sent to

the client computer as a cookie. When the client makes a request the cookie is returned to establish the client's guest status. After a period of time the guest username and password would automatically expire.

CGI

Common Gateway Interface (CGI) is a standard for interfacing other application systems (within the Web server site) to Web servers. Essentially, it provides a general technique whereby a request from a Web client can initiate execution of any program on the server system. If, for example, you wished to make a database accessible to anyone on the Web you would write a CGI program that communicates with the database. The CGI program would be referenced in the associated Web page and when this page is requested by a client the CGI program executes and provides access to the database. CGI programs can be written in any language that can be executed on the server computer; commonly used languages for this purpose are C/C++, Perl and even UNIX shell scripts.

The main difficulty with CGI is that it is inefficient – every client request will initiate a new execution of the CGI program. If several hundred clients access the site simultaneously, the server system would be overloaded with processes. However, it is possible to alleviate this somewhat by the use of a CGI application server; a database application program runs continuously in the server computer. The CGI executable (activated by the client request) just dispatches the request to the database program rather than accessing the DBMS engine directly.

Alternatives to CGI have appeared, notably NSAPI (Netscape Application Programmer's Interface) and ISAPI (Internet Server API) from Microsoft. These work in a similar fashion but are more efficient in system resources. However, other products have appeared that offer more radical solutions. These products consist of bridging software that operates as an intermediary between the Web server and the database system. Typical products of this type are Symantec's dbAnywhere, Microsoft's Visual InterDev and Borland's Intrabuilder. These systems operate in a three-tier mode as illustrated in Figure 11.7.

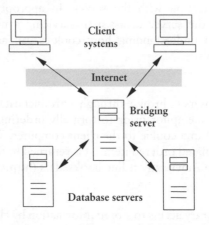

Figure 11.7   Three-tier architecture.

In this architecture, the application programs are written in Java and JDBC and execute on the client computers. Client queries are managed initially by the bridging software and converted into requests to the database servers.

Summary

This chapter has reviewed some of the important aspects of using databases in conjunction with networks. The main topic has been distributed database systems; the main point to note in this regard is that the principal justification for the use of distributed databases is the reduction in network traffic and increased local access times. The topics that have been covered in this section include

- Client-server systems
  - Advantages of client-server approach
  - Peer-to-peer systems

- Distributed databases
  - Homogeneous and heterogeneous
  - Partitioned, horizontal and vertical
  - Replication
  - Transparency
  - Schema management
  - Query processing

- Date's 12 Objectives

- Advantages and disadvantages of distributed databases

- Other network technologies
  - ODBC
  - JDBC
  - Databases on the Web

Answers to in-text questions

11.1 In a client-server environment, the client is an application system that requires some service to be provided, such as obtaining data from a database. The server is the software system on the same or another computer that responds to the request.

11.2 The property code could consist of a 'branch code' followed by a sequence number within that branch. For instance, a property code of AB01234 refers to property 1234 within branch AB; property code AD01234 refers to property 1234 within branch AD. The fragmentation would then be based on the branch code.

11.3 (a) The row would need to be added specifically to the database fragment at the site that 'owns' the row, as determined by the row key value. For instance, in the estate agent example, if the new property code was AD0345 then the new row would be written to the fragment at branch AD. Note that, on the basis of locality of reference, this new row is likely to originate at branch AD but not necessarily.(b) Separate rows, consisting of projections of the full row, would need to be written to the sites holding vertical fragments.

11.4 Without transparency, distributed systems would be much less useful. If applications were obliged to take the location, fragmentation and replication into account, then application development would be much more complex and would involve incorporating distribution information into the application program code. This would make subsequent modification of the system structure very difficult as it would necessitate extensive amendment of applications.

11.5 DBMS independence would be beneficial in circumstances where databases which have been separately developed need to be connected. This can happen when new computer systems are being introduced at some sites of a company but not at all. Also, when companies merge, they are often faced with uniting different systems. It also prevents a company being constantly tied to one system vendor to avoid compatibility problems.

REVIEW QUESTIONS

Answers in Appendix C.

1 Explain what is meant by a 'client-server system'.

2 What is meant by saying a database is 'distributed'?

3 List the various ways in which a database can be distributed.

4 What is meant by 'database replication'?

5 In the context of distributed databases what is meant by 'transparency'?

6 What are ODBC and JDBC used for?

7 How is CGI used in Web systems?

EXERCISES

Answers to exercises flagged wth an asterisk appear in Appendx D.

1 Identify the problems inherent in performing database queries within a distributed database environment.

2 *Discuss the advantages and disadvantages of distributed database systems.

3 Explain what is meant by transparency in the context of distributed databases, identifying the different forms of transparency.

4 *Explain the purpose of the ODBC and JDBC technologies.

5 Why is it desirable to be able to connect a database to a Web server site? Describe some of the techniques used for this purpose.

Beyond the relational model

Introduction

Relational databases are currently the most popular form of database in general use. The older database models, such as the network, are still in use but largely restricted to 'legacy' systems, i.e., systems developed some time ago but still operational and whose importance prevents them from being immediately replaced. In the light of this level of success, it is reasonable to assume that the relational model possesses certain advantages over other systems; these advantages are identified in this chapter.

However, the relational model is not without its problems and, while it has gained total dominance in commercial type applications, there are other applications where it is less effective. The limitations of relational systems are also discussed herein.

Advantages and limitations of relational databases

Advantages

The advantages of the relational model can be summarised as described below.

Simplicity of concept
The relational model is based on the essentially simple concept of a two-dimensional table; this has provided several benefits. The simplicity has enabled non-specialist users to become familiar with the idea and has facilitated the development of convenient supporting software packages.

Good theoretical basis
Prior to the relational system, databases (hierarchical, network) were not based on any formal model. The underlying mathematical base of the relational model has facilitated research into databases that has assisted their development. For instance, normal forms and SQL are products of such research.

Data independence
The relational database provides a much higher degree of data independence than earlier databases. This arises because the data descriptions (schema) are maintained independently of the data itself, unlike earlier systems where physical links existed within the data records.

Improved security and integrity
The organisation of the data into tables and the use of high-level languages such as SQL facilitates the maintenance of better security and integrity.

Suitable for high-level languages
The simple structure has facilitated the use of declarative type languages such as SQL and other high-level 4GL languages and interactive non-programming environments found in current software.

Limitations of the relational database

The limitations of relational database systems can be summarised as shown below.

Proliferation of tables
Even relatively simple applications seem to produce a disproportionate number of separate tables. Most are logically acceptable since they correspond to real-world entities but many are created to satisfy first normal form or simply to interlink other tables.

Processing overheads
A consequence of having to use many tables is that it is necessary to gather information from several tables to satisfy the requirements of a query. This is potentially a very processor and disk-intensive operation and is only made feasible in the general case by the use of indexes and the application of search optimising techniques.

Lack of semantic power
The term 'lack of semantic power' means, first, that the relational database holds only limited information about the 'meaning' of its data and also that it is limited in its ability to express certain data relationships. These two points are pursued futher in the following three sections.

1. The normalisation process fragments the 'natural' expression of the data into multiple tables; at the same time, the original connections between the parts of the data are not preserved automatically. For instance, related tables have to be joined by explicit operations at run time. Note, however, that some current systems do permit the specification of relationships; Microsoft Access provides a graphical interface to identify links between tables and the current SQL standard provides for definition of foreign keys. These features, although helpful, do not avoid the need for run-time joining of the tables.

2. It is difficult or awkward to express sub-typing (i.e. a specialisation relationship) using relational tables. Consider the example of an Employee database; this could be viewed as a hierarchical structure as illustrated in Figure 12.1.

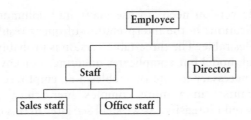

Figure 12.1   Sub-typing.

Considering only the first level of sub-typing:

The general Employee details are:	Employee No, Name, Address, Age, etc.
The Staff entries would include:	Department, Salary, Responsible-to, etc.
The Director entries would include:	Responsibility, etc.

This can be implemented in two ways, neither very satisfactory:

- as a single table with nulls where the attribute is not applicable; for instance, a director's entry would look like

Employee number	Name	Address	Age	Dept	Salary	Resp-to	Responsibility
1234	Jones	London	49	NULL	NULL	NULL	Sales

while data for a Staff member would look like this

Employee number	Name	Address	Age	Dept	Salary	Resp-to	Responsibility
2987	Smith	Bristol	31	Sales	28000	3002	NULL
3002	Brown	London	48	sales	46000	1234	NULL

- three tables; employee, staff, director.

Employee

Employee number	Name	Address	Age
1234	Jones	London	49
2987	Smith	Bristol	31
3002	Brown	London	48

Staff

Employee number	Department	Salary	Responsible-to
29874	Sales	28000	3002
3002	Brown	46000	1234

Director

Employee number	Responsibility
1234	Sales

The single-table version needs to use many null columns; use of nulls can produce complications in the interpretation of query results and is generally regarded as undesirable. The three-table version is probably more in the spirit of the relational model but complicates querying. For any particular type of employee, it is necessary to join two tables, i.e., employee-staff or employee-director. Of course, in a more complex hierarchical application, these complications would intensify. As we shall see later in this chapter, sub-typing can be more readily modelled using inheritance in an object-oriented database.

12.1 Would it ever be necessary to join all three of the tables shown above?

3. It is not possible to use user-defined types. In particular, you cannot invent types using aggregate data items or array elements. The ability to design sub-types would enable systems with fewer tables to be designed. This point is discussed in more detail later in these notes. To some extent, sub-range types, such as the Pascal style 1..100, can be simulated for the purposes of data validation by using validation filters but this is not a complete answer.

Unsuitable for long transactions
The transaction systems used in relational databases, using Commit, Rollback and locking are appropriate only where transactions are 'short'; in some applications, notably in CAD/CAM systems, transactions could be very long, possibly hours. This arises when, for instance, a design is being developed; parts of the design will be in an incomplete state for long periods while being amended which, using a relational database, would require extensive locking of tables and rows, effectively preventing any other users from gaining access.

Example
The first three of the above points (i.e., proliferation of tables, processing overheads and lack of semantic power) are interrelated. The following example illustrates these points. Consider the data required for a bibliographic database system.

    Reference Num
    Title
    Authors
    Publisher
    Date
    Keywords
    etc.

The 'Authors' probably consists, in the majority of cases, of a single name; however, allowance must be made for the general case where there might be two, three or possibly many names. Hence, in terms of first normal form, a separate table is required for the authors. A similar argument applies to the keyword values – another separate table is required, producing three tables as shown below.

Reference table

Reference number	Number,
Title	char(30),
Publisher	char(20)

Author table

Reference number	Number,
Author	char(20)

Keyword table

Reference number	Number,
Keyword	char(15)

Note that, producing tables in this form, there are no inherent linkages between the tables; such linkages have to be re-established using join operations. This seems an excessively complicated solution for a simple problem. Essentially, it would be convenient to be able to use a 'set attribute', but this is not possible for relational systems. (This point is pursued further in the next section in relation to extended relational systems.)

In terms of programming languages and database facilities, such an arrangement would need some additional mechanism to enable processing of the set members. There have been some research prototypes based on ideas such as these and commercial systems are now appearing on the market.

? **12.2** With reference to the above example, would it not be sufficient to assemble the keywords as a single string containing a comma-separated list of words?

Extended relational systems

The relational database has been so successful and effective for most applications that it makes sense to attempt to extend its capability to address its perceived limitations and drawbacks. This section describes some developments in this direction.

Multimedia attributes

Many applications now utilise multimedia data such as photographic images, sound, video, etc. For instance, a personnel system might include photographs of employees in addition to the more conventional textual information. Modern relational databases generally provide for storage of such information. In Microsoft Access, for instance, one or more columns of a table can be designated as type 'OLE Object'. Object linking and embedding (OLE) is a Microsoft technique that allows 'objects' from one application to be stored within a document of another application.

Common usages of OLE are to include spreadsheets or graphical images within word processing documents. In terms of database usage, columns typed as 'OLE Object' can be used to store any OLE compliant data for each row of the table. The OLE data can be displayed using a form or report.

While being an effective and useful facility within a relational database, multimedia provision does not extend the general capabilities of the relational mechanism. From the point of view of the relational database, the object is a 'black box'; the internal structure and data are not usable or accessible to the querying system for instance. Objects stored in this way are often called 'blobs' (binary large objects). A more fundamental extension would be the ability to use a much wider range of attribute types. Some of the possibilities in this direction are described below.

Type extensions

Conventional relational databases provide a fixed range of column attribute types, each of which (with the exception of OLE objects) are simple non-complex values, such as text and numbers. In particular, users are unable to devise their own types as is possible in many conventional programming environments. This suggests that the descriptive and semantic power of the database could be enhanced by allowing extended types to be used. Two possibilities are (a) to provide more complex 'built-in' types and (b) to allow arbitrary user-defined types. These are discussed further below. Note that these ideas are theoretical only and do not describe any current system.

Complex types

A specific idea here is to provide 'set-based' facilities, i.e., to allow multi-valued attributes in the form of a set or a list of basic values. There are many examples where this would be helpful. In the bibliography application introduced earlier, it would be convenient to express the authors and keywords as a set of text values; in a 'pseudo-SQL', this might look like this:

```
CREATE  TABLE  Reference
(
        Title           CHAR(30),
        Publisher       CHAR(20),
        Authors         SETOF  CHAR(20),
        Keywords        SETOF  CHAR(15)
)
```

In a personnel table, the names and dates of birth of dependants could be represented as sets:

```
CREATE TABLE Personnel
(
        EmployeeNo      CHAR(6),
        Name            CHAR(15),
        ChildNames      SETOF  CHAR(12),
        ChildDOB        SETOF  DATE
)
```

Note that, in the above two examples, we have reduced the number of necessary tables (in the relational sense) from three to one. This would have the benefit of avoiding joins of these tables and of providing a more logical and compact representation. Presumably, the internal storage of such data would facilitate rapid retrieval of all the components. Given an Employee Number, all associated Child data would be accessible without further index references or joining.

User-defined types

The ultimate enhancement to the basic relational model would be the ability to define one's own attribute data types. Essentially, this would provide the generality available in 3GL languages such as Pascal and C. The typical mechanisms that would be employed in this respect would be definition of structured types (including arrays which could serve as sets) and sub-range types. A structured type is an aggregation of basic (or possibly other user-defined) types. For instance, in the Personnel table example above, the 'children' information could be formed into one unit. This is illustrated below in a 'pseudo-SQL' format:

```
CREATE TYPE Child
(
      Name  CHAR(12),
      DOB    DATE
)
```

then the Personnel table would be defined as

```
CREATE TABLE Personnel
(
      EmployeeNo     CHAR(6),
      Name           CHAR(15),
      Children       SETOF  Child
)
```

Specification of a new data type implies not only defining the structure but also the functionality of objects of the type. For instance, basic input and output and validation of the Child data would have to be specified. This raises many difficulties, both in how the functionality should be specified (e.g., implementation language) and in how to handle the user interface. Interactive user interfaces in database systems such as Microsoft Access typically provide automatic generation of forms and reports. This raises problems about how a user-defined data item would be mapped onto a form for input and how it would be formatted on a report.

? **12.3** Devise an address datatype (based on the general ideas shown above) consisting of two address lines and a postcode. Show how this datatype might be used in a customer table.

Current developments in extended/object relational systems

Oracle version 8

Oracle's latest version has introduced some significant extended relational facilities. These include:

- ability to store an array in a column
- nested tables, i.e., a column can include a table
- user defined datatypes; this effectively allows the use of a CREATE TYPE command similar to that described earlier in this chapter. Oracle's approach is to base the type design on an object specification in the manner of an object-oriented language, e.g.,

```
CREATE TYPE Person AS OBJECT
(
    Name           CHAR(12),
    DOB            DATE,
    MEMBER FUNCTION getname
        RETURN Name
)
```

Note that the object definition specifies both the data elements and the functionality of the type as is the usual procedure in object-oriented systems. For more complex functions, the code can be implemented in PL/SQL (Oracle's procedural language that is integrated with SQL) or in a 3GL language, probably C/C++.

The new type can then be used as an attribute in the design of tables:

```
CREATE TABLE Employee
(
    Name           CHAR(12),
    Dept           CHAR(10),
        . . .
    Spouse         Person
)
```

The elements of the new type can be referenced using the dot notation: Employee.Spouse.Name

UniSQL

UniSQL is a new system that effectively implements the kinds of extensions discussed above. It permits the specification of user-defined classes which can be used as column attribute types. If no such classes are defined, the system reduces to a conventional RDB. Internally, the data is mapped into conventional RDB tables.

Informix

The Informix relational database company markets a product called Informix Universal Server incorporating a technique called Datablades. This system allows users to add data types to the system by means of code modules written in SQL and C. The user can specify the conversion of the external data to its internal format.

SQL3

Another SQL standard called SQL3 is currently being developed. The design intention of SQL3 is to provide a system of SQL commands that can be applied in any database context, including relational, extended relational and true object-oriented databases. This means that the language has to bridge the relational and object-oriented paradigms. The target date for the publication of the SQL3 standard is 1999 and it will be later still before implementations appear on the market.

Object-oriented databases

Overview

An object-oriented database (OODB) is a database that provides for storage and retrieval of data in the form of objects, as the term is used in object-oriented programming languages such as C++ and Smalltalk.

OODBs are based on the object model of data, as opposed to the relational model used by relational databases. There are some similarities between these two models; the relational model uses the concept of an entity to model real-world 'things' whereas the object model uses the term 'object'. Entities/objects are linked together by various forms of association. The principal distinctions between the relational model and the object model are

- The object model includes a definition of the functionality of the object, i.e., an object definition will include functions that can be used to access and modify the object.
- An object can have an arbitrarily complex data structure; the relational model uses simple two-dimensional tables.
- The object model incorporates a number of other concepts such as classes; these are covered in this section.

The richer data structures possible with OO systems permit the representation of modelling associations such as generalisation/specialisation (subtyping) and aggregation which are not easily modelled in a relational system.

We begin this section with an introduction to the principles of object-orientation. The following section then examines how these ideas are applied in object-oriented databases.

Introduction to the principles of object-orientation

Basic principles

The OO philosophy views the world as a set of objects which communicate with each other. This view is applied to the design of computer systems that model and service real-world applications.

An object is a representation of a real world entity (e.g., person, component, company, etc.) which takes part in a computer application. This representation consists of data and procedures. The object data defines the state of the object at any time (hence are often called the state variables) and the procedures, usually called methods in this context, provide a set of allowable operations on the data.

An object

data 1	State
data 2	Variables
...	
method 1	
method 2	Object
method 3	Methods
...	

Note that, conceptually, the only way to access and/or modify object variables is by using the object methods. This provides a high degree of encapsulation which is considered desirable in programming terms since it isolates the object data from the rest of the program. In this respect, OO may be considered an extension to the concept of modularity, but OO extends the notion of encapsulation far beyond that found in conventional programming. This potentially provides several benefits:

- The object may be modified, with less danger to the program as a whole, as long as the external 'effect' of the object remains the same.
- Since the object performs some complete self-contained role, it could be reused in another application.
- Each object has a clearly defined interface which facilitates programming.

12.4 Why is the reuse of software considered a benefit?

In addition to the basic object concept, OO philosophy encompasses a number of other important concepts that are important in programming and database development. These concepts are listed below and described in subsequent sections.

- Messages; objects are viewed as communicating by the sending of messages to each other.

- Classes; generic specification of object design.
- Identity; all objects are given a system-wide unchangeable code that uniquely and permanently identifies each object.
- Inheritance; derivation of more specific object classes from existing classes.
- Polymorphism; technique whereby different object classes respond differently to the same message.

Object examples

OO techniques are commonly applied to graphical programs. About the simplest graphical object is a point, which could be described as follows:

```
POINT:
     State variables
          X-pos, Y-pos     - point coordinates
          Visible          - boolean indicating whether the point is visible
     Methods
          Move point
          Show Point
          Hide Point
          Where            i.e., return current X-pos, Y-pos values
```

Note that, even to find out the position of the point, it is necessary to invoke an object method (called 'Where' in the above example).

In a simulation program, we may wish to model the behaviour of a vehicle. An object specification for this might appear as shown below:

```
VEHICLE:
     State variables
          X-pos, Y-pos
          Speed
          Direction
     Methods
          Start
          Accelerate
          Brake
          Change direction
          Where          i.e., return current location
          What Speed     i.e., return current speed
```

Hence, an OO program takes the form of a large number of objects which communicate with each other. In general, there have to be 'active' objects which initiate communication, often by themselves receiving 'outside' stimulus, such as data input from the program user.

The communication between objects is viewed as a process of 'message passing'; this concept is dealt with in the next section.

Messages

If one object wants to make another perform some action, it sends a message to the other which causes the invocation of one of the recipient object's methods. In some systems, a system of actual encoded messages is employed; for example, in Windows, moving the mouse causes a series of messages to be sent from the mouse driver to the object representing the current window. These could form a queue of messages which are processed in sequence by the Windows software.

In other, simpler, systems, message passing is more of a metaphor; the calling object simply invokes the method by means of a conventional procedure or function call. This is the case in C++ for example, which is one of the principal OO languages.

Classes

Real-world objects are typically not one-offs. In the simulation suggested above, for example, we would typically have many vehicles, not just one. An object can be viewed as one item belonging to a set of such items. The term 'class' is used to refer to the generic specification of a set of objects; essentially, the class is a template which defines the structure and behaviour of each object of that type. It is similar in many ways to the notion of type (e.g., char, int) used in Pascal and other languages. Types, however, are built-in to the language and have a fixed pre-defined behaviour; for instance, we can use arithmetic operators and functions with int and real variables but not char variables. Classes, on the other hand, are user-defined, with modifiable behaviour.

In OO programming languages, we first define the classes we wish to use in our application. Within the application programs, we can then declare objects which are 'instances' of these classes. The process of creating objects of a defined class is called instantiation.

The descriptions given above for POINT and VEHICLE in effect constitute class outlines. An instance of class VEHICLE would represent a specific vehicle with a set of current state values for each of its variables.

In general discussion, the terms object and class can be used somewhat interchangeably; in particular, object is often used when class would be more appropriate. No confusion should arise from this usage if you are aware of the problem and if you remember that a class is purely a template or description (it is not stored in memory) while an object is similar to a program variable – it takes up space in memory.

Object identity

Real-world things that are modelled by objects in an object-oriented programming environment are considered to have a separate and unique identity so that different objects can be distinguished from each other. On creation, each object is assigned an Object ID, a system-generated value that is unique to the object and which is never changed or reused. This contrasts with the relational model wherein the role of identification is provided by the primary key concept. However, the primary key is usually one attribute (or combination of attributes) that is unique for the relation involved and is generally a value used in the actual application. The possibility exists that the primary key could be changed which could have serious repercussions for database integrity. In object-oriented systems, the object id not used and is generally unseen in applications. The object ids are used to interconnnect objects; object A can be linked to (or refer to) another object B by holding the value of B's object id in A.

?   **12.5** In what circumstances could a primary key value (in a relational database table) change?

Inheritance

In an example earlier, we defined a 'point' object class. Typically, a graphics program will require more complex graphical objects, such as lines, rectangles, circles, etc. However, these objects typically share a number of common features such as position. The OO inheritance mechanism enables more complex objects to be derived from simpler, previously defined objects. For example, a rectangle could be derived from a point object; a rectangle also has a position (of one corner, say) and can be visible or not. However, a rectangle also requires two lengths for the sides. We could define a rectangle class, for example, by inheriting the point class and adding to it and/or overriding certain variables and methods.

```
RECTANGLE: Inherit from POINT
State Variables
     SideX Length
     SideY Length
Methods
     Show              these are methods which are overridden from
     Hide              the POINT version
     SetFillColor      these are methods peculiar to RECTANGLE
     ChangeSize
     . . .
```

In effect, inheritance provides a system of specialisation and generalisation and enables us to define a hierarchy of classes. For example, consider the following taxonomy of workers employed in a company:

```
EMPLOYEE
     OFFICE EMPLOYEE
          OFFICE MANAGER
          SECRETARIAL
               SUPERVISOR
               SECRETARY
          . . .
     WORKS EMPLOYEE
          LINE SUPERVISOR
          WELDER
          FITTER
          . . .
```

SALES EMPLOYEE
AREA MANAGER
SALESPERSON
...

etc.

Descending through such a hierarchy produces increasing specialisation, while ascending produces increasing generalisation. Another way of looking at this is to say that it expresses an 'IS-A' relationship, e.g., an Office Manager IS-AN Office Employee, an Office Employee IS-AN Employee. A specialisation-generalisation can best be recognised by applying this IS-A test.

This, of course, is the sub-typing modelling concept which as we saw earlier presents some complications for relational databases. The benefits of being able to use inheritance are

- it permits a more natural representation of sub-typing relationships that exist in the application
- it potentially saves coding effort because code implemented at a higher level can be reused at a lower level.

Using inheritance structures makes it possible to develop programs in terms of routines dealing with the general cases, qualified and complemented by routines for the various specialised cases. For example, a simple routine to print the employee's name and address would be common to all and would be defined at the EMPLOYEE level; however, in a payroll system, office staff and works staff would all be paid under different terms and conditions (e.g., monthly salary, weekly salary, hourly paid, etc.) and would have specialised program routines defined for each class of staff such as WORKS EMPLOYEE, OFFICE EMPLOYEE, etc. Within WORKS EMPLOYEE, the supervisor might differ from line workers, and so on.

The overall expectation is that object-oriented design should minimise the amount of specialised coding and should facilitate reuse of more general routines.

Polymorphism

The Greek derivation of this word means 'many forms'. In the field of programming, it refers to the ability of a language to use the same identifier (e.g. function or procedure name) to perform different operations depending on the class of the variables involved. For instance, we might want a method called Print whose role is to display the contents of objects presented to it as parameter values. The actual effect of Print will depend on which object is involved. In the absence of polymorphism, a separate method would be required for each different object class. Note that polymorphism is utilised in inherited classes; in the POINT/RECTANGLE example above, the Show method of the POINT class is overridden with a method of the same name. If we use the call Show(pointobject) it will execute the POINT Show method; if we use the call Show(rectangleobject) it will execute the RECTANGLE method.

The benefit of this facility is that programs can be written to deal with objects dynamically, i.e., the precise effect of a command is determined only at run-time when the methods 'discover' the class of objects being passed to them.

General principles of OODBs

In essence, an object-oriented database enables objects, as described in the foregoing sections, to be stored within a database. The objct database management system (ODBMS) would be expected to provide the same range of facilities as a relational DBMS in terms of security, concurrency, etc.

In order to be able to specify the structure functionality of an object that is to be stored, some form of programming language is required. In practice, OODBs tend to be based on an OO language, most commonly, C++ or Java. Within a C++ program, the user can define classes and instantiate objects which exist within the program while the program is running but which are lost when the program terminates. Hence there is a need for data persistence as in any other programming environment. One option would be to use a relational database; however, the complexity of data often required in OO programs for applications such as CAD does not convert very readily to the strict 'flat' table layout of relational databases. This difficulty is sometimes referred to as an 'impedance mismatch' (borrowing an expression from electrical theory!) meaning that there is a mismatch between the internal data structures in C++ and the structures provided by a relational database. In contrast, an OODB enables the programmer to store the data as an object without conversion of their basic structure. Figure 12.2 illustrates this point.

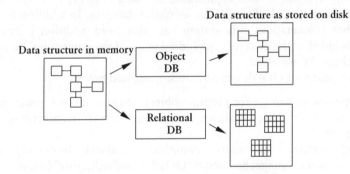

Figure 12.2   RDB and OODB comparison.

Figure 12.2 shows that if the C++ programmer uses a relational database, it is necessary to convert the internal data structures used in their programs into tabular form for storing in the database. Such conversions involve more work for the programmer and are often awkward to implement. The OODB provides the programmer with the ability to make the data 'persistent', i.e., it is transparently held on disk and survives the end of the program execution. This is achieved without any conversion operations.

Because they are essentially a programming tool, OODBs currently tend to be used directly by programmers and not end users, as is the case with RDBs. The simplicity of the relational model (e.g. basic data types, 2D tables, standard query language) facilitates a simple user interface, but the potential complexity of objects makes a standard user interface difficult to implement. There is no equivalent, therefore, of Microsoft Access in the OODB world.

Another factor that distinguishes object and relational systems is the fact that relational systems are based on relations that consist of a set of rows. This structure is convenient for dealing with the types of applications that commonly employ relational databases, i.e., essentially record-based systems. The object model does not prescribe a standard structure corresponding to the relation and object database applications often deal with single instances of objects. However, data structures of arbitrary complexity can be represented in the object model so that it can readily simulate a relation as a (collection) set of objects. The term 'extent' is sometimes used in the context of a set of objects used in a similar fashion to a relation.

There is considerable controversy about the relative performance of OODB and RDB systems. Early expectations about the relative performance of OODBs were perhaps not realised in practice, possibly in part due to the continuing improvements in relational database technology. It appears that, in general, OODB systems are faster in access time than RDBs and are increasingly so as the volume of data increases. This is due to the distinct ways in which the two systems store data: RDBs need to perform joins, the time for which rises exponentially with increasing table sizes; OODBs tend to use data which is naturally stored and linked together. Access time therefore tends to be simply proportional to the volume of data. However, updating of RDBs is faster due again to the simple table structure. A typical example of an OODB system is the American on-line 'Yellow Pages' system which is built on the ObjectStore OODB. In this application, the data is large, relatively static and requires fast access – an ideal profile for an object database. In addition to the basic phone number information, this system can also hold additional data on the companies included in the directory, including maps of the companies' locations and 'how to get there' information.

The main features of OODB systems are summarised below

- Provide persistent storage for program objects, mostly in C++ programs.
- Provide usual database facilities: multi-user access, transactions, locking, indexing, etc.
- Querying systems are more complex; products frequently use the implementation language. See under 'OODB Standardisation' below.
- Generally utilised by programmers rather than 'end-users'.
- Suited to large applications requiring fast access and/or complex data.

12.6 Why are object-oriented databases used mostly by programmers rather than end users?

OODB standardisation

Current OODB products have tended to emerge from independent lines of research and development and hence show considerable divergence of approach and facilities. The first attempt to produce a statement of definition for an object database was presented by the 'Object-Oriented Data Systems Manifesto' (Atkinson 1990). More recently, a number of database vendors have formed a consortium called the Object Data Management Group to address the standardisation of object database systems.

Information on ODMG work can be found in Cattell (1997) and on the ODMG Web site (http://www.odmg.org). Two specific concepts introduced by the ODMG standards, namely, ODL, the Object Definition Language and OQL, Object Query Language. These standards are intended to provide for object databases, facilities similar to DDL/DML and SQL as applied in relational databases.

Object definition language (ODL)

ODL is used to define the schema for an object database, i.e., it specifies the structure of objects to be stored in the database. ODL is defined in a programming-language independent manner and specifies object types, attributes, relationships and operations. It is intended that the ODL schema is stored within the datbase itself.

In practice, programmers would produce an ODL for a particular database using a 'language binding' – an expression of the ODL using the syntax of a chosen implementation language such as C++, Smalltalk or Java. For instance, the ODL/C++ binding consists of a set of C++ classes that provides constructs corresponding to the basic ODL constructs.

Object query language (OQL)

The OQL was devised to provide a standard language for object database querying. In the absence of OQL, OODB products tend to use the implementation language (e.g., C++) or a proprietary language for the purposes of querying. OQL was designed to be as similar to SQL as possible but is necessarily more complex due to the richer data facilities of object-oriented compared with relational systems. In spite of this, OQL has many similarities with SQL, both in syntax and in its relationship with other components of the database environment. OQL is similar to SQL in that it is not 'computationally complete' which means that it cannot resolve arbitrarily complex computations so that it will typically be used in conjunction with another language system. Also, like SQL, it can be used as a free-standing query language or embedded in another language.

OQL's object features include facilities to handle object identity, complex objects, inheritance, object collections and navigational queries.

Current object databases

Object database concepts have been under development since the end of the 1980s but have been slow to gain momentum. The causes of this are probably, in the first instance, the reluctance of developers to commit themselves to a new and radical technology and secondly the relative satisfaction with relational databases for most applications.

However, object databases are now developing apace and several vendors report success in contributing to many new projects based on their object database product. Table 12.1 indicates the market leaders in the area, together with their Web site addresses. The latter are a useful source of technical and product information.

Table 12.1

Product	Company	Web site
ObjectStore	Object Design Inc.	www.odi.com
O²	Ardent Software	www.02tech.co.uk
Versant	Versant inc.	www.versant.com
Objectivity	Objectivity Inc.	www.objectivity.com
Poet	Poet Software Inc.	www.poet.com

A good description of object database principles can be found in Eaglestone (1998).

Summary

In this chapter we have identified some of the shortcomings of the traditional relational database and described alternatives in the form of the extended-relational and object-oriented databases. The following lists the more important points in the chapter.

- Limitations of relational databases
  The principal limitations are lack of semantic power (including problems with sub-typing and lack of user-defined types) and processing overheads.

- Extended relational databases
  These are based on the relational database but have facilities for complex or user-defined datatypes.

- Object databases
  These are radically different from relational systems and are based on the object model. They promise faster access and more general specification of data structures.

Answers to in-text questions

12.1 Yes. To obtain a full listing of all information about all employees, all three tables would need to be joined.

12.2 Although this would be possible, the keywords would not be amenable to searching with a query language. For instance, if a keyword string contained the value 'computing, database, relational' it would be difficult to search for the word 'database' since it is embedded in the middle of the string. This would require a sub-string search which is not generally provided for in language such as SQL.

12.3 A possible definition might be

```
CREATE TYPE Address_type
(
        Address1        CHAR(20),
        Address2        CHAR(20),
        Postcode        CHAR(10)
)
```

This could then be used in a Customer table

    CREATE TABLE Customer
    (

CustId	CHAR(6),
Name	CHAR(25),
Address	Address_type,
. . . etc.	

)

12.4 The ability to utilise pre-written and, significantly, pre-tested software enables new applications to be built on previous work. This facilitates more rapid development of programs with greater reliability.

12.5 Since primary key values are often used in the application system, it is always possible that they may require some revision. For instance, two companies might merge and wish to rationalise their Product codes. This could necessitate extensive modification of many tables that use or refer to Product codes.

12.6 Object databases do not have the simplicity of relational database that can be viewed as two-dimensional tables. Also, they tend to be based on high-level languages such as C++ which are more the realm of the professional programmer.

REVIEW QUESTIONS

Answers in Appendix C.

1 Outline the main advantages of relational databases.

2 Outline the main limitations of relational databases.

3 What are the principal innovations of extended-relational databases?

4 In the object model, what is meant by (a) classes; (b) object identity; (c) inheritance?

EXERCISES

Answers to exercises flagged with an asterisk appear in Appendix D.

1 Explain what is meant by saying that the traditional relational database model is limited in semantic power. In particular, identify the problems involved in representing a sub-typing association in the relational model using a suitable example.

2 A common feature of extended relational databases is the ability to design user-defined types. Explain this term and describe how user-defined types can assist in the design of database tables.

3 Describe the principal characteristics of an object-oriented database.

4 *The introduction of post-relational databases into the marketplace has been very slow. Discuss the problems that a vendor faces in introducing new database technology.

5 *Using the CREATE TYPE command described in the chapter, design a user-defined type to represent an item in a Sales Order. It should have attributes Order Number, Product Number, Quantity. Using the suggested SET notation show how the item objects could be contained in an Order object.

13

SQL tutorial notes

Introduction

In Chapter 2, we saw how relational algebra can be used to express queries that extract data from relational databases. While it would be possible in principle to implement an interpreter for relational algebra, for practical use it is more convenient to use a more English-like language to express queries. This is the role played by Structured query language, SQL, in today's relational database environment. A knowledge of SQL is an important requirement for today's database practitioners.

SQL is by far the most important standard within the modern-day relational database market. It provides a measure of standardisation in an area crowded with competing and divergent technologies. A significant application of SQL in modern database usage, for example, is its role as a communication language that enables systems using different database technologies to operate successfully together. In particular, it facilitates use of client-server techniques for database access.

While SQL presents a somewhat primitive command-driven user interface, this is not too important because it is rarely used in this mode in practice. As noted in Chapter 8, SQL is mostly employed within some other language system, such as COBOL or C or 4GL languages (e.g., Oracle PL/SQL, Informix 4GL) or as a communication language in a client-server environment. For the purposes of learning the syntax, however, a command interpreter is ideal and these notes will be most beneficial if the student has access to such a facility.

This chapter provides an introductory description of the principal features of the SQL language, with minimal practical exercises. Accompanying the book is a set of tutorials with extensive practical query exercises; these are intended to provide the student with the practice essential in developing competence in the language. Both this chapter and the tutorials consist of a series of related sessions to provide a convenient subdivision of the work involved in studying the language and in doing laboratory exercises. In addition, each tutorial session contains a brief résumé of the SQL commands and techniques used in that section.

It should be noted that we are providing here a general introduction to the more common features and facilities of SQL, conforming as far as possible to the currrent SQL standard. Practical systems, such as IBM DB2 or Oracle, will typically provide a much richer set of SQL commands designed to manage and optimise that particular system. Note also that there are variations in the interpretation of SQL commands by the various proprietary systems; these notes have been prepared using Oracle's SQL*Plus interpreter and hence will generally reflect Oracle's implementation, although some reference is made to standard SQL features not implemented by Oracle.

For further reading in SQL refer to Bowman (1996) and Groff (1994). Both provide excellent practical treatment of the subject.

Background

As noted in Chapter 8, SQL is a declarative command language that enables you to perform a range of operations on relational tables. These operations are traditionally divided into three categories as indicated below. Note that although these categories are referred to as languages, they are all part of the one SQL language.

- Data definition language: commands that
  - create a table
  - amend a table
  - specify integrity checks
  - delete a table
  - build an index for a table
  - define a virtual table (view).

- Data manipulation language: commands that
  - query the database to show selected records
  - insert, delete and update rows of the table
  - control transactions when updating a database (transactions are covered in Chapter 10).

- Data control language: commands that control access rights to parts of the database.

We will cover all these operations in this chapter, starting with the DML, since this contains the most frequently used commands and presents the most complex problems for the student.

The following sections are divided into sessions corresponding to the sessions used in the set of tutorials accompanying this chapter that are contained in the lecturer's supplement. The narrative in this chapter and the tutorials are based on a simple set of tables described below. They describe personnel within a company that has a number of separate branches. The employee information is held in the table employee; a separate related table, branch, contains information on company branches. Interpretation of the tables is quite straightforward and requires only a few points of clarification:

1. The 'departments' are deemed to exist within the branches, i.e., the Sales department for branch 01 is different from the Sales department of branch 02.

2. The Supervisor column refers to the Employee ID (EMP_ID) of the person's supervisor.

3. The budget column of the branch table is expressed in thousands of pounds.

The exercises have been carried out in the SQL*Plus interpreter of Oracle 7, however, most of the command formats illustrated are sufficently basic that they will run on most interpreters.

The format and content of the two tables is shown below. Note that in displaying output, the SQL interpreter often truncates part of the heading. Please note the full names given in the table descriptions below. In some instances, the headings have been edited to clarify the text.

The lecturer's supplement contains a file of SQL statements that can be used to create these tables.

Employee table

```
Name               Null?           Type
----------------------------------------------
EMP_ID             NOT NULL        VARCHAR2(4)
NAME                               VARCHAR2
POSITION                           VARCHAR2(12)
HIRE_DATE                          DATE
SALARY                             NUMBER(7,2)
BRANCH_CODE        NOT NULL        VARCHAR(2)
DEPARTMENT                         VARCHAR2(10)
SUPERVISOR                         VARCHAR2(4)
```

EMP_ID	NAME	POSITION	HIRE_DATE	SAL	BRANCH CODE	DEPART	SUPERV
1001	Kennedy	Director	16-JAN-84	50000	01		
1045	Smith	Salesman	12-MAY-94	18000	04	Sales	3691
1271	Steward	Clerk	30-APR-89	16000	03	Accounts	3255
1534	Bell	Supervisor	28-NOV-95	20000	01	Admin	3876
1653	Walker	Secretary	03-AUG-87	15500	04	Admin	3876
2244	Chung	Programmer	09-APR-96	21500	01	Technical	7663
3255	Young	Manager	19-MAR-92	30000	01	Accounts	1001
3691	Adams	Supervisor	01-OCT-86	23000	04	Sales	4206
3876	Hill	Manager	27-JAN-90	27000	04	Admin	
4206	Gomatam	Manager	23-JUL-97	31000	02	Sales	
4936	Moore	Salesman	30-JUN-85	19500	02	Sales	4206
5833	Bradley	Technician	08-SEP-88	14500	03	Technical	7663
6223	Hamilton	Accountant	21-FEB-88	20000	01	Accounts	3255
7663	Newman	Manager	15-AUG-92	28000	03	Technical	
8253	Evans	Salesman	13-JUN-93	17500	02	Sales	4206
9743	Fletcher	Chief Clerk	29-OCT-87	18000	03	Accounts	3255
2906	Stein	Supervisor	04-FEB-89	15500	03	Sales	
3198	Roxburgh	Salesman	21-SEP-84	20000	01	Sales	3255
4218	Cohen	Engineer	25-AUG-92	21000	04	Technical	
4102	Monaghan	Clerk	13-JUN-93	17000	02	Admin	4206
9743	Nicholson	Chief Clerk	09-JUL-90	15000	04	Accounts	3255

Branch table

```
Name                 Null?         Type
-------------------------------------------
BRANCH_CODE          NOT NULL      VARCHAR2(2)
BRANCH_NAME                        VARCHAR2(10)
CITY                               VARCHAR2(12)
MANAGER_ID                         VARCHAR2(4)

BR  BRANCH_NAM   CITY       MANA    BUDGET
-------------------------------------------
01  SOUTH        London     1001    300
02  WEST         Liverpool  4206    250
03  EAST         York       7663    350
04  NORTH        Aberdeen   3876    200
05  EUROPE       Paris
```

Session 1: Simple queries

Introduction

The most important SQL command is the SELECT command. SELECT enables you to perform queries against the database. The full SELECT command is quite elaborate, so we start with an abbreviated version that will suffice for our purposes in this session.

> SELECT *column-list* FROM *table-name*
> [WHERE *condition*]
> [ORDER BY *column-list*]

To describe the format of command within this chapter, we use a notation that helps to describe the allowable components of valid statements. Words shown in UPPER CASE are SQL-reserved words that have a specific meaning in that context. Words in *italics* indicate where an entry or entries must be supplied by the user. Clauses in square brackets are optional, i.e., they provide additional functionality which may or may not be needed.

Note that although the SQL keywords such as SELECT are highlighted here in upper case, in practice SQL is insensitive to the case of keywords and user-supplied names. Literal values in single quotes, however, are NOT case insensitive and must be consistently used. (See Query 1.2 below.)

The SELECT command extracts rows from the table specified by *table-name*. The rows selected are defined by *condition*. The parameter *column-list* specifies the columns of the table to be shown on the output. *Column-list* can be the special value * (asterisk) that indicates that ALL columns are to be shown.

Query 1.1
Show a list of the names and postions of all employees in branch 03.

SQL: SELECT name, position FROM employee WHERE
        branch_code = '03'

Result:

```
NAME            POSITION
-------------   ------------
Stewart         Clerk
Bradley         Technician
Newman          Manager
Fletcher        Chief Clerk
Stein           Supervisor
```

> **Query 1.2**
> Show all details for employees working in Admin departments.
>
> SQL: SELECT * FROM employee WHERE department = 'Admin'

Result:

EMP_	NAME	POSITION	HIRE_DATE	SALARY	BR	DEPARTMENT	SUPE
1534	Bell	Supervisor	28-NOV-95	2000	01	Admin	3876
1653	Walker	Secretary	03-AUG-87	1550	04	Admin	3876
3876	Hill	Manager	27-JAN-90	2700	04	Admin	
4102	Monaghan	Clerk	13-JUN-93	1700	02	Admin	4206

Note that the literal value used in the condition is case sensitive so that the case of letters must match *exactly* with the table data, for instance, using . . . WHERE department = 'ADMIN' would produce no rows in the answer.

Conditions

The WHERE clause in the SELECT command specifies a condition that each row selected must satisfy. Conditions can be expressed in a number of ways; the most common is a simple comparison of values as used in Queries 1.1 and 1.2.

Comparative operators

The usual comparative operators are available:

- = equal to
- > greater than
- < less than
- >= greater than
- <= less than or equal to
- <> not equal to

> **Query 1.3**
> Show all details for employees earning more than 20000.
>
> SQL: SELECT * FROM employee WHERE salary > 20000

Result:

EMP_	NAME	POSITION	HIRE_DATE	SALARY	BR	DEPARTMENT	SUPE
1001	Kennedy	Director	16-JAN-84	50000	01		
2244	Chung	Programmer	09-APR-96	21500	01	Technical	7663
3255	Young	Manager	19-MAR-92	30000	01	Accounts	1001
3691	Adams	Supervisor	01-OCT-86	23000	04	Sales	4206
3876	Hill	Manager	27-JAN-90	27000	04	Admin	
4206	Gomatam	Manager	23-JUL-97	31000	02	Sales	
7663	Newman	Manager	15-AUG-92	28000	03	Technical	
4218	Cohen	Engineer	25-AUG-92	21000	04	Technical	

Query 1.4

Show the names, hire dates and department of employees hired on or before 1st Jan 1990.

SQL: SELECT name, hire_date, department FROM employee
       WHERE hire_date <= '1-Mar-90'

Result:

NAME	HIRE_DATE	DEPARTMENT
Kennedy	16-JAN-84	
Stewart	30-APR-89	Accounts
Walker	03-AUG-87	Admin
Adams	01-OCT-86	Sales
Hill	27-JAN-90	Admin
Moore	30-JUN-85	Sales
Bradley	08-SEP-88	Technical
Hamilton	21-FEB-88	Accounts
Fletcher	29-OCT-87	Accounts
Stein	04-FEB-89	Sales
Roxburgh	21-SEP-84	Sales

Note from Query 1.4 that dates can be compared; earlier dates are 'less than' later dates.

Other forms of condition

BETWEEN .. AND ..
    Range test; tests specified column for values in given range. Handy for dates.

IN (*list*)   Set membership test; tests for a value in a specified list

IS NULL   Test for null values

LIKE   Pattern Matching Test; selects values with a specified pattern, typically using wildcard characters. The wildcard character % matches zero or more characters; the wildcard character _ (underscore) matches a single character.

Examples of these conditions follow:

BETWEEN

> **Query 1.5**
> Show the names and department of employees hired between 12th March 1992 and 1st Jan 1997.
>
> SQL: SELECT name, department FROM employee
>   WHERE hire_date BETWEEN '12-Mar-92' AND '1-Jan-97'

IN

> **Query 1.6**
> Show all details of employees in Accounts, Sales and IT departments.
>
> SQL: SELECT * FROM employee WHERE department IN
>   ('Account', 'Sales', 'IT')

IS NULL

> **Query 1.7**
> Show the names and departments of employees with no assigned supervisor.
>
> SQL: SELECT name, department FROM employee WHERE supervisor IS
>   NULL

LIKE

> **Query 1.8**
> Show the names of all employees with names begnning with B.
>
> SQL: SELECT name FROM employee WHERE name LIKE 'B%'

Result:

```
NAME
-------
Bell
Bradley
```

> **Query 1.9**
> Show the names of all employees with 5 letter names beginning with C.
>
> SQL: SELECT name FROM employee WHERE name 'C____'

Note: The value in quotes includes four underscores.

Logical operators

Logical operators allow you to produce more elaborate conditions involving combination and negation of conditions. The available operators are

AND   Selects rows meeting BOTH specified conditions.
OR   Selects rows meeting EITHER specified condition.
NOT   Negate; used with other condition tests to negate the sense of the
          condition. Not can be used with any other condition format.

There are many traps for the unwary in the use of logical operators; particular attention should be paid to the extra notes supplied below.

AND

> **Query 1.10**
> Show the names of all employees in Sales departments earning more than 18000.
>
> SQL: SELECT name, department FROM employee
>   WHERE department = 'Sales' AND salary > 18000

OR

> **Query 1.11**
> Show the names of all employees in Accounts and Sales departments.
>
> SQL: SELECT name, department FROM employee
>   WHERE department = 'Accounts' OR department = 'Sales'

Result

```
NAME                DEPARTMENT
----------          ----------
Smith               Sales
Stewart             Accounts
Young               Accounts
Adams               Sales
Gomatam             Sales
Moore               Sales
Hamilton            Accounts
Evans               Sales
Fletcher            Accounts
Stein               Sales
Roxburgh            Sales
Nicholson           Accounts
```

> ### Notes
>
> 1. The above example is worthy of close study. Query 1.11 is expressed in normal English, using the 'and' connective: we want a list of all the Accounts staff and all the Sales staff. However, the correct logical definition uses the OR operator, as shown in the SQL answer. If we expressed this as
>
>   WHERE department = 'Accounts' **AND** department = 'Sales'
>
>   SQL would be looking for rows where the department value was equal to both 'Accounts' and 'Sales' simultaneously, clearly impossible.

2. The second point to note is that, again conflicting with English usage, we have to repeat the 'department =..' bit for the second comparison. That is –

   WHERE department = 'Accounts' OR 'Sales' – is **invalid**.

3. Note that the IN type of query is essentially a form of OR. Use of IN instead of explicit ORs is generally neater and safer. Refer to Query 1.6 above.

NOT

Query 1.12
Show the names of all employees NOT in the Accounts or the Sales departments.

SQL: SELECT name, department FROM employee
       WHERE department NOT IN ('Accounts', 'Sales')

Result:

```
NAME            DEPARTMENT
---------       ----------
Bell            Admin
Walker          Admin
Chung           Technical
Hill            Admin
Bradley         Technical
Newman          Technical
Cohen           Technical
Monaghan        Admin
```

Multiple logical operators

You can employ two or more ANDs and/or ORs in one command.

Query 1.13
Show the names and salaries of all employees in Accounts departments, who were hired since the beginning of 1990 and earning less than 20000.

SQL: SELECT name, salary FROM employee
       WHERE department = 'Accounts'
       AND hire_date>= '1-Jan-90'
       AND salary <20000

Notes

Operator precedence

1. If you use both AND or OR in one command, it is important to be aware that a rule of precedence applies, namely, that the ANDs are evaluated before the ORs. Failure to take this into account can produce serious errors that can be easily overlooked.

2. You can modify the effect of the default precedence by using brackets to associate conditions together. Bracketed conditions are evaluated as an independent unit (i.e., yielding either true or false) and the result combined with the rest of the conditions.

These points are illustrated in the examples shown below.

Query 1.14

Show the names, department and salaries of all employees in the Accounts or Sales departments, earning less than 18000.

WRONG VERSION

SQL: SELECT name, department, SALARY FROM employee
       WHERE DEPARTMENT = 'Accounts'
       OR department = 'Sales'
       AND salary < 18000

This query as it stands will select

- all staff in Accounts (from *department = 'Accounts'*)
- staff in Sales earning < 18000 (from *department = 'Sales' AND salary < 18000*), not what the query asked for. The erroneous table shown below is produced. Note that it includes staff earning more than 18000.

Result

NAME	DEPARTMENT	SALARY
Stewart	Accounts	16000
Young	Accounts	30000
Hamilton	Accounts	20000
Evans	Sales	17500
Fletcher	Accounts	18000
Stein	Sales	15500
Nicholson	Accounts	15000

Query 1.15

Show the names, department and salaries of all employees in the Accounts or Sales departments, earning less than 18000.

CORRECT VERSION

SQL: SELECT name, department, SALARY FROM employee
       WHERE (department = 'Accounts'
       OR department = 'Sales')
       AND salary < 18000

Result

```
NAME            DEPARTMENT      SALARY
----------      ----------      ------
Stewart         Accounts        16000
Evans           Sales           17500
Stein           Sales           15500
Nicholson       Accounts        15000
```

Order by

The ORDER BY clause can be used to control the sequence of output of the result. Normally, the output will be produced in the physical sequence of the stored rows. If you want to see the output in some more useful sequence, the ORDER BY clause specifies a column or columns that govern the sorted output

> **Query 1.16**
> Show the names and salaries of all employees in sequence of their name.
>
> SQL: SELECT name, salary FROM employee ORDER BY name

The ORDER BY column need not be part of the output. Also, the sequence can be reversed by use of the DESC (=descending) keyword.

> **Query 1.17**
> Show the names, departments and salaries of employees in the Sales department in order of salary, from greatest to smallest.
>
> SQL: SELECT name, department, salary FROM employee
>   WHERE department = 'Sales' ORDER BY salary DESC

Result

```
NAME            DEPARTMENT      SALARY
---------       ----------      ------
Gomatam         Sales           31000
Adams           Sales           23000
Roxburgh        Sales           20000
Moore           Sales           19500
Smith           Sales           18000
Evans           Sales           17500
Stein           Sales           15500
```

It is possible to sort on multiple columns.

> **Query 1.18**
> Show the names, positions, branch code and department of all employees in sequence of name within each branch and department.
>
> SQL: SELECT name, position, branch_code, department FROM
>   employee ORDER BY branch_code, department, name

Result

```
NAME          POSITION        BR    DEPARTMENT
----------    ----------      --    ----------
Hamilton      Accountant      01    Accounts
Young         Manager         01    Accounts
Bell          Supervisor      01    Admin
Roxburgh      Salesman        01    Sales
Chung         Programmer      01    Technical
Kennedy       Director        01
Monaghan      Clerk           02    Admin
Evans         Salesman        02    Sales
Gomatam       Manager         02    Sales
Moore         Salesman        02    Sales
Fletcher      Chief Clerk     03    Accounts
Stewart       Clerk           03    Accounts
Stein         Supervisor      03    Sales
Bradley       Technician      03    Technical
Newman        Manager         03    Technical
Nicholson     Chief Clerk     04    Accounts
Hill          Manager         04    Admin
Walker        Secretary       04    Admin
Adams         Supervisor      04    Sales
Smith         Salesman        04    Sales
Cohen         Engineer        04    Technical
```

Notes

1. Note that the ORDER BY columns are listed in 'major' to 'minor' sequence, i.e., the branch codes (major sequence) are in sequence, within each branch the departments are in sequence and finally within each department the names are in sequence.

2. If two or more columns are used in the ORDER BY, it makes no sense to use a column that has unique (or almost unique) values as a major sequence key. For instance, in the clause

    ... ORDER BY emp_id, department

    the 'department' component is redundant since emp_id values on every row are all distinct.

Set operations

If the result of individual SELECT queries is viewed as a set of values it is possible to combine such sets using operators based on the relational algebra. As in other parts of SQL, there is some divergence between the standard and the various implementations. The SQL/92 standard defines UNION, INTERSECT and EXCEPT; some systems only support UNION which is the most useful. In these notes we use the Oracle offering which has UNION, INTERSECT and MINUS (same as the standard EXCEPT).

The operators described here are subject to the restriction that the two operands (i.e., the output from the component SELECTs) must be identical in structure, i.e., they have the same number of columns and corresponding columns are of the same type. This restriction arises from the nature of the set operations which are defined only for identically structured relations.

The UNION operator combines the results of two queries; the rows of the first query and the second query are 'ORed' together into one relation.

> **Query 1.19**
> Show the names, branches and departments of employees who are in branch 02 or who earn at least 20000.
>
> SQL: SELECT name, branch_code, department, salary FROM employee
>   WHERE branch_code = '02'
>   UNION
>   SELECT name, branch_code, department, salary FROM employee
>   WHERE salary >= 20000

Result

```
NAME              BR      DEPARTMENT      SALARY
---------         --      ----------      ------
Adams             04      Sales           23000
Bell              01      Admin           20000
Chung             01      Technical       21500
Cohen             04      Technical       21000
Evans             02      Sales           17500
Gomatam           02      Sales           31000
Hamilton          01      Accounts        20000
Hill              04      Admin           27000
Kennedy           01                      50000
Monaghan          02      Admin           17000
Moore             02      Sales           19500
Newman            03      Technical       28000
Roxburgh          01      Sales           20000
Young             01      Accounts        30000
```

The trained eye will notice that the same result could be obtained more simply using the condition:

> WHERE branch_code = '02' OR salary > 20000

Accordingly, the UNION operator would not be used in this fashion. However, if the SELECTs referred to different tables, a UNION would be necessary. The following query is a somewhat contrived example, using the employee and branch tables.

> **Query 1.20**
> Show the branch code of employees who earn more than 25000 and the branches with a budget greater than 6000.

> SQL: SELECT branch_code FROM employee
>   WHERE salary > 29000
>   UNION
>   SELECT branch_code FROM branch
>   WHERE budget > 300

Result

```
BRANCH
------
01
02
03
```

The resultant relations from these two SELECTs have the same structure (a single column called branch_code) and hence can be 'UNIONed'.

Note that the two component queries could potentially yield the same row; the action of SQL in this instance is to eliminate duplicate rows from the answer. If you really want to preserve duplicate rows you change the operator to UNION ALL.

Session 2: Calculations and functions

Calculations

In addition to columns from database tables, an SQL query can also refer to values calculated by arithmetic expressions and by the application of functions. The expressions use the basic arithmetic operators found in programming languages, namely + –/(divide) and * (multiply).

The *column-list* in the SELECT command can include arithmetic expressions.

> **Query 2.1**
> Show the names and *monthly* salaries of all employees in the Accounts department. (Note: the salary column stores annual values).
>
> SQL: SELECT name, salary/12 FROM employee WHERE department = 'Sales'

Result

```
NAME        SALARY/12
-------     ---------
Smith            1500
Adams       1916.6667
Gomatam     2583.3333
Moore            1625
Evans       1458.3333
Stein       1291.6667
Roxburgh    1666.6667
```

The display of decimal places can be controlled by the use of functions. These are described shortly.

The WHERE clause can also use expressions.

> **Query 2.2**
> Show the names of all employees whose monthly salary exceeds 2000 by more than 100.
>
> SQL: SELECT name, salary FROM employee
>   WHERE salary/12–100>2000'

Result

```
    NAME          SALARY
    -------       ------
    Kennedy       50000
    Young         30000
    Hill          27000
    Gomatam       31000
    Newman        28000
```

Note that the usual precedence of arithmetic operators applies: multiplication and division are done first, then addition and subtraction. The precedence can be altered by the use of brackets.

> **Query 2.3**
> The annual salaries of all Technical employees is to be increased by £400 this month plus a further 5% next month. Show the names and new annual salaries.
>
> SQL: SELECT name, (salary+400) * 1.05 FROM employee WHERE
>   department = 'Technical'

Result

```
    NAME          (SALARY+400)*1.05
    -------       -----------------
    Chung         22995
    Bradley       15645
    Newman        29820
    Cohen         22470
```

Note that date columns can be computed arithmetically. If you add a number *d* to a date it produces a new date *d* days after the specified date. Subtraction works similarly. If you subtract two date values, the result is the number of days between these dates.

Functions

> ### Revision
>
> A **function** is a program module that accepts zero or more input values and produces a *single value* answer. The input values are called the **parameters** of the function. A function is called by using the function name as a value; this value will be of some type, i.e., numeric, text, date, etc. The general function call format is *function-name (parameter-list)*. All this will become clearer when we have tried a few examples.

Note that the current standard for SQL (namely SQL2) specifies a number of 'built-in' functions, but individual implementations such as Oracle, DB2, etc., appear to conform to these only rather loosely. The same functionality is often provided but with altered syntax and with many extensions.

The examples provided here are just that; they illustrate how functions are used and the general range of facilities available. The reference manuals should be consulted for the system you are using to determine the functions available for that system.

Numeric functions

These are functions that operate on numeric data items. The **ROUND** function rounds a data item to the nearest value having a specified number of decimal places. For instance, to round a column *Amount* to two decimal places, we would use the expression ROUND(Amount, 2). The items in the brackets are parameters; they are the 'input' values to the function.

> **Query 2.4**
> Show the weekly salary of employee Smith, unrounded and rounded to two decimal places.
>
> **SQL:** SELECT salary/52, ROUND(salary/52, 2) FROM employee
> WHERE name = 'Smith'

Result

```
SALARY/52      ROUND(SALARY/52,2)
---------      ------------------
346.15385                 346.15
```

In Query 2.4, the parameters of ROUND are **salary *12 /52** and **2**.
Other common numeric functions are

ABS(A)	returns the 'positive' value of A, regardless of whether A is positive or negative.
POWER(A, n)	returns the value A to the power n.

Another large group of numeric functions are available that operate on groups of rows (instead of single rows). These are described later when the notion of groups has been covered.

Character functions

These functions operate on text data items. The most common of these are described below.

UPPER(T)	converts the text item **T** to upper case.
LENGTH(T)	returns the length (in characters) of the text item **T**. Note that the input to this function is character but the return value is numeric.
LTRIM(T,'c')	Removes leading 'c' characters from the text item **T**. This would most frequently be applied to the removal of leading spaces in text fields.
RTRIM(T,'c')	as for LTRIM but for *trailing* characters.

Examples

Query 2.5
List the department names in upper-case characters.

SQL: SELECT DISTINCT UPPER(department) FROM employee

Result

```
UPPER(DEPARTMENT)
-----------------
ACCOUNTS
ADMIN
SALES
TECHNICAL
```

Note that the DISTINCT keyword causes SQL to suppress the output of duplicate values; if this were not done there would be a result row produced for every row of the table.

Query 2.6
List the names of employees whose names are longer than six characters.

SQL: SELECT name FROM employee WHERE LENGTH(name) > 6

Result

```
NAME
----------
Kennedy
Stewart
Gomatam
Bradley
Hamilton
Fletcher
Roxburgh
Monaghan
Nicholson
```

Note
The operation of the LENGTH function is dependent on the implementation of the column data type. Some CHAR(n) types actually define a fixed width column, such that the LENGTH function would return the maximum value (n) regardless of the content of the column.

Date functions

Handling of dates is the most implementation-dependent area of SQL. Systems differ in the range of date formats they support and hence in the behaviour of date functions. Presented here are the date functions provided by Oracle SQL; other systems will generally offer comparable facilities.

ADD_MONTHS(date, num)	Returns a date obtained by adding **num** months to **date**
MONTHS_BETWEEN(date1, date2)	Returns a *number* equal to the months between date1 and date2.
LAST_DAY(date)	Returns the date of the last day of the current month.
TO_CHAR(date, 'format')	Returns a *text* value obtained by formatting the given **date** to the pattern specified by **format**.

Also necessary in the context of date handling is some way of representing today's date; the SQL standard suggests a parameter-less function called **CURRENT_DATE**. The Oracle version is the global variable **SYSDATE**.

Examples

> **Query 2.7**
> Calculate the number of months that Smith has been employed.
>
> SQL: SELECT MONTHS_BETWEEN(SYSDATE, hire_date) FROM
>   employee WHERE name = 'Smith'

Note

The answer to Query 2.7 yields a column heading directly obtained from the SELECT item. You can output tidier headings by using **alias column name**. An alias is specified simply by providing a name after the SELECT item. If aliases are supplied, these are used as the column headings. We can restate Query 2.7 as follows, using an alias of MONTHS.

Query 2.7a
Calculate the number of months that Smith has been employed.

SQL: SELECT MONTHS_BETWEEN(SYSDATE, hire_date)
        MONTHS FROM employee WHERE name = 'Smith'

Result

```
MONTHS
---------
49.859547
```

Note that this query (probably) produces a fractional answer. To round this to the nearest month, we can additionally apply the ROUND function.

Query 2.8
Calculate, to the nearest whole number, the number of months that Smith has been employed.

SQL: SELECT ROUND(MONTHS_BETWEEN(SYSDATE, hire_date))
        MONTHS FROM employee WHERE name = 'Smith'

Result

```
MONTHS
------
    50
```

As previously mentioned, date operations are very implementation dependent. The Oracle TO_CHAR function is a case in point. The **'format'** string specifies a wide range of date representations usable in the Oracle system. Examples of format strings are shown below. The examples assume an SQL statement of the form

SELECT TO_CHAR(hire_date, *'format-string'*) FROM employee

Format string	Result
DD/MM/YY	27/01/97
Dy DD Month, YYYY	Mon 27 January, 1997
Day "the" ddth "of" Month	Monday the 27th of January
Day Mon YYYY	27 Jan 1997

> ### Helpful hint
>
> If you are experimenting with date functions (or indeed any functions) it is convenient to be able to output single item answers without reference to a real table. However, the SELECT syntax insists that a 'FROM *table*' clause be used. The way round this is to use a dummy table that has only one row and one column with meaningless content. Oracle SQL provides for this purpose a special table called (rather mysteriously) DUAL, but you could define your own table if your system does not provide one. You could use DUAL like this
>
> SELECT TO_CHAR(SYSDATE, 'DD/MM/YY') FROM DUAL
>
> This will produce a single value equal to today's date.

Other functions

A number of other functions are often available that work with a range of datatypes. These include

GREATEST(A, B, . . .)   Returns the 'largest' of the parameter values; these can be of any datatype, but all values after the first are automatically converted (if possible) to the type of the first.

LEAST(A, B, . . .)   Sim. to GREATEST but selecting the smallest.

NVL(A, B)   **Null Value Conversion.** If **A** is null, this function returns the value **B** else the value **A** is returned. This function is used to express a null value in a more meaningful manner.

Examples

> **Query 2.9**
> Show the greater of Smith's salary and £17000.
>
> SQL: SELECT GREATEST(salary, 17000) FROM employee
>   WHERE name = 'Smith'

Result

```
GREATEST(SALARY,17000)
----------------------
                 18000
```

> **Query 2.10**
> List the name of each employee in the Sales department, together with their supervisor's number. If no supervisor code is present (i.e., it is null), output "NONE".
>
> SQL: SELECT name, NVL(supervisor, 'NONE') FROM employee
>   WHERE department = 'Sales'

Result

```
NAME         NVL (
--------     -----
Smith        3691
Adams        4206
Gomatam      NONE
Moore        4206
Evans        4206
Stein        NONE
Roxburgh     3255
```

Session 3: Groups and group functions

Introduction

The queries and functions we have covered thus far all deal with the individual rows of a table. Another important aspect of queries is to derive information about the characteristics of *groups* of rows. For example, you might want to know the average of the salaries in the employee table. This query, by its nature, produces a *single answer* for the whole group of rows being examined.

For the average salary query suggested above, the group is the whole table. However, we may wish to subdivide the table into smaller groups, based on commonality of some attribute. For instance, we may want to know the average salary for each of the departments. In this case, we form sub-groups of rows, each member of each group having a common department name. The salary query would now yield *n* rows in the output, where *n* is the number of departments.

These ideas will become clearer when we deal with specific examples later in this session. However, be warned that group queries can often be quite difficult to understand and formulate and hence it is important that the underlying concepts be well understood before attempting complex queries.

Group functions

The list below shows the most common of the group functions. The parameter **N** in these functions must be the name of a numeric column.

AVG(N)	Returns the average of the values in column N of the group.
COUNT(A)	Counts the number of rows in the group. If the value in column A is null, that row is not counted. If A is *, all rows are counted.
MAX/MIN(A)	Returns the largest/smallest of the values in column A of the group.
SUM(N)	Returns the total of all values in column N of the group.
STDDEV(N)	Returns the standard deviation of all values in column N of the group.
VARIANCE(N)	Returns the variance of all values in column N of the group.

The following examples show the use of group functions applied to the 'whole table'. Note that this does not prevent us from being selective about the rows being examined. That is, we can still use the WHERE clause. We provide only a limited number of examples at this stage; it becomes more interesting when we deal with sub-groups of the table.

Examples

Query 3.1
Calculate the average salary and total salary of all employees.

SQL: SELECT AVG(salary), SUM(salary) FROM employee

Result

```
AVG(SALARY)        SUM(SALARY)
-----------        -----------
  21809.524            458000
```

Note that there is only *one line* in the answer because we are treating the whole table as one group. Note also that it would be incorrect to try to refer to any column names in this query; for instance:

SQL: SELECT Name, AVG(salary), SUM (salary) FROM employee

is *invalid* (try it) because if we use a group function (such as AVG or SUM) we are committed to working with a group, not individual rows.

Query 3.2
Output the number of employees in the company.

SQL: SELECT COUNT(*) FROM employee

Result

```
COUNT(*)
--------
      21
```

The * parameter in the COUNT statement caused *all* rows to be counted. Compare this with the next query.

Query 3.3
Output the number of employees in the company.

SQL: SELECT COUNT(department) FROM employee

Result

```
COUNT(DEPARTMENT)
-----------------
               20
```

One missing! When the COUNT parameter is a column name, null values in this column are not counted. In this instance, the Director has a null in the department column.

We can apply a WHERE clause in conjunction with group functions; this simply filters the table, excluding rows from examination that do not meet the condition.

> **Query 3.4**
> Find out the highest salary in any Sales department.
>
> SQL: SELECT MAX(salary) FROM employee
>   WHERE department = 'Sales'

Result

```
MAX(SALARY)
-----------
      31000
```

Group by clause

In Query 3.1, we obtained the average salary for the whole company. Suppose now that we wanted to obtain the average salary for each department. We could of course simply do each department in turn:

>   SELECT AVG(salary) FROM employee WHERE department = 'Sales'
>   SELECT AVG(salary) FROM employee WHERE department = 'Accounts' ...
>   etc

but this is rather laborious.

A better way is to use the GROUP BY clause. This clause notionally subdivides the table into groups based on a nominated column (or columns). Members of each group have the same value of the nominated column.

Examples

> **Query 3.5**
> Find out the highest salary in a Sales department.
>
> SQL: SELECT department, MAX(salary) FROM employee GROUP BY
>   department

Result

```
DEPARTMENT    MAX(SALARY)
----------    -----------
Accounts      30000
Admin         27000
Sales         31000
Technical     28000
              50000
```

Here, our nominated GROUP BY column is 'department' so that the rows of the table are notionally organised into groups, one group per department. Note that the result has one row per group. Note also that we can output the department name in the query because this is the 'grouping' column, i.e., the department is constant within each group. A full listing of the table divided into these groups will help in understanding all of this. For this we use the instruction:

> SQL: SELECT name, department, salary FROM employee ORDER BY
>   department

Result

```
NAME          DEPARTMENT    SALARY
----------    ----------    ------
Stewart       Accounts      16000
Young         Accounts      30000    <- maximum for Accounts
Fletcher      Accounts      18000
Nicholson     Accounts      15000
Hamilton      Accounts      20000

Bell          Admin         20000
Monaghan      Admin         17000
Hill          Admin         27000    <- maximum for Admin
Walker        Admin         15500

Smith         Sales         18000
Moore         Sales         19500
Roxburgh      Sales         20000
Stein         Sales         15500
Evans         Sales         17500
Adams         Sales         23000
Gomatam       Sales         31000    <- maximum for Sales

Chung         Technical     21500
Newman        Technical     28000    <- maximum for Technical
Bradley       Technical     14500
Cohen         Technical     21000
Kennedy                     50000
```

The most important point to note when working with the GROUP BY clause is that we are dealing with the characteristics of the *groups* and not the individual *rows*. To be specific, when we use the GROUP BY clause, the data that we can select (i.e., items in the SELECT list) must be one of the following:

1. A column (or columns) value that is *constant* within the group; this must be the GROUP BY column(s). Note that if more than one GROUP BY column is used, any individual column may be output.

2. A value computed over the whole group; i.e., aggregate functions such as AVG, SUM, COUNT.

3. Expressions involving combinations of the above.

As an example of the pitfalls that you can fall into in this area, we might be tempted to extend Query 3.4 to supply the name of the person with the highest salary:

Query 3.6
Find out the name and salary of the employee with the highest salary in each department.

SQL: SELECT name, MAX(salary) FROM employee GROUP BY
       department   **WRONG**

Result

Oracle produces the following error message:

```
SELECT name, MAX(salary)  FROM employee  GROUP BY   department
       *
ERROR at line 1:
ORA-00979: not a GROUP BY expression
```

This query produces an error because 'name' does not conform to any of the above categories of allowable items although the 'sense' of the query is arguably clear. This query can be answered but not in this way – it requires a **subquery**. Subqueries are described in Session 5.

If you think about it, the GROUP BY rules are quite reasonable, since they emerge purely from the nature of forming groups. However, in some situations they appear to be over-restrictive. In particular, SQL takes no account of functional dependencies within the tables. We will return to this point later, after table joining has been covered, since a suitable example requires that two or more tables be involved.

HAVING clause

The WHERE clause is used to select or reject specific *rows* that participate in a normal query; in a similar fashion, the HAVING clause is used to select/reject *groups* involved in a GROUP BY query. The syntax of the HAVING clause is similar to WHERE, in terms of the use of comparative operators etc., however, expressions in a HAVING condition are subject to the same restrictions as discussed above for the SELECT list. That is, the HAVING clause condition can involve only the three classes of data listed in the previous section.

Examples

> **Query 3.7**
> List the branches with more than five employees.
>
> SQL: SELECT branch_code, COUNT(*) FROM employee GROUP BY
>   branch_code HAVING COUNT(*)>5

Result

BRANCH	COUNT(*)
01	6
04	6

> **Query 3.8**
> List the branch departments whose highest salaries exceed £22000.
>
> SQL: SELECT branch_code, department, MAX(salary) FROM employee
>   GROUP BY branch_code, department
>   HAVING MAX(salary)>22000

Result

BR	DEPARTMENT	MAX(SALARY)
01	Accounts	30000
01		50000
02	Sales	31000
03	Technical	28000
04	Admin	27000
04	Sales	23000

Session 4: Joining tables

Introduction

In the preceding sessions, we have utilised only one of the tables (the employee table) defined at the start. In this section we enrich our SQL experience considerably by introducing the second table into our queries.

The theory and the process of joining tables was covered in Chapter 2; to recap, relational databases use tables to represent entities and relationships within the application domain. To satisfy queries against the database, tables have to be 'joined', i.e., a new table is formed by uniting columns drawn from the component tables of the database.

Tables are joined on the basis of primary and foreign keys; i.e., one table contains a column (a foreign key) that holds values referring to the primary key column of the other table. When performing joins in SQL, it is essential to remember that this *join condition* must be specified; some very strange (=wrong) results are obtained if you forget this.

Join definition

Note that there are two ways of defining join conditions; the 'traditional' way that uses a simple variation of the SELECT statement and an alternative method defined by SQL92 that uses an explicit JOIN keyword. Not all SQL implementations support the new format, including Oracle 7. We will describe the traditional method first; the SQL92 method is described later, after the OUTER join has been covered.

If we want to issue a query that requires data from more than one table, the relevant tables must be declared in the SELECT command. The basic SELECT command format given at the start of this chapter is modified to the following:

> SELECT *column-list* FROM *table-names*
>   WHERE *join-conditions* [AND *select-conditions*]
>   [ORDER BY *column-list*]

Notice that the FROM clause now contains two or more table-names, being the tables involved in the join. Note also that the WHERE clause is now mandatory since it must at minimum define the join conditions for the tables. Optionally, as before, there may be additional conditions that select specific rows from the joined tables.

Time for an example. We can utilise the second table (branch) that we defined at the start of this chapter but which, until now, has been languishing on the shelf. The branch table holds information about the company branches. The employee table has a foreign key column of *branch_code* that refers to the same-named branch table primary key. Thus, the 'join condition' for these tables is:

> Employee table branch_code = Branch table branch_code

We emphasise again that any query using both of these tables *must* include the join condition.

Example

> **Query 4.1**
> List the names of each employee and the *name* of the branch they work in.
>
> SQL: SELECT name, branch_name FROM employee, branch
>   WHERE employee.branch_code = branch.branch_code

Result

```
NAME          BRANCH_NAME
---------     -----------
Kennedy       SOUTH
Bell          SOUTH
Young         SOUTH
Chung         SOUTH
Hamilton      SOUTH
Roxburgh      SOUTH
Gomatam       WEST
Evans         WEST
```

```
Monaghan      WEST
Moore         WEST
Stewart       EAST
Stein         EAST
Bradley       EAST
Fletcher      EAST
Newman        EAST
Smith         NORTH
Nicholson     NORTH
Adams         NORTH
Hill          NORTH
Cohen         NORTH
Walker        NORTH
```

Note
Query 4.1 produces a **natural** join, i.e. the join column (branch_code) appears only once in the output. If the * indicator is used as the select list, then an **equijoin** is produced – all columns will be shown including two identical branch_code columns. This does not appear to have any practical purpose.

This query requires data from both tables and hence they have been joined. Note the format of the join condition: **WHERE employee.branch_code = branch.branch_code**. Because the 'branch_code' column name is used in both tables, it is necessary to qualify the column names by prefixing them with the table names, as shown. This applies to any column names used anywhere in the query; if the name is not unique (across all the joined tables) it must be prefixed with the appropriate table name.

Note
The need to use table name prefixes as indicated above often makes the query rather long-winded. This can be relieved to some extent by the use of **table aliases** (similar to the column aliases introduced earlier). A table alias is an alternative name defined for a table with an SQL statement. It is defined within the FROM clause and makes Query 4.1 look like this:
Query 4.1   List the names of each employee and the *name* of the branch they work in.
SQL: SELECT name, branch_name FROM employee E, branch B   WHERE E.branch_code = B.branch_code
The aliases E and B are arbitrary choices; any valid names can be used, but with regard to the purpose of these names, short ones are best.

If the query includes other conditions, the WHERE clause can be extended.

Query 4.2
List the name of each employee, department and the name of the branch
they work in for all employees in Sales departments.

SQL: SELECT name, branch_name, department FROM employee E,
       branch B
       WHERE E.branch_code = B.branch_code
       AND department = 'Sales'

Result

```
NAME              BRANCH_NAM      DEPARTMENT
--------          -----------     ----------
Roxburgh          SOUTH           Sales
Gomatam           WEST            Sales
Moore             WEST            Sales
Evans             WEST            Sales
Stein             EAST            Sales
Smith             NORTH           Sales
Adams             NORTH           Sales
```

We can also combine a join with a GROUP BY operation. This incidentally yields a
problem alluded to in the previous session.

Query 4.3
List the name of each branch and the number of people employed in it.

SQL: SELECT branch_name, COUNT(*) FROM employee E, branch B
       WHERE E.branch_code = B.branch_code
       GROUP BY branch_name

Result

```
BRANCH_NAM        COUNT(*)
----------        --------
EAST              5
NORTH             6
SOUTH             6
WEST              4
```

Now for the problem. Suppose we want list the branch_code as well as the branch
name. We might be tempted to try

SQL: SELECT E. branch_code, branch_name, COUNT(*) FROM
       employee E, branch B
       WHERE E.branch_code = B.branch_code
       GROUP BY branch_name   **WRONG**

Oracle produces the following error message:

```
SELECT E.branch_code, branch_name, COUNT(*) FROM employee E,
       *
ERROR at line 1:
ORA-00979: not a GROUP BY expression
```

What is the problem here? Well, the SELECT list item branch_code does not qualify as a GROUP item – it is not a GROUP BY column and not a group function. However, since branch_name is functionally dependent on branch_code, it is clear that within each branch_name group the branch_code will also be constant. We can fix this problem simply by extending the GROUP BY parameter to include the branch_code:

> **Query 4.3a**
> List the code and name of each branch and the number of people employed in it.
>
> SQL: SELECT E.branch_code, branch_name, COUNT(*) FROM
>   employee E, branch B
>   WHERE E.branch_code = B.branch_code
>   GROUP BY E.branch_code, branch_name

Result

```
BR     BRANCH_NAM    COUNT(*)
--     ----------    --------
01     SOUTH         6
02     WEST          4
03     EAST          5
04     NORTH         6
```

In effect, the branch_code entry here is redundant but it keeps SQL happy! Note also that the branch_code column name has to be prefixed with a table name because it is not a unique name – it occurs in both tables. Either table name would do.

Inner and outer joins

There are a number of variations of the joining principle which are described in this section. The examples above in fact illustrate *inner natural joins*. To recap on the principle involved here, the inner join ignores rows in any of the tables being joined that do not meet any of the join conditions. For instance, in the previous query, there are no rows in the result that refer to branch code 05 although branch code 05 appears in the branch table. However, there are no matching rows in the employee table, i.e., there are no rows in the employee table for which branch_code = 05. In real-world terms, this situation could arise if a new branch were built but had not yet been occupied by staff.

If we want to see the details from the unmatched row (in this case, the information about the 05 branch), we need to use an *outer join*. An outer join enables data pertaining to unmatched rows to be output; columns of the output corresponding to unavailable data are set to null.

Note
The notation used to specify outer joins is very implementation dependent; the technique given here is that used by Oracle.

Query 4.2 re-expressed using an outer join appears as shown in Query 4.4.

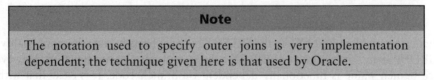

Query 4.4
List the names of each employee and the name of the branch they work in for all employees *including branches with no employees.*

SQL: SELECT name, branch_name FROM employee E, branch B
       WHERE E.branch_code(+) = B.branch_code

Result

```
NAME              BRANCH_NAM
----------        -----------
Kennedy           SOUTH
Bell              SOUTH
Young             SOUTH
Chung             SOUTH
Hamilton          SOUTH
Roxburgh          SOUTH
Gomatam           WEST
Evans             WEST
Monaghan          WEST
Moore             WEST
Stewart           EAST
Stein             EAST
Bradley           EAST
Fletcher          EAST
Newman            EAST
Smith             NORTH
Nicholson         NORTH
Adams             NORTH
Hill              NORTH
Cohen             NORTH
Walker            NORTH
                  EUROPE        <- this entry caused by outer join
```

Note the use of the (+) notation; this tells SQL to treat the associated table (employee in this case) as though it had an extra row of null columns. Any unmatched rows from the branch table are automatically matched with this null row. Note that, depending on the context, the (+) device can be on either side of the WHERE condition (and, theoretically, on both sides although this rarely has any practical value).

Question
What would be the effect of Query 4.4 if the (+) symbol were placed on the other side of the condition, i.e.,

SELECT name, branch_name FROM employee E, branch B
    WHERE E.branch_code = B.branch_code(+)

Answer

The answer would include a row for any employee branch_code with no matching branch_code in the branch table. No such row exists so the answer will be identical with that for Query 4.1. Note that the presence of such a row would imply lack of referential integrity, i.e., a foreign key in the employee table refers to a primary key that does not exist in the branch table.

SQL92 JOIN formats

As mentioned earlier, the SQL92 standard introduced a new generalised method of dealing with joins by means of extensions to the SELECT command. The new syntax was probably introduced to resolve the variations in implementation found in different products. It enables explicit definition of the type of join at the expense of additional keywords but does not provide any effect not achievable by the 'traditional' syntax. The new syntax is not implemented on every version of SQL.

As there are a number of variations in the new syntax, it is helpful to see the full picture in the form of syntax diagrams. The new options are effectively extensions to the FROM clause, i.e., a SELECT command is of the form

SELECT *Column-list* FROM *Join-Expression* . . .

where *Join-Expression* can be of two forms, which we will refer to as the *Natural Form* and *On/Using Form*.

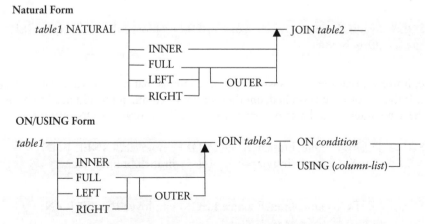

Figure 13.1   SQL92 Join formats.

The following notes explain the principles involved in this syntax.

1. The diagrams are intended to show the valid paths through the various combinations of options. For instance, the group of keywords INNER, FULL, LEFT, etc., are all optional and can be skipped by traversing the line between *table1* and JOIN *table2*. This should become clearer when we cover a few examples.

2. In the Natural version, the join columns are automatically assumed to be the columns of the two tables *with the same name(s)* so no explicit join conditions are required.

3. The keyword INNER is assumed by default (so it is essentially a 'noise' word) unless one of FULL, LEFT or RIGHT is used.

4. The keyword OUTER is also a noise word; it is assumed if FULL, LEFT or RIGHT is used.

5. Using the ON option, the join condition is expressed as in the 'traditional' version.

6. The USING option allows you to supply a list of 'join columns' which must occur in all tables being joined.

We can now repeat some of the earlier queries using this new syntax.

Inner joins

> **Query 4.1**
> List the names of each employee and the name of the branch they work in.
>
> SQL: SELECT name, branch_name FROM employee NATURAL JOIN branch

This is certainly a neater version of the original answer, exploiting the fact that the join column has the same name in both tables. The noise word INNER can be used if desired:

> SQL: SELECT name, branch_name FROM employee, NATURAL INNER JOIN branch

Note, however, that these joins would use *all* columns that had the same name in each table. If this is not what is wanted, another format of command would need to be used.
The same query could also be expressed using the USING or ON options.

> SQL: SELECT name, branch_name FROM employee, INNER JOIN branch ON employee.branch_code = branch.branch_code

> SQL: SELECT name, branch_name FROM employee INNER JOIN branch USING (branch_code)

The question could be asked: why might one choose to use the USING format rather than the NATURAL format? The answer is that the NATURAL format will use *all* similarly named columns in the two tables; although the USING format also uses similarly named columns, it allows you to select specific columns.

Outer joins

The Outer Joins are intrinsically more complicated than the Inner since it has to cope with three different ways of joining the two tables. In each example below, the keyword OUTER is used but it should be remembered that this word is always optional.

A 'LEFT' join means that the table on the left of the JOIN keyword is 'null-extended', i.e., unmatched rows of this table will be shown. This is equivalent to using the (+) notation on the left of the join condition.

Similarly, a 'RIGHT' join implies a null-extended row in the table on the right of the JOIN keyword.

For example, these two SQL lines are equivalent:

```
SQL:   SELECT name, branch_name FROM employee E, branch B
       WHERE E.branch_code(+) = B.branch.code

SQL:   SELECT name, branch_name FROM employee NATURAL LEFT
       OUTER JOIN branch
```

(The NATURAL option works as for inner joins – all matching column names are used in the join.)

Alternative forms of this query are

```
SQL:   SELECT name, branch_name FROM employee LEFT OUTER
       JOIN branch USING (branch_code)

SQL:   SELECT name, branch_name FROM employee LEFT OUTER
       JOIN branch ON employee.branch_code = branch.branch_code
```

Similarly, the following RIGHT joins are equivalent:

```
SQL:   SELECT name, branch_name FROM employee E, branch B
       WHERE E.branch_code = B.branch.code (+)

SQL:   SELECT name, branch_name FROM employee NATURAL RIGHT
       OUTER JOIN branch
```

and similarly for the ON and USING options.

Finally, FULL joins follow the same pattern:

```
SQL:   SELECT name, branch_name FROM employee E, branch B
       WHERE  E.branch_code(+) = B.branch_code(+)

SQL:   SELECT name, branch_name FROM employee NATURAL FULL
       OUTER JOIN branch
```

Multi-table joins

Our join examples thus far have involved only two tables but in practice joins over three or more tables are not uncommon. The general principle is simple; for n tables $n - 1$ joins are required. For example, for three tables two joins are necessary.

Using the basic join conventions, this means that we require an extra join condition to be specified for each extra table. As an example, assume that we have another table called Warehouse that describes company warehouses. Each warehouse is associated with a particular branch and hence contains a foreign key of branch_code referencing the branch table. There can be more than one warehouse per branch. If we assume that the format of the Warehouse table is as follows then we can try a three-table join example.

```
Warehouse Code    VARCHAR2(4),
Name              VARCHAR2(15),
Branch_code       VARCHAR2(2),
Address           VARCHAR2(20)
```

Query 4.5
List the names of each manager, the branch he/she manages and the names and addresses of warehouses connected to the branch.

```
SQL:   SELECT E.name, B.branch_name, W.name FROM employee E,
       branch B, Warehouse W
       WHERE manager_id = emp_id            (join employee – branch)
       AND     B.branch_code = W.branch_code (join branch – warehouse)
       AND     position = 'Manager'
```

Session 5: Subqueries

Consider the following query and an erroneous attempt at an answer.

Query 5.1
Find out the name, position and salary of the employee wth the highest salary.

```
SQL:   SELECT name, position, salary FROM employee
       WHERE salary = MAX(salary)      **WRONG**
```

Oracle produces the following error message:

```
WHERE salary = MAX(salary)
                    *
ERROR at line 2:
ORA-00934: group function is not allowed here
```

This is invalid because we are mixing a group function (MAX) with non-group columns. Use of group functions like MAX (in the absence of a GROUP BY clause) tells SQL to treat the whole table as a group; this is inconsistent with our use of individual columns (name, position and salary) that are not constant within the table.

In order to answer this query, we need firstly to find out what the maximum salary is and then to check each row of the table for this value. Notionally this involves two queries:

SELECT MAX(salary) FROM employee – and, using the answer from this (50000) do

SELECT name, position FROM employee WHERE salary = 50000

Passing a value 'manually' from one query to another is clearly unsatisfactory and SQL provides an alternative – **subqueries**. A subquery is a query that yields an answer within the WHERE (or HAVING) clause of a main query. The above query then becomes

Query 5.2
Find out the name, position and salary of the employee with the highest salary.

SQL: SELECT name, position, salary FROM employee
       WHERE salary = (SELECT MAX(salary) FROM employee)

Result

```
NAME         POSITION      SALARY
-------      --------      ------
Kennedy      Director      50000
```

We can also use a nested query within a HAVING clause:

Query 5.3
Find out the name of the department with the most employees.

SQL: SELECT department FROM employee
       GROUP BY department
       HAVING COUNT(*) = (SELECT MAX(COUNT(*)) FROM
                                employee GROUP BY department   )

Result

```
DEPARTMENT
----------
Sales
```

Note that the subquery must be on the 'right-hand side' of the comparison, e.g., you cannot use

WHERE (SELECT MAX(salary) FROM employee) = salary   ** WRONG **

This is not really a restriction because you can can always reverse the sense of the operator, although sometimes the resultant statement does not 'read' quite right.

How SQL interprets a subquery

It is important to appreciate how SQL handles a query containing a subquery. Essentially, the subquery should be executed for every row of the main query. However, in many cases, the subquery is independent of the main query, i.e., it will produce the same answer regardless of the row being processed by the main query. In Queries 5.1 and 5.2, for instance, the subquery simply produces a fixed single answer. To execute the subquery for every row in the main query in these circumstances would be very wasteful in processing time. Fortunately, SQL interpreters are smart enough to recognise this situation and will take a shortcut by evaluating the subquery once and using this answer for all the main query rows.

However, in some cases, the subquery is affected by the main query; this is called a **Correlated Subquery**. In effect, the subquery is dependent on the current row of the main query and hence must be executed for every main query row.

> **Query 5.4**
> List employees'names and salaries for employees who earn more than the average for their branch.
>
> SQL: SELECT name, salary FROM employee Emp
>   WHERE salary > (SELECT AVG(salary) FROM employee
>   WHERE branch_code = Emp.branch_code)

Result

```
        NAME          SALARY
        --------      ------
        Kennedy       50000
        Young         30000
        Adams         23000
        Hill          27000
        Gomatam       31000
        Newman        28000
        Cohen         21000
```

Notice use of the 'Emp' alias for the employee table in the main query; this enables the subquery to refer to the branch_code currently being processed in the main query.

Let us look in detail at what is happening here. The main query 'scans' the employee table row by row, so it looks first at row 1:

```
EMP NAME     POSITION HIRE_DATE SALARY BRANCH DEPARTMENT SUPERVISOR
ID                                     CODE
---- ------- -------- --------- ------ ------ ---------- ----------
1001 Kennedy Director 16-JAN-84  50000 01
```

The subquery is now executed using the branch_code from this row; the subquery scans *the full table* but only takes into account rows meeting the condition *branch_code = Emp.branch_code*, which resolves to *branch_code = '01'*. For such rows the average salary is calculated, yielding the value 26917. This is then compared with the salary value in the current main row (50000) and, since it is greater than 26917, the name and salary are displayed. The main query then moves on to the next row and the process repeats.

The previous query used only one table, but it is possible for the main and subqueries to use different tables. The same principles apply; columns named in the subquery not found in the subquery table are assumed to refer to the table in the main query. The next example uses two tables and also shows the use of grouping within the main query – this query is quite complex but worth some study!

> **Query 5.5**
> List those departments whose total salary is greater than 20% of the budget for the branch it is in. (Note: the budget figure in the table is in thousands.)
>
> SQL: SELECT SUM(salary), branch_code, department FROM employee E
> HAVING SUM(salary) > (SELECT budget* 1000*0.2 FROM branch
> WHERE branch_code = E.branch_code)
> GROUP BY branch_code, department

Result

```
SUM(SALARY)      BR     DEPARTMENT
-----------      --     ----------
68000            02     Sales
42500            04     Admin
41000            04     Sales
```

Note that the GROUP BY clause uses two columns, branch_code and department; this is necessary since the departments are effectively 'within' each branch, e.g., there is a Sales department in more than one branch.

Subqueries yielding multiple rows

If the subquery yields a single value answer (as in the above examples), you can use any of the usual operators (= < > <= >= <>) when comparing with the subquery answer. If the subquery may produce more than one row, then these operators cannot be used on their own. Instead, you must use other additional qualifiers that are designed to work with sets of values. These qualifiers are ANY, ALL. Additionally, there are two other operators, IN and EXISTS, that can be applied to multiple row answers. These keywords are described below; first the qualifiers.

ANY – compares a value with each of a set of values; the left-hand side value is compared (using the given comparison operator) with each of the subquery result values. It returns true if, and only if, the comparison is true for any row of the subquery.

ALL – compares a value with all of a set of values; the left-hand side value is compared with each of subquery result values. It returns true if the comparison is true for all rows of the subquery.

The IN operator is called the **Set Membership** test. Note that we have already met this operator in Session 1 where it was used to test for membership of a fixed list of values. It is actually just a convenient alternative to =ANY; similarly, NOT IN is equivalent to <>ALL. In practice, the IN operator is much more intuitive than ALL/ANY and should be used in preference. However, we will look at both usages.

> **Query 5.6**
> List branches that do not employ any Clerks.
>
> SQL: SELECT DISTINCT branch_code FROM employee E
>   WHERE 'Clerk' <> ALL (SELECT position FROM employee
>   WHERE branch_code = E.branch_code)
>
>   SELECT DISTINCT branch_code FROM employee E
>   WHERE 'Clerk' NOT IN (SELECT position FROM employee
>   WHERE branch_code = E.branch_code)

Either of these queries would produce the result show below.

Result

```
BRANCH
------
01
04
```

Note that this query uses a correlated subquery. For each row of the main query, the inner select effectively produces a single column relation containing the positions within the branch indicated in the main query. The position value of the current row of the main query is tested against this list and will not be reported if a match occurs.

The EXISTS operator checks to see whether a subquery yields any rows as an answer. In contrast to the other subquery operators, EXISTS is not concerned with the actual values returned, only whether there are any! Here is a (somewhat contrived) example.

> **Query 5.7**
> List the names of branches where there are at least two salesmen.
>
> SQL: SELECT branch_name FROM branch B
>   WHERE EXISTS (SELECT * FROM employee
>   WHERE position = 'Salesman' AND
>   B.branch_code = branch_code
>   GROUP BY branch_code
>   HAVING COUNT (*) >=2)

Result

```
BRANCH_NAME
-----------
WEST
```

Since the actual values derived from the subquery are irrelevant, the 'SELECT *
FROM employee' could be replaced by any other select, such as 'SELECT name
FROM employee'. Traditionally, the asterisk is used to avoid implying some other
intent in the clause.

Subqueries producing multiple columns

It is possible to compare multiple columns with a subquery result as long as the
column pattern is identical on both sides of the comparison

> **Query 5.8**
> List the names and position of employees who are earning the highest salary
> for each position.
>
> SQL: SELECT name, position FROM employee, branch
>   WHERE (position, salary) IN (SELECT position, MAX(salary)
>   FROM employee
>   GROUP BY position)

Result

```
NAME          POSITION
---------     -----------
Hamilton      Accountant
Fletcher      Chief Clerk
Monaghan      Clerk
Kennedy       Director
Cohen         Engineer
Gomatam       Manager
Chung         Programmer
Roxburgh      Salesman
Walker        Secretary
Adams         Supervisor
Bradley       Technician
```

> **Note**
>
> This facility is catered for in the SQL standard, but is not implemented
> in every version of SQL.

Use of this technique is relatively rare; it possibly makes certain queries, like Query
5.7, easier to follow but in fact this Query could be implemented more simply by

> SQL: SELECT name, position FROM employee
>   WHERE salary IN (SELECT MAX(salary)
>   FROM employee
>   GROUP BY position)

The subquery creates a single column of 'MAX' salaries, one row per position. The main query only reports those rows whose salary column matches one of the subquery rows.

More complex subquery constructions

Subqueries can be utilised in a variety of different ways, subject to the general rule that the subquery must yield an answer that is admissible on the 'right-hand side' of a WHERE or HAVING condition. For instance, although it might seem a good idea in some situations, you cannot use a subquery as an item in the SELECT column list. This section explores two variants in subquery usage.

Multiple levels of nesting

Previous examples have used one subquery within a main query but it is possible for the subquery itself to include a subquery and so on for several levels. This yields an outline structure as shown below:

SELECT *column-list* FROM *table*
    WHERE *value* = (SELECT *column-list* FROM *table*
            WHERE *value* = (SELECT *column-list* FROM *table*
                    WHERE *value* = (SELECT ...)))

The number of permissible levels is implementation dependent but will generally be more than it is realistic to need in practice. Multiple subquery levels arise in queries that effectively need a series of separate queries to evaluate.

Example

> **Query 5.9**
> Find the names of employees whose salary is more than the maximum salary of anyone working at the same branch as Walker.
>
> SQL: SELECT name FROM employee
>   WHERE salary > (SELECT MAX(salary)
>   FROM employee
>   WHERE branch_code = (SELECT branch_code
>   FROM employee
>   WHERE name = 'Walker'))

Result

```
NAME
-------
Kennedy
Young
Gomatam
Newman
```

This query breaks down into three steps:

1. Find out Walker's branch_code (=04).
2. Find out the maximum salary in this branch (=27000).
3. Find out who is earning more than this salary, as shown in output result.

Logical connectives

If a WHERE or HAVING condition requires to use AND or OR connectives, subqueries can be used in each component of the condition.

Query 5.10
Find the names of employees whose salary is more than the average of those working in branch 02 and who are in the same postion as Young.

SQL: SELECT name FROM employee
        WHERE salary > (SELECT AVG(salary)
                        FROM employee
                        WHERE branch_code = '02')
        AND position = (SELECT position FROM employee
                        WHERE name = 'Young')

Result

```
NAME
-------
Young
Hill
Gomatam
Newman
```

Session 6: Data definition language (DDL)

Introduction

The earlier sessions have all utilised a set of database tables that already exist; in this session we are concerned with DDL – the part of the SQL language that provides facilities for table creation and maintenance. There are a number of activities included in this area:

- creating a table schema and 'empty' table
- changing the structure of a table
- adding data to a table
- deleting data from a table
- amending data in a table
- deleting a whole table
- creating and deleting indexes.

It is worth noting again that there are considerable variations in the facilities offered by the various implementations (and in the standard) in this area. In particular, the range of permissible data types and the facilities offered by the ALTER TABLE command are subject to considerable variations. Most implementations claim to be supersets of the standard (i.e., they include all of the standard and provide additional facilties) but this is often not the case. As before, we note that these notes have been prepared using Oracle Version 7 and the syntax given reflects this version. Some additional references are made to significant elements of the SQL standard.

Table names, column names and other items created within the DDL must conform to the rules for the formation of SQL identifiers; these are summarised below. Note that there may be some variations in these rules in particular implementations.

- A name must begin with a letter and must consist of letters, numbers or the underscore character.
- A name may be up to 128 characters long; this is likely to be implementation dependent but all products will support names of sufficient length for practical use.
- Within one context, all names must be unique. For instance, within one table all column names must be unique but two tables can contain columns with the same name.
- You cannot use any SQL keyword as an identifier, e.g., you cannot name a table 'SELECT' or 'WHERE'.
- The case of an identifier is insignificant; the names EMPLOYEE, Employee and employee are all considered identical.
- While it is possible to have identifiers with embedded spaces, it is necessary to enclose them (for every occurrence) in double quotes, e.g., "Date of Birth" (the quotes are part of the identifier) is valid. However, such usage is not recommended.

Creating tables

Creating a database table requires that you assign a name to the table and that you define the names and data types of each of the columns of the table. Additionally, each column description may include other supplementary clauses concerned with validation and integrity.

The command used to create a new database table is CREATE TABLE which has the basic format shown below.

> CREATE TABLE   *tablename*
> (*column-definition-list*)

where *column-definition-list* consists of a comma-separated list of column definitions each with the format:

column-name   type   [additional clauses]

The square brackets indicate optionality. The *additional clauses* are concerned with validation and integrity and are mostly dealt with later. One clause, however, is sufficiently common that it deserves mention here. The NOT NULL option applied to a column indicates that the column must always have a value; SQL will not insert a row in the table if no value is supplied for a NOT NULL column. The NOT NULL restriction should always be applied to primary key columns and optionally to other columns where the application demands a valid value.

Query 6.1
Create the employee table used in this chapter.

SQL: CREATE TABLE employee
        (
                Emp_id   VARCHAR2(4) NOT NULL,
                Name   VARCHAR2(10)
                Position   VARCHAR2(12)
                Hire_Date   DATE,
                Salary   NUMBER(7,2)
                Branch_Code   VARCHAR2(2) NOT NULL,
                Department   VARCHAR2(10),
                Supervisor   VARCHAR2(4)

)

VARCHAR2, DATE and NUMBER are the data types used in this table. The first column description for instance, defines the first column of the table to be Emp-id with a data type of VARCHAR2; this being the primary key of the table, it is also qualified with NOT NULL. Note that the NOT NULL qualifier does not *make* this column a primary key. Within the format of the basic CREATE statement used here there is no way to identify a primary key.

The data type of the column governs the nature of the data to be stored in the column. In effect, it determines how the data is handled on input and output and what the domain of the stored data is. The SQL standard defines a range of data types but again implementations differ in terms of the types offered. Table 13.1 shows the most commonly used data types and those used within this text.

Table13.1

Type	Description
CHAR(n)	Fixed length text string of n characters
CHAR	A single text character
VARCHAR(n)	Variable length text string of maximum length n characters.
VARCHAR2(n)	Oracle extension; similar to VARCHAR
NUMBER	Floating point value
NUMBER(n, p)	Fixed point value with total width n digits of which p are decimal places
DATE	Date value

Creating a table from an existing table

It is possible to create a new table by copying from all or part of an existing table. In effect, the new table is derived from the result of executing a SELECT query on the current table.

> **Query 6.2**
> Create a new table containing the emp_id, name, postion and salary from the employee table for all employees in the02 branch.
>
> SQL: CREATE TABLE Employee2
>   AS
>   SELECT emp_id, name, position, salary FROM employee
>   WHERE branch_code = '02'

This would create a table with the following structure and content:

```
EMP_ID NAME          POSITION          SALARY
------ ----------    ------------      ---------
  4206  Gomatam      Manager            31000
  4936  Moore        Salesman           19500
  8253  Evans        Salesman           17500
  4102  Monaghan     Clerk              17000
```

Note that, while a basic CREATE TABLE command just defines the table format, the CREATE .. AS command also populates the new table with data from the source table.

Changing the structure of a table

If it becomes necessary to alter the structure of a table, due to an error or because the design has changed, the ALTER TABLE command may help, although it is subject to certain restrictions. The basic formats of the ALTER command are defined below.

    ALTER TABLE *tablename*
    ADD (*column-name type* [NOT NULL])

or

    ALTER TABLE *tablename*
    MODIFY (*column-name   type* [NOT NULL])

The first format allows you to add a new column to a table. The column will initially contain nulls.

> **Query 6.3**
> Add a new 'department' column to the employee2 table, defined as in the original employee table.
>
> SQL: ALTER TABLE employee2
>   ADD (department VARCHAR2(10))

The new column will be filled with nulls.

The second format is used primarily to increase the width of a column; most implementations will not allow you to reduce the width of a table unless the whole column is empty (i.e., the table is empty or the column contains nulls). Also, changing the type of the column, say from CHAR to NUMBER is generally not possible. An example of a MODIFY operation is shown below.

> **Query 6.4**
> Change the size of the name column in employee2 table to 20 characters.
>
> SQL: ALTER TABLE employee2
>   MODIFY (name VARCHAR2(20))

> ### Implementation note
>
> The MODIFY option is not now part of the current standard but still supported by many implementations. The standard has an ALTER TABLE ... ALTER COLUMN option but its only action is to change the default value for the column.
>   Conversely, the standard defines a DROP COLUMN option that is not provided in Oracle.

Deleting a whole table

If it becomes necessary to remove a table from a database completely, the DROP command is used. This has a simple syntax, illustrated below:

> **Query 6.5**
> Delete the employee2 table.
>
> SQL: DROP TABLE employee2

The commands covered in next three sections describe how table data can be processed by SQL, i.e., adding, deleting and amending rows of data.

Adding rows to a table

The SQL INSERT command can be used to add one row of data to a table. The syntax of the INSERT command is shown below:

INSERT INTO *tablename* [(*column-name-list*)]
VALUES (*data-value-list*)

The optional column-name-list is used if you want to supply data only for selected columns. Columns not specified in this list would be set to null. Normally, data for all columns is supplied and the column list can be omitted. The data-value-list consists of a comma-separated list of values each of which correspond to one column of the table.

Query 6.6
Add a new row of data to the employee table.

SQL: INSERT INTO employee VALUES
       ('6752', 'Ross', 'Programmer', '12-May-95', '18000', 'Technical', '7663')

If we list the full table again, we can see the new row:

```
EMP_ NAME          POSITION        HIRE_DATE    SALARY BR DEPARTMENT SUPE
---- ------------  --------------  ---------  --------- -- ---------- ----
1001 Kennedy       Director        16-JAN-84      50000 01
1045 Smith         Salesman        12-MAY-94      18000 04 Sales      3691
1271 Stewart       Clerk           30-APR-89      16000 03 Accounts   3255
1534 Bell          Supervisor      28-NOV-95      20000 01 Admin      3876
1653 Walker        Secretary       03-AUG-87      15500 04 Admin      3876
2244 Chung         Programmer      09-APR-96      21500 01 Technical  7663
3255 Young         Manager         19-MAR-92      30000 01 Accounts   1001
3691 Adams         Supervisor      01-OCT-86      23000 04 Sales      4206
3876 Hill          Manager         27-JAN-90      27000 04 Admin
4206 Gomatam       Manager         23-JUL-97      31000 02 Sales
4936 Moore         Salesman        30-JUN-85      19500 02 Sales      4206
5833 Bradley       Technician      08-SEP-88      14500 03 Technical  7663
6223 Hamilton      Accountant      21-FEB-88      20000 01 Accounts   3255
7663 Newman        Manager         15-AUG-92      28000 03 Technical
8253 Evans         Salesman        13-JUN-93      17500 02 Sales      4206
9743 Fletcher      Chief Clerk     29-OCT-87      18000 03 Accounts   3255
2906 Stein         Supervisor      04-FEB-89      15500 03 Sales
3198 Roxburgh      Salesman        21-SEP-84      20000 01 Sales      3255
4218 Cohen         Engineer        25-AUG-92      21000 04 Technical
4102 Monaghan      Clerk           13-JUN-93      17000 02 Admin      4206
9743 Nicholson     Chief Clerk     09-JUL-90      15000 04 Accounts   3255
6752 Ross          Programmer      12-MAY-95      18000 03 Technical  7663
```

Note that the items in the value list correspond to the columns of the table in sequence and type. Only one row of data can be handled by one INSERT.

Row data may be drawn from another table; a SELECT query is used to define the data. More than one row may be added by this means.

Query 6.7
Add to the employee2 table data from the rows of the employee table that refer to the Sales department.

SQL: INSERT INTO employee2
       SELECT emp_id, name, postion, salary FROM employee
       WHERE department = 'Sales'

Table employee2 is now as shown:

```
EMP_ NAME          POSITION           SALARY
---- ----------    ------------       ---------
4206 Gomatam       Manager              31000
4936 Moore         Salesman             19500
8253 Evans         Salesman             17500
4102 Monaghan      Clerk                17000
1045 Smith         Salesman             18000
3691 Adams         Supervisor           23000
4206 Gomatam       Manager              31000
4936 Moore         Salesman             19500
8253 Evans         Salesman             17500
2906 Stein         Supervisor           15500
3198 Roxburgh      Salesman             20000
```

Updating data in tables

To update data in a current table, we use the UPDATE command, with syntax:

> UPDATE *table-name*
> SET *column-name = expression or subquery*
> [WHERE *condition*]

The condition is optional but if not included the change will be applied to every row. A more typical example is shown below.

> **Query 6.8**
> Increase the salary of everyone in the Technical department of the employee table by 10%.
>
> SQL: UPDATE employee
>   SET salary = salary * 1.1
>   WHERE department = 'Technical'

Deleting rows from a table

The syntax of this command is quite simple:

> DELETE FROM *tablename* [WHERE clause]

> **Query 6.9**
> Delete rows from the employee table that relate to Smith or Moore.
>
> SQL: DELETE FROM employee
>   WHERE name = 'Smith' OR name = 'Moore'

If you want to delete all the rows from a table, omit the WHERE clause. Note that this is different from the DROP TABLE command; in addition to deleting the data, the DROP TABLE command also removes the table definition from the schema whereas the DELETE FROM simply leaves an empty table.

Session 7: Additional SQL features

Introduction

In this session we describe a number of SQL features that have not fitted into any of the categories dealt with in the earlier sessions. These features include

- Views
- GRANT and REVOKE commands
- Transactions
- Constraints

Views

Views have already been described in Chapter 2. To recap, a view is a virtual relation that appears to the user to be a real table. It is derived from a query on 'real' tables. In a sense, any query produces a result which is a temporary relation; the difference a view makes is that the query definition is recorded as a named entity that can be referenced later, as if it were a table.

A view is defined by the CREATE VIEW command, illustrated below:

> **Query 7.1**
> Create a view called emp_view that shows the emp_id, name and position of all employees.
>
> SQL: CREATE VIEW emp_view
>   AS
>   SELECT emp_id, name, postion, salary FROM employee

The view emp_basic can now be used as if it were a table:

> **Query 7.2**
> List the emp_id, name and position of all salesmen.
>
> SQL: SELECT * FROM emp_view
>   WHERE postion = 'Salesman'

Result

```
EMP_ NAME          POSITION        SALARY
---- ----------    ------------    ---------
1045 Smith         Salesman            18000
4936 Moore         Salesman            19500
8253 Evans         Salesman            17500
3198 Roxburgh      Salesman            20000
```

A view can be defined based on any valid query; in particular, the query may use group functions:

> **Query 7.3**
> Create a view representing the average salary of each branch-department.
>
> SQL: CREATE VIEW emp_average
>   AS
>   SELECT branch_code, department, AVG(salary) avg_salary FROM
>   employee GROUP BY branch_code, department
>
>   SELECT * FROM emp_average

Result

```
BR DEPARTMENT AVG_SALARY
-- ---------- ----------
01 Accounts      25000
01 Admin         20000
01 Sales         20000
01 Technical     21500
01               50000
02 Admin         17000
02 Sales         22667
03 Accounts      17000
03 Sales         15500
03 Technical     21250
04 Accounts      15000
04 Admin         21250
04 Sales       20999.5
04 Technical     21000
```

(Note that the column alias 'avg_salary' is required so that the view column has a conventional column name.)

There are some caveats that must be noted when working with views. Firstly, because a view is based on a query, reference to a view will require re-evaluation of the query if the underlying real table(s) have been amended. For small tables, such as our employee table, this is not a problem; however, if the table has 100,000 rows the performance implications are more serious. This is not to say that the view mechanism increases the querying time; if the application requires the answer to a query over a large table, it does not matter whether a view or the underlying view query is used. The potential problem with a view is that the apparent simplicity of a query based on a view can obscure the processing overheads involved in rebuilding the view.

Another view difficulty is its 'updatability'; a view looks like a real table but can it be updated like a real table? Clearly, since a view does not exist physically, a data amendment must be propagated through to the underlying source tables. However, this is not always possible because of, first, restrictions in the DBMS implementation and second, natural limitations due to the way views are formed.

Taking the latter point first; if you look at view emp_view above, it is clear that there is a one-to-one relationship between view rows and table rows. In this case, there is no theoretical restrictions on view updating; if you amend row *n* of the view, the corresponding row of the real table is amended.

> **Query 7.4**
> Using emp_view, change the salary of employee Bell to 22000.
>
> SQL: UPDATE emp_view
>   SET salary TO 22000

However, if we consider view emp_average, things are not so simple. The rows of the view correspond to a *group* of rows of the underlying employee table. The view salary figures (avg_salary), for instance, are averages of several table rows, hence an amendment to avg_salary cannot be propagated as a unique change in the employee table.

The original ANSI SQL standard specifies a list of conformance rules for view updatability; these tended to be too restrictive and many vendors' products exceeded the standard. The current standard is less prescriptive and allows for variations between products. Accordingly, the best reference for the rules in this respect lies in your DBMS documentation. As an example, you cannot update a view in Oracle SQL if the view definition query contains any of the following constructs:

- a join
- a set operator
- group function
- GROUP BY clause
- DISTINCT operator

GRANT and REVOKE

In Chapter 9 we covered the topic of database security where the notion of access privileges was described. This section describes the SQL commands concerned with this topic.

The GRANT and REVOKE commands are used to control the granting and revoking of system and data privileges to/from database users. These commands form the basis for SQL-controlled database security. This is an area where there is substantial variation between DBMS products; also, practical systems such as Oracle provide a wealth of different options designed to cater for many operating environments. In this section we can provide only a general indication of the range of facilities one might find in a real product, with examples drawn from Oracle. For specific details, consult your own DBMS documentation.

System privileges

System privileges refers to the right 'to do things' (such as creating tables, amending tables, etc.) on the database. The command format (simplified) in this respect is

GRANT *system-privilege* TO   *user*   [WITH ADMIN OPTION]

The identifier *user* is the name by which the person being granted the privilege is known to the DBMS. If the option WITH ADMIN OPTION is used, the privilege recipient (*user*) can then bestow this privilege on others. The range of available system privileges is extensive; here are a few typical examples.

ALTER ANY TABLE	allows the grantee to alter the structure of a table.
ALTER USER	allows the grantee to modify the system details (such as password, disk quotas) of other users.
CREATE ANY TABLE	allows the grantee to create a table in any schema.
CREATE TABLE	allows the grantee to create a table in their own schema.
CREATE ANY VIEW	allows the grantee to create a view in any schema.
CREATE SESSION	enables the grantee to logon to the database.
DROP ANY TABLE	allows the grantee to drop any table.
INSERT ANY TABLE	allows the grantee to insert rows into any table.
SELECT ANY TABLE	allows the grantee to issue select queries on any table.
UNLIMITED TABLESPACE	allows the grantee to use an unlimited amount of tablespace on disk.

Examples

> **Query 7.5**
> Allow user gordon to logon to the database.
>
> SQL: GRANT CREATE SESSION TO gordon

> **Query 7.6**
> Allow user gordon to create tables within his own schema.
>
> SQL: GRANT CREATE TABLE TO gordon

Data privileges

The (simplified) general format for data privileges (called Object Privileges in Oracle) is

GRANT *data-privilege* ON *data-object* TO *user* [WITH GRANT OPTION]

The *data-privilege* can be the value ALL (or ALL PRIVILEGES) or any combination of the following: ALTER, DELETE, EXECUTE, INDEX, INSERT, REFERENCES, SELECT or UPDATE.

In general, the grantee is bestowed the right to perform the given command on the specified object. The EXECUTE privilege allows the grantee to execute the procedure or function specified by *data-object*. The REFERENCES privilege allows the grantee to create a constraint that refers to the table named by *data-object*.

Examples

> **Query 7.7**
> Allow user gordon to delete rows from the employee table.
>
> SQL: GRANT DELETE ON employee TO gordon

> **Query 7.8**
> Allow user karen to issue queries on, and update the branch table.
>
> SQL: GRANT SELECT, UPDATE ON branch TO karen

The REVOKE command does the reverse of the GRANT – it removes privileges from users. The formats of the command are very similar to GRANT:

> REVOKE *system-privilege* FROM *user* [WITH ADMIN OPTION]

and

> REVOKE *data-privilege* ON *data-object* FROM *user* [WITH GRANT OPTION]

This operates as one might expect – the privileges previously granted are revoked from the specified user.

Transactions

Transactions, including SQL facilities, were described in Chapter 9. In this section, we wish only to reinforce the concepts involved by illustrating transaction commands using our example tables.

To recap, the COMMIT command finalises a transaction and the amendments (since the start of the transaction) are written to disk. The ROLLBACK command aborts the current transaction and reverts the database to its state at the start of the transaction. Before commencing the following test, it would be advisable to issue a COMMIT command to commit all previous work on the current session.

First of all, we run through a sequence of commands that amends the employee table.

1.   change Adams salary to 25000

> UPDATE employee SET salary = 25000 WHERE name = 'Adams'

2.   change Adams position to Manager

> UPDATE employee SET position = 'Manager' WHERE name = 'Adams'

If we now do a listing of the tables we can see these changes.

> SELECT * FROM employee WHERE name = 'Adams'

EMP_	NAME	POSITION	HIRE_DATE	SALARY	BR	DEPARTMENT	SUPE
3691	Adams	Manager	01-OCT-86	25000	04	Sales	4206

If we were to do a COMMIT command at this point, these changes would become permanent. However, if we now do a ROLLBACK command, these changes are reversed.

EMP_	NAME	POSITION	HIRE_DATE	SALARY	BR	DEPARTMENT	SUPE
3691	Adams	Supervisor	01-OCT-86	23000	04	Sales	4206

Constraints

The topic of constraints was described in Chapter 9 in the context of database integrity. This is another area of SQL that is very implementation dependent. In this section we will highlight only a few facilities that are provided by the Oracle DBMS.

The constraints provision in Oracle is quite complex. In effect, it allows you to specify rules that restrict the allowable values for one or more columns of a table. Constraints can be applied using the CREATE command (i.e., when the table is being initially created) or using ALTER on an existing table.

Constraints can be applied at the table level or at column level. The two most important and most used constraints are those used to specify the primary and foreign keys of a table. As an example we will apply these constraints to the employee table; the primary key of this table is emp_id and column branch_code.

If the constraints were defined when the table is created, then the following column definitions would be used:

```
CREATE employee
(   emp_id VARCHAR2(4)  PRIMARY KEY,
    . . .
    branch_code VARCHAR2(2) REFERENCES branch(branch_code),
    . . .
)
```

To apply table constraints to an existing table, we would issue the following commands:

```
ALTER TABLE employee ADD PRIMARY KEY (emp_id)
```

```
ALTER TABLE employee ADD FOREIGN KEY (branch_code) REFERENCES
branch
```

Appendix A: B-Trees

Correct design and usage of indexes in a database application does not require knowledge of the internal structure of indexes. However, a brief examination of the principles of underlying mechanisms can be useful in understanding some of the finer points of indexes.

The vast majority of relational database systems today use indexes based on some version of a data structure called a B-Tree (not be confused with binary tree). A B-Tree is a balanced arrangement of nodes that hold index key values, associated record number references and links to other nodes in the tree. The best way of explaining this is by means of a diagrammatic example.

There are two kinds of nodes; index set nodes and sequence set nodes. The sequence set holds values for every index key value, i.e., in the example, the set of key values 2, 9, 13, 17, 24, 29 . . . are *all* the values that appear in the data table. Also, the sequence set nodes contain references to the associated data table records. The sequence set enables the records of the table to be read in the indexed sequence.

The index set forms a tree of linked references that enable the system to navigate through the key values to find a particular key in the sequence set. The index set nodes contain key values and pointers to other nodes that contain greater or lesser key values; refer to Figure A.1. In order to find a particular key value, say 75, the process starts at the 'top' of the tree, the so-called root node. The search value 75 is compared with the node keys scanning from the left and the following action ensues:

Test	Result	Action
75 <= 51	No	No further keys; follow right pointer
75 <= 66	No	Go to next node key (78)
75 <= 78	Yes	Follow left pointer
75 <= 69	No	Next key
75 <= 71	No	Next key
75 <= 75	Yes	Key found! Follow data pointer.

The example shows an index with three keys per node. In practice, rather more keys per node than this would be used, depending on the length of the keys, say 20 or 30. Also, the nodes would typically not be full as shown but would have room for insertion of new keys, caused by insertion of new data records into the table. When an index node become full, it is necessary to create a new node and to spread the keys across both nodes appropriately. The process involves a splitting of the node and consequent adjustment of the parent node. This creates a performance overhead.

However, the B-Tree has the advantage that it is a *balanced system*, i.e., all keys are at *the same depth* of search through the tree which guarantees a fairly consistent performance in terms of retrieval speed.

Deletion of database records requires keys to be removed from the index. This has the effect of vacating 'slots' in the nodes; nodes that become too empty can be deleted and the remaining keys in that node distributed to other nodes. This can cause a series of changes that propagate up the tree.

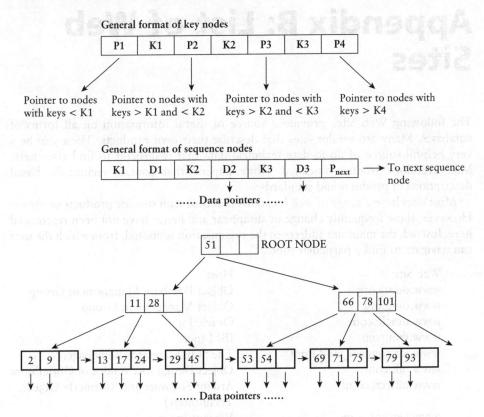

General format of key nodes

P1	K1	P2	K2	P3	K3	P4

Pointer to nodes with keys < K1

Pointer to nodes with keys > K1 and < K2

Pointer to nodes with keys > K2 and < K3

Pointer to nodes with keys > K4

General format of sequence nodes

| K1 | D1 | K2 | D2 | K3 | D3 | P_next | → To next sequence node |

...... Data pointers ......

...... Data pointers ......

Figure A.1 Structure of B-Trees.

Appendix B: List of Web Sites

The following Web Sites provide a source of useful information on all forms of databases. Many are vendor sites that describe their own products. These can be a very helpful source of up-to-date technical data that is difficult to find elsewhere. Many vendors produce so-called 'white papers' that contain technically based descriptions of products and standards.

Most sites have a range of web locations that deal with specific products or topics. However, these frequently change or disappear and hence have not been referenced here. Instead, the main site address of the organisation is quoted, from which the user can navigate to find a particular topic.

Web Site	Host
www.odmg.org	Object Database Management Group
www.omg.org	Object Management Group
www.oracle.com	Oracle Inc.
www.ibm.com	IBM Inc.
www.jcc.com/sql_stnd.html	The SQL Standards homepage.
www.odi.com	Object Design Inc, vendor of ObjectStore
www.o2tech.co.uk	Ardent Software Inc. (formerly Object Technology)
www.versant.com	Versant Inc.
www.objectivity.com	Objectivity Inc.
www.poet.com	Poet Software Inc.
www.microsoft.com	Microsoft.
www.sybase.com	Sybase Inc.
www.informix.com	Informix Inc.
davecentral.com/cgidata.html	Independent software resource link site.
www.inquiry.com/techtips/thesqlpro/	Independent software resource link site.
www.dbpd.com/	Database Programming and Design magazine.
www.webtechniques.com/	Web Techniques magazine.

Appendix C: Answers to review questions

Chapter 1

1 A table consists of a fixed number of columns (each of which holds one attribute of the table) and a variable number of rows.

2 The rows of the table each describe one instance of the entity class that the table models.
Each column describes one attribute of the entity instance and must be a simple single-valued data item.

3 A schema is a description of the structure of the tables within a database.

4 The main elements consist of facilities that enable

  - the design and maintenance of database tables
  - the formulation of queries
  - the design of forms
  - the design of reports
  - the construction of macros and programs.

Chapter 2

1 - Columns in the relation are all single values, i.e., arrays of values or other compound structures are not allowable.
  - Entries in any column are all of the same data type, e.g., integer, real number, character, data, etc.
  - No two rows of the relation are identical.
  - The order of the rows in the table is immaterial.
  - The order of the columns in the table is immaterial.
  - Each table contains an identifying column or columns (the ruling part or primary key).

2 A candidate key is one or more attributes that can serve as a primary key (because each has a unique value in each row). The primary key is one of the candidate keys that is chosen to act as the unique identifier for the table. A foreign key is an attribute in one table that refers to the primary key of another table. This is the basic linking mechanism used to associate tables together.

3 If attribute B is functionally dependent on attribute A, then every instance of a specific value of A automatically determines a specific value of B. If A has value x in one row and B has value y in that row, then every row containing A = x will also have B = y.

4 Nulls are used to 'fill' attribute values where an actual attribute value is unavailable for some reason, e.g., the value is not known or is not applicable for that row instance. A null is not a value but the 'state of having no value' and should not be confused with a space character in a text attribute or a zero in a numeric attribute.

5 Referential integrity is concerned with the correctness of foreign key to primary key links between the database tables. Every foreign key value must have a matching value which is a primary key in one of the database tables.

6 A view is a virtual table whose content is defined by a query specification. Since it has the characteristics of a relation, it can be treated in many respects like a real table. However, the data values of the view are not stored in the database, only the query definition; the query is re-executed when the view data is required.

Chapter 3

1 'Entity' is a term used to refer to any 'thing' – object, person, concept – which you wish to model in an ER diagram. An entity set is the set of all instances of the kind of entity being modelled. An ER diagram represents the entity set.

2 One-to-one, one-to-many and many-to-many.

3 By a 'crowsfoot', i.e., a splayed group of three lines.

4 It means that for one (or both) entity sets involved in the relationship there may be some instances of the entity that do not have related entity in the other entity set. For instance, in the relationship WORKS ON between entity sets ENGINEER and PROJECT, the relationship is optional if one or more engineers are not necessarily working on any project and/or one or more projects do not necessarily have any engineers working on it.

5 This conveys the same notion as optionality described in the previous answer but expressed differently. Using the example given in Answer 4, the Engineer entity set is said to have partial participation if there are some engineers not working on a project. The optionality or participation depends on the 'rules' of the application, not on the chance values in specific entity sets.

6 A weak entity is one that cannot exist without another, related, entity. A hospital appointment cannot exist without a patient since it has no logical interpretation.

7 A unary relationship is one in which members of an entity set are related to other members of the same set. For example, in a Employee entity set, a Supervises relationship relates one employee (a supervisor) to one or more other employees.

Chapter 4

1 • Convert each relation to a table.
   • Create tables for certain relationships that need to be represented by a separate table.
   • Establish links between tables using suitable foreign key to primary key pairings.

2 A many-to-many relationship always requires a separate table containing foreign keys linking to the two original tables.

3 Although one-to one relationships can be represented by combining the two tables, retaining two table clarifies the entity table representation and makes the tables easier to amend.

4 When the entity has partial participation in the relationship.

5 It requires the generation of a separate table each of which holds one of the attribute values.

6 It requires the generation of a separate table, each row of which holds one instance of the value(s) per specific time.

Chapter 5

1 Normalisation is the process of converting the design of database tables so that they conform to a set of defined criteria that lead to an optimal design.

2 A normalised set of tables exhibits minimal redundancy and freedom from update anomalies.

3 • First NF: remove repeating values of attributes. Create a new table to hold the repeating values linked to the original.
   • Second NF: Remove attributes with partial dependencies (i.e., dependent only on part of the primary key) to a separate relation.
   • Third NF: Remove attributes dependent on non-key attributes to a separate relation.

4 A relation is in BCNF if every determinant in the relation is a candidate key.

5 It is the 'ultimate' normal form: no further normal forms are possible or necessary. However, its practical significance is limited.

Chapter 6

1 The main factors are:
   • scale
   • performance
   • support for data types
   • connectivity
   • processing complexity.

2 The main datatypes are
- Text (character): alphanumeric data
- Numeric: various formats in two main categories of integer and real (floating point)
- Date and time
- Boolean (logical value)
- Sequence number (counter, autonumber): automatically generated numerical sequence number.

Other common types are Binary: large unstructured data allocation; Object: binary object in standard application format, e.g., OLE.

3 Indexing provides faster access to specific rows and enables the table data to be displayed in a specific sequence.

4 Introducing redundancy is used to improve the performance of querying especially if joining of large tables is avoided.

5
- general-purpose 'window' to underlying tables
- management of application transactions
- menu construction.

6 The report will involve one or more columns that are being totalled and other columns simply being listed. Also one or more columns will act as a grouping key; the key could be 'sales area' and the value being totalled is the sales amount per sales area. A report example is given in the chapter text.

Chapter 7

1
- schema manager
- forms generator
- query processor
- report generator
- programming interface.

2 Typically, it should be possible to index on any number of columns or combinations of columns and to specify either unique or non-unique index values.

3 Physical data management and accessing including
- Index management
- View management
- Accessing of Data Dictionary
- Concurrency control
- Security: access rights
- Integrity: validation, referential integrity, transactions, recovery.

4 A passive data dictionary is used purely for system documentation. An active data dictionary is accessed by the database engine and is used in working with the database.

Chapter 8

1 These are categories applied to languages used in databases. DDL = Data Definition Language is language elements used in the definition of table schemas. DML = Data Manipulation Language is language elements used to process and query the database. DCL = Data Control Language is used in aspects of database control such as access rights.

2 Essentially, a query language is a database language used to extract or derive data from a database. However, in general use, a query language can also process and update a database.

3 The most significant query language is Structured Query Language (SQL).

4 SQL commands can be incorporated into program code of other languages. SQL is used to query the database and extract required data. The other language code is then used to process the data.

5 4GL stands for Fourth Generation Language which refers to a high-level language offering more advanced facilities than 3GL languages such as Pascal and C. Generally, 4GLs are associated with a database and have intimate communication with the database engine.

6 Event handling languages such as VBA (Visual Basic for Applications) is used to write program code that responds to events at the user interface. For instance, if a text field on a form is updated this can 'fire' an event handler to check the validity of the update.

Chapter 9

1 A constraint is a definition of a limitation or restriction on the admissible values of data items in the database.

2 Possible threats are: hardware failure, software errors, operator errors, physical damage, concurrency errors, breach of confidentiality.

3 Data validation refers to the checking of data as it is entered into a database to ensure that it conforms to specified limits.

4 Datatypes define the domain of data items, i.e., the bounds of acceptable values for the items. An attribute of a given type cannot hold values not in the domain of that type.

5 An assertion is a general declarative statement of a database constraint that must be applied wherever and whenever the data concerned is altered. A trigger is a trap for a specific condition or event.

6 A transaction is a series of database operations 'bracketed' together. The DBMS treats the transaction as an atomic unit – either all the operations are carried out or none is carried out.

7 A transaction log is used to record all updates applied to a database over a period of time so that the update can be re-applied in the event of a database failure.

8 GRANT is used to bestow access, update and other rights on specified users of the database. REVOKE is used to remove these rights.

Chapter 10

1 The possibility arises of two users working on the same data (or data held in the same disk block). This can cause interference between the work of the two users resulting in possible loss of updates and other problems.

2 Lost update: effect caused by interference of concurrent transactions whereby a user submits a database update that appears to be actioned but is in fact overwritten by another update. Uncommitted dependency: concurrency error caused by one transaction updating uncommitted data that is later rolled back, causing database corruption. Inconsistent analysis: occurs when a database query produces an erroneous result due to another changing the data while it is being read by the query transaction.

3 If transactions were all executed in sequence, without concurrency, then no concurrency errors would arise. Serialisation refers to techniques that allow concurrent transactions but produce the same result as if the transactions were serially executed.

4 Locking of a part of a database (row, block, etc.) by one transaction prevents read and/or write access to the data by other transactions. Locking is used to achieve serialisation.

5 Two-phase locking is a locking technique that uses two phases – the growing phase (during which locks can be acquired) and the shrinking phase (when locks are released). This avoids the problems listed in Question 2.

6 Granularity of locking refers to the unit of storage locked in one lock operation. Can be database, table, block or row with block being the most common.

7 A deadlock occurs when two (or more) transactions are waiting for the release of locks when the release will not occur due to a circular wait situation. Caused by each transaction holding one lock while requesting a data item that is locked by another.

8 The methods are prevention (acquiring all locks at the same time) and detection (allowing deadlock to occur but then clearing it by rolling back a transaction).

Chapter 11

1 A technique used in networked system where some computers (the servers) provide a service to other computers (the clients).

2 A distributed database is physically stored at two or more separate locations connected by a network rather than at a single location.

3 Possibilities are:
- tables stored separately
- tables split into groups of rows (horizontal distribution)
- tables split into groups of columns (vertical distribution)
- combinations of these.

4 Database replication refers to the storing of one or more copies of a database at other network locations.

5 Transparency refers to an objective of distributed systems whereby the user of the system need not be aware of the distribution and/or replication of the database they are using.

6 ODBC and JDBC are application program interfaces designed to enable programs to access database systems in a platform independent way. ODBC is C language based and JDBC is based in the Java language.

7 CGI (Common Gateway Interface) is a technique used in Web systems which enables a client HTML script to activate and execute a program on the server system. This is used, among other things, to allow access to a server database.

Chapter 12

1
- simplicity of concept
- data independence
- good theoretical basis
- improved security and integrity
- suitable for high-level languages.

2
- Applications frequently require large numbers of tables.
- Processing overheads can be large and increase disproportionately with increasing database size.
- Lack of semantic power.
- Unsuitable for complex transactions.

3 These are based on some relaxation of the relational model. Principal extensions are composite attributes and user-defined datatypes.

4 (a) generic specification of 'object type' (b) system generated permanent identification code for each object (c) derivation of a new class from an existing one.

Appendix D: Answers to chapter exercises

Chapter 2

1 (a) Union of A and B

Order number	Company	City
A1002	Rentokil	London
A3333	Eurotunnel	Paris
B0987	Kwikfit	Glasgow
C7521	BT	Edinburgh
E0102	Halifax plc	Halifax
D2489	Hanson	London

(b) Difference A−B

Order number	Company	City
A1002	Rentokil	London
A3333	Eurotunnel	Paris
C7521	BT	Edinburgh

(c) Difference B−A

Order number	Company	City
D2489	Hanson	London

(d) Intersection of A and B

Order number	Company	City
B0987	Kwikfit	Glasgow
E0102	Halifax plc	Halifax

Chapter 3

1 (a) One consultant treats many patients.
One patient is treated by one consultant.
One consultant specialises in one topic.
One topic is specialised in by many consultants.

2

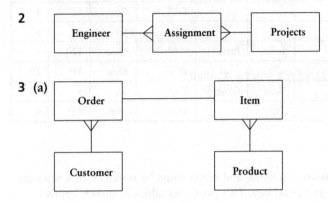

3 (a)

Chapter 4

1 This process is explained in some detail in the text. In summary, the main points are as follows:

- All entities are converted to tables with a primary key chosen for each table.
- For relationships
  - One-to-one: consider merging of the tables since this can be done with no loss of detail. However, it is often best to preserve the separate representation for clarity. One of the tables would require a foreign key to link to the other table.
  - One-to-many: Can be achieved with the two entity tables. The table at the 'many' side of the relationship would have a foreign key linking to the other primary key. Three tables can also be used in the same fashion as many-to-many.
  - Many-to-many: a new relationship table is necessary. It will contain a foreign key to each of the entity tables.

2 (a) Table Student: MatricNumber, name, Course Code, . . .
Table Course: Course Code, Title, DeptCode, . . .
Table Module: Module Code, Title, . . .
Table Department: Dept Code, Name, . . .
Relationship table Composition: Course Code, Module Code, . . .

Chapter 5

1 The original table is:

Ord no	Date	Cust no	Name	Address	Prod no	Desc	Price	Qty
1	05-01-96	22	Smith	London	A95	Jacket	55	4
					G17	Coat	120	8
					K10	Suit	90	5
2	19-01-96	47	Jones	Paris	G17	Coat	120	9
					D77	Shirt	35	20
3	27-03-96	25	West	Glasgow	E30	Tie	5	25
					D77	Shirt	35	4

1NF:
The rightmost four columns are repeating and hence must be removed to a separate table together with OrdNo as partial key. This produces tables as shown below:

Order

Ord no	Date	Cust no	Name	Address
1	05-01-96	22	Smith	London
2	19-01-96	47	Jones	Paris
3	27-03-96	25	West	Glasgow

OrderItem

Ord no	Prod no	Desc	Price	Qty
1	A95	Jacket	55	4
1	G17	Coat	120	8
1	K10	Suit	90	5
2	G17	Coat	120	9
2	D77	Shirt	35	20
3	E30	Tie	5	25
3	D77	Shirt	35	4

2NF:
The only 2NF candidate is table OrderItems since it has a composite key. The description and the price are dependent only on the product code and hence must be separated into another table with key ProdNo. The OrderItem table therefore decomposes into:

OrderItem

Ord no	Prod no	Qty
1	A95	4
1	G17	8
1	K10	5
2	G17	9
2	D77	20
3	E30	25
3	D77	4

Product

Prod no	Desc	Price
A95	Jacket	55
G17	Coat	120
K10	Suit	90
G17	Coat	120
D77	Shirt	35
E30	Tie	5
D77	Shirt	35

3NF:

In the Order table, we can see that Name and Address depend only on the CustNo and not on the table primary key. We can decompose the table into:

Order

Ord no	Date	Cust no
1	05-01-96	22
2	19-01-96	47
3	27-03-96	25

Customer

Cust no	Name	Address
22	Smith	London
47	Jones	Paris
25	West	Glasgow

4

Project number	Project name	Employee number	Employee name	Department	Hours spent
1	Apollo	1001	Smith	Engineering	127
1	Apollo	1003	Jones	Accounts	45
2	Mercury	1002	Stewart	Marketing	70
3	Venus	1001	Smith	Engineering	21

Inspecting the table, we see that we have redundancy in respect of the Project number to Project name dependency and Employee number to Employee name and Department dependency. The natural key of the table is Project number–Employee number so the table is not in 2NF. The following anomalies could arise:

- Delete anomaly: If Stewart is deleted then information about project Mercury is lost.
- Insert Anomaly: A new employee cannot be introduced until asigned to a project.
- Update anomaly: If employee Smith changes department, then all rows pertaining to Smith must be amended.

Chapter 6

1

Order Table

Ord no	Customer no	Order date	Total order value

Order Item Table

Ord no	Product no	Product description	Product price	Quantity

In the Order Item table, the key is Order no. – Product no. Product description and Product price conflict with 2NF since they depend only on Product no. This is not likely to be of any merit. It would appear to avoid having to use a Product table but would take up more space and would be subject to update anomalies.

In the Order table, the column Total order value does not conflict with normalisation rules but is redundant since it can be calculated from the Order Item table. This uses minimal extra storage and could save considerable processing time (in calculating the value from a query). Hence, it is likely to be a viable option.

4 (a)

Product code	Branch	Total sales
B342	North	350
B342	South	300
C100	North	250
C100	South	100
E501	North	400
E501	South	150

Chapter 7

1 A DBMS is the software system that provides the functionality of the database. It provides the following main functions:

1. the user interface
2. the database engine: the system that manages the storage and accessing of the physical data
3. the data dictionary.

The user interface consists of a number of elements including

1. schema manager, i.e., design and usage of tables
2. forms generator
3. query processor
4. report generator
5. menu generator
6. programming interfaces.

Chapter 8

1 SQL is used extensively in modern database systems. In most programming environments, it is generally used to resolve queries before further processing of the data. Since it is standardised it is used frequently in inter-database communication. In other words, SQL is an indispensable requirement in any modern database.

The various ways in which SQL can be applied are:

1. As a command-based interpreter.
2. Embedded in a conventional language such as COBOL or C++.
3. Embedded (or incorporated) in a 4GL such as Oracle PL/SQL.
4. Other systems such as event handling languages can hold SQL as text strings which are sent as a request to a database server.

Chapter 9

1 A transaction is a series of database steps (such as adding, deleting or amending rows of the database) that is to be treated as an atomic unit. This means that either the whole series of commands are carried out successfully or none of them are.

A single operation in an application using a database (such as entering a sales order or booking a holiday) generally involves several changes to the database tables. These changes are related in the sense that the operation is not complete unless all of the changes are made. For instance, if you enter a sales order and record the sales details but do not amend the stock level, then the database has lost integrity. Enclosing the series of steps within one transaction guarantees that it is not possible for only some of the steps to be carried out.

In order to provide for transactions, a database system must support two essential operations, commit and rollback. The commit operation is issued on completion of a series of updates that constitute a transaction and has the effect of terminating the transaction and making permanent the changes included in the transaction. The rollback operation has the effect of aborting the current transaction and returning the state of the database to that before the start of the transaction.

Chapter 10

1 The final result would depend on the sequence of the transactions. If A occurred before B then the accounts would change as follows:

Transaction A
Reduce balance in ACC1:   ACC1 = 3000   ACC2 = 5000
Increase balance in ACC2:   ACC1 = 3000   ACC2 = 6000

Transaction B
Increase balances by 1.5%:   ACC1 = 3045   ACC2 = 6090

If transactions occurred in sequence B–A:

Transaction B
Increase balances by 1.5%:   ACC1 = 4060   ACC2 = 5075

Transaction A
Reduce balance in ACC1:   ACC1 = 3060   ACC2 = 5075
Increase balance in ACC2:   ACC1 = 3060   ACC2 = 6075

The actual changes would be:

Transaction A
Reduce balance in ACC1   ACC1 = 3000   ACC2 = 5000

Transaction B
Increase balances by 1.5%   ACC1 = 3045   ACC2= 5075

Transaction A
Increase balance in ACC2   ACC1 = 3045   ACC2 = 6075

Note that the result does not conform to either valid sequence. The problem arises because transaction A releases the lock on ACC1 too soon allowing transaction B to intercede. Use of two-phase locking would avoid this error. To comply with two-phase locking transaction A must hold the lock on ACC1 until ACC2 is locked and the full update is carried out. Both locks can then be removed without a problem.

Chapter 11

2

Advantages of distributed databases
In discussing the advantages of distributed databases it is necessary to make clear what the alternative is. We can assume that the enterprise operating the database has two or more locations, so that if a distributed system were not used then two possibilities exist:

- a centralised database is used with network connections to this from the other sites.
- separate databases are employed.

The second alternative is not feasible unless the various sites do not need to 'pool' their information and transactions. Otherwise it would be complex trying to keep the databases aligned. The first alternative is the more likely; the problems created by this are that the single database has to cope with the full load of the enterprise and considerable network traffic is created focused again on the central site. Also, the access time for data will incur network delays. Lastly, the whole system is sensitive to failure of the central site both in terms of the database and of the network.

Further advantages of distributed databases are that

- Data can be stored near to where it is most commonly used.
- The access time for that data will be much faster.
- Network traffic will be reduced.
- Failure of any one site will not cause total system failure.

Disadvantages

- Complexity; requires advanced software and management skills.
- If the 'whole' database is viewed as all the distributed parts combined, then failure of any site or network connection will render the database partly unavailable.
- Specific technical problems in query processing, schema management and concurrency.
- More complex database design.

4 ODBC and JDBC are application programming interfaces (API) designed to enable programmers to write programs that are capable of communicating with any database for which the API is enabled. This generally consists of having available a function library (often in the form of a dynamic link library) that implements the API function calls. Using ODBC/JDBC it is possible to use a standard set of instructions for 'talking' with any database. The programming system does not have to be specific to the particulat database used. So, for example, a C program using ODBC written to access an Oracle database would look the same if it were to access an Informix database. Also, both types of database could be accessed in the one program. ODBC is based on the C/C++ language while JDBC is based on the Java language.

Chapter 12

4 The principal problems arise from the difficulty in persuading customers to adopt the new technology. The reluctance of companies in this respect is based on the following factors:

- Incompatibility with current systems, e.g., SQL, programming environments. The extended relational systems require new SQL interpreters and other programming tool extensions.
- Lack of current standardisation.
- Investment in current technology; the company probably is running current systems using conventional relational database technology. Adopting another system would require some investment in conversion. This could include new software and re-training costs.
- Novel technologies require the weight of a large vendor behind them. Companies are reluctant to invest in new ideas unless the vendor has considerable market presence.
- Unproven benefits. Many developers remain to be convinced of the need for, or the significant advantage of, extended relational systems.
- True object systems serve the needs of many new applications.

Like most new developments of this type, extended relational systems will advance when the large vendors show enthusiasm for them and when some measure of stardardisation is achieved.

5

```
CREATE TYPE ITEM
(
        OrderNumber       CHAR(6),
        ProductNumber     CHAR(5),
        Quantity          NUMBER(5)
)

CREATE TABLE ORDER
(
        OrderNumber       CHAR(6),
        CustomerNo        CHAR(6),
        Items             SET OF ITEM
)
```

Bibliography

Atkinson M. *et al* (1990) 'The Object-Oriented Database Manifesto' in *Deductive and Object-Oriented Databases*, Kim, W. *et al*. Elsevier. 1990.

Bowman J.S., Emerson S.L. and Darnovsky M.D. (1996) *The Practical SQL Handbook* 3rd edn Addison-Wesley.

Cattell R.G.C., ed. (1997) *The Object Database Standard: ODMG 2.0* Morgan Kaufman, San Francisco, 1997.

Chen P.P. (1976) 'The entity-relationship model: towards a unified view of data' *ACM Trans. on Database Systems* 1:1, 1976.

Codd E. F. (1971) 'A relational model of data for large shared data banks' *Comm. ACM*, **13**, 6.

Database Language SQL (ISO 9075:1992(E)). International Standards Organisation.

Eaglestone B. and Ridley M. (1998) *Object Databases – an Introduction* McGraw-Hill.

Fagin R. (1981) 'A Normal Form for Relational Database that is Based on Domain Keys' in *ACM Transactions on Database Systems*, September 1981.

Groff J.R. (1994) *LAN Times Guide to SQL* McGraw-Hill.

G. Hamilton (1997) *JDBC Database Access from Java* Addison Wesley.

Kroenke D. M. (1992) *Database Processing* Macmillan.

Smith R. and Sussman D. (1997) *Beginning Access 97 Programming* Wrox.

Ullman J.D. and Widom J. (1997) *A First Course in Database Systems* Prentice-Hall.

Zloof M. M. (1977) 'Query-By-Example: A database language' *IBM Systems Journal*, **16**, 4.

Index